Quality Education for All

REFERENCE BOOKS IN INTERNATIONAL EDUCATION
VOLUME 38
GARLAND REFERENCE LIBRARY OF SOCIAL SCIENCE
VOLUME 1105

QUALITY EDUCATION FOR ALL
COMMUNITY-ORIENTED APPROACHES

EDITED BY
H. DEAN NIELSEN AND
WILLIAM K. CUMMINGS

GARLAND PUBLISHING, INC.
NEW YORK AND LONDON
1997

Library of Congress Cataloging-in-Publication Data

Quality education for all : community-oriented approaches / edited by H. Dean
    Nielsen and William K. Cummings.
            p.   cm. — (Garland reference library of social science ; v. 1105.
    Reference books in international education ; v. 38)
        Includes bibliographical references and index.
        ISBN 0-8153-2378-6 (alk. paper)
        1. Critical pedagogy—Case studies.   2. Postmodernism and education—Case
    studies.   3. Community and school—Case studies.   4. School management and
    organization—Case studies.   5. Educational change—Case studies.   I. Nielsen,
    H. Dean.   II. Cummings, William K.   III. Series: Garland reference library of
    social science ; v. 1105.   IV. Garland reference library of social science. Refer-
    ence books in international education ; vol. 38.
    LC196.Q35   1997
    370.11'5—dc21   97-1995
                                                                          CIP

Contents

Series Editor's Foreword   vii

Preface   ix

Introduction

1. **The Limits of Modern Education**   5
   William K. Cummings

2. **The Last Frontiers of Education for All: A Close-Up of Schools in the Periphery**   25
   H. Dean Nielsen

Strategies

3. **Improving School-Community Relations in the Periphery**   37
   James H. Williams

4. **School-Language Policy Decisions for Nondominant Language Groups**   79
   Zeynep F. Beykont

5. **School Curriculum in the Periphery: The Case of South India**   123
   Prema Clarke

6. **Teachers Working in the Periphery: Addressing Persistent Policy Issues**   139
   Maria Teresa Tatto

7. **School and Classroom Organization in the Periphery: The Assets of Multigrade Teaching**   183
   S. Dunham Rowley, Jr., and H. Dean Nielsen

Managing Change

8. **Management Initiatives for Reaching the Periphery**   215
   William K. Cummings

9. **Reaching the Periphery: Toward a Community-Oriented Education**   247
   H. Dean Nielsen and Zeynep F. Beykont

Index   267

Series Editor's Foreword

This series of scholarly works in comparative and international education has grown well beyond the initial conception of a collection of reference books. Although retaining its original purpose of providing a resource to scholars, students, and a variety of other professionals who need to understand the role played by education in various societies or world regions, it also strives to provide accurate, relevant, and up-to-date information on a wide variety of selected educational issues, problems, and experiments within an international context.

Contributors to this series are well-known scholars who have devoted their professional lives to the study of their specializations. Without exception these men and women possess an intimate understanding of the subject of their research and writing. Without exception they have not only studied their subject in dusty archives, but have lived and traveled widely in their quest for knowledge. In short, they are "experts" in the best sense of that often overused word.

In our increasingly interdependent world, it is now widely understood that it is a matter of military, economic, and environmental survival not only that we understand better what makes other societies tick, but also that we make a serious effort to understand how others, be they Japanese, Hungarian, South African, or Chilean, attempt to solve the same kinds of educational problems that we face in North America. As the late George Z.F. Bereday wrote more than three decades ago: "[E]ducation is a mirror held against the face of a people. Nations may put on blustering shows of strength to conceal public weakness, erect grand façades to conceal shabby backyards, and profess peace while secretly arming for conquest, but how they take care of their children tells unerringly who they are" (*Comparative Methods in Education*, New York: Holt, Rinehart and Winston, 1964, p. 5).

Perhaps equally important, however, is the valuable perspective that studying another education system (or its problems) provides us in understanding our own system (or its problems). When we step beyond our own limited experience and our commonly held assumptions about schools and learning in order to look back at our system in contrast to another, we see it in a very different light. To learn, for example, how China or Belgium handles the education of a multilingual society; how the French provide for the funding of public education; or how the Japanese control access to their universities enables us to better understand that there are reasonable alternatives to our own familiar way of doing things. Not that we can *borrow* directly from other societies. Indeed, educational arrangements are inevitably a reflection of deeply embedded political, economic, and cultural factors that are unique to a particular society. But a conscious recognition that there are other ways of doing things can serve to open our minds and provoke our imaginations in ways that can result in new experiments or approaches that we may not have otherwise considered.

Since this series is intended to be a useful research tool, the editor and contributors welcome suggestions for future volumes, as well as for ways in which this series can be improved.

Edward R. Beauchamp
University of Hawaii

Preface

Whereas children in every community within a nation have the right to quality education (*World Declaration on Education for All*), current educational systems everywhere have built-in limitations in reaching out to peripheral groups. Peripheral groups, as we define them, are those with limited access to basic goods and services, usually due to their small numbers or geographic isolation, their low position in the status hierarchy, and/or their history of unfavorable relations with dominant groups. This definition broadens earlier conceptualizations of periphery that focus on geographic separation and remoteness from the center. The complexities of demographic change over the past fifty years, including patterns of rural-urban and international migrations, have necessitated a more inclusive definition. Such a definition calls attention to peripheral groups in every nation, including highly prosperous ones such as the United States, Norway and Japan, as well as poorer ones such as Bolivia, Bangladesh and Burundi. Peripheral groups are found in urban centers and remote areas, in large metropolitan areas and small villages, in squatter communities and refugee camps. They can be in the minority or majority in their ethnic, racial, linguistic, or religious affiliations.

Throughout this book we try to emphasize this more inclusive definition. However, since our authors, and the writers they draw upon, have generally had more direct experience with peripheral groups from rural and remote areas, our examples and case studies tend to overrepresent such groups. It is our hope that our analyses and conclusions will still be found relevant to the other kinds of peripheral groups.

We have compiled this volume to critically review existing programs of education in the periphery and to offer an alternative vision. Our criticisms are rooted in the theories of center-periphery relations of Edward Shils (1975) and the more contemporary critical theories concerning cultural elite, social domination and political legitimacy of Henry Giroux, Donaldo Macedo and Hans Weiler. Post-modernist thinking has also influenced our views, particularly in our discussions of the limits of modern education and centralized government planning and our calls for the reconceptualization of schooling in the periphery. We reject deterministic and ideological formulations such as those found in dependency and world-systems theories. Instead our analyses are grounded in field studies and oriented towards the pragmatic concerns of policy adjustment and improved practice.

Our vision for the future is also colored by the movement of *new communitarian thinking* which quickly gained momentum in the United States during the writing of this book under the leadership of Amatai Etzioni. Our support for a community-oriented approach to education of periphery groups reflects the spirit and optimism of this movement.

The various chapters in this book examine specific ways in which current educational systems actually hinder peripheral groups' access to quality education. In particular, policies and practices regarding school-community relations, language of instruction, school curriculum, teacher policy, school/classroom organization, and school system management are critically reviewed. Whereas each of these factors can present barriers to quality education in the periphery, we demonstrate how the *interconnections* among them often create formidable impediments to positive learning outcomes among children who live on the margins of society. Our book concludes with calls for systemic education reform that goes beyond piecemeal changes in the existing system. We urge a community-oriented approach in which community and center participate as equal partners in educational decisions to create a balance between the needs of the nation-state and those of the community. Offering a quality education for *every* child should be the ultimate goal of education.

H. Dean Nielsen
Zeynep Beykont
Honolulu and Cambridge
August, 1996

QUALITY EDUCATION FOR ALL

Introduction

CHAPTER 1

The Limits of Modern Education

William K. Cummings

"To enlighten the people is to destroy kings"—Alexis de Tocqueville

Modern education, conceived in the late eighteenth to early nineteenth century to promote enlightenment and social equality, may finally be nearing its institutional limit. Over the past decade, following nearly a century of steady gains, there has been little further advance in the diffusion of modern education. The modern system has proved effective in serving the interests of the established core of contemporary society, but ineffective in "reaching for the periphery." This, in our view, is wrong and needs to be set right.

The core chapters of this book outline a set of strategic shifts that will enable education to reach the periphery. But as a first step, it is necessary to understand what constrains modern education. We propose here that modern education, despite its egalitarian rhetoric, was never designed to provide equal or even appropriate education for all.

EDUCATION FOR ALL

"Liberty, Equality, and Fraternity" is perhaps the most memorable slogan of the modern period, shouted as the citizens stormed the Bastille in 1789. The French Revolution symbolizes a worldwide process of reform that aspired to liberate all of the human race from bondage and slavery into a common condition of freedom, and ultimately to the status of equality and citizenship in a new world order. The reform movement of the nineteenth century gradually expanded the concept of citizenship to include first human rights, then political rights, and finally social rights.

Among these social rights was the guarantee of a basic education. Myron Weiner (1991), in a fascinating analysis of contemporary Indian attitudes toward compulsory education, notes that the debate over education is closely intertwined with the debate over child labor. On the ideological right are those who argue that the economy needs cheap child labor in order to be competitive, while on the left are those who argue that child labor is exploitative. In several of the early European cases, the balance was tilted by Protestant religious leaders who argued that young people needed a basic education so they could read the Bible and thereby discover the path to salvation (and, moreover, become more productive). With the French

Revolution, this religious reform movement was adopted by progressive political leaders who insisted that the modern state should provide education for all.

According to Weiner, as early as 1524, "Martin Luther sent a letter to German municipalities insisting it was their duty to provide schools, and the duty of parents to educate their children." (1991: 111.) Protestant influence also was behind the early progress of mass education in Scotland and eventually throughout Europe. For example, in Sweden a royal decree of 1723 told parents and guardians to "diligently see to it that their children applied themselves to book reading and the study of lessons in the Catechism." Japan's modernizing Meiji government, only four years after overthrowing the feudal Tokugawa regime, issued the Fundamental Code of Education, which insisted "every guardian, acting in accordance with this, shall bring up his children with tender care, never failing to have them attend school." (Passin, 1965: 209-211.)

Thus by the turn of the twentieth century, education for all was a firm plank in the political fabric of most independent states. As other nations became independent, particularly following World War II, they usually adopted this plank, and introduced selective policies for its promotion. The United Nations Charter of 1946, with its declaration of the Human Right of Literacy, was another important symbolic step on the road of educational progress.

Particularly since the late fifties, universal education has become an important concern of the international donor community. A recent indication was the much-heralded World Conference on Education for All (EFA) that took place in Jomtien, Thailand, March 5-9, 1990. This conference, attended by chief ministers of education and delegates from over 130 nations, prepared a World Declaration on Education for All as well as a Framework for Action (UNDP, UNESCO, UNICEF, and World Bank, 1990). These documents once again affirmed the commitment of the world's educational leaders to the noble goal of universal literacy through a combination of national, regional, and international initiatives.

But neither these words nor the various actions that are supposed to follow will be enough. For what is envisioned in the current EFA campaign is more of the same: Modern education designed by the center to serve, first and foremost, the interests of the center. The Jomtien initiative, while using the phrase "for all," in fact only proposes to reach 85 percent of the world's young people by the turn of the century; and while it makes reference to such groups as the poor and the disabled, it nowhere suggests that these groups require preferential treatment, relative to the advantaged who reside in the societal center. Without setting educational policies on their head, without developing new strategies that favor the periphery over the center, it will be impossible to realize the dreams that inspired the modern educational revolution.

MODERN EDUCATION IS CREATED BY AND FOR THE CENTER

There is little reason to doubt the sincerity of the eminent national and world leaders who have promoted modern education, and who recently reiterated their concerns in the EFA Declaration. But we will argue that their efforts inevitably face an upper limit, simply because they, as representatives of the central institutions of the modern system, have proposed policies that favor the center, over the periphery.

To introduce this argument, it is useful to gain some understanding of the nature of the center, and of the centripetal forces in social interaction. Edward Shils (1975), who has perhaps done more than any other thinker to enhance understanding of the center-periphery relation, writes:

> Society has a center. There is a central zone in the structure of society. This central zone impinges in various ways on those who live within the ecological domain in which the society exists. . . . The central zone is not, as such, a spatially located phenomenon. It almost always has a more or less definite location within the bounded territory in which the society lives. Its centrality has, however, nothing to do with geometry and little with geography.
>
> The center, or the central zone, is a phenomenon of the realm of values and beliefs. It is the center of the order of symbols, of values and beliefs, which govern the society. . . . One of the major elements in any central value system is an affirmative attitude toward established authority. . . .
>
> The central value system thus . . . legitimates the existing distribution of roles and rewards to persons possessing the appropriate qualities which in various ways symbolize degrees of proximity to authority. (Shils, 1975: 14)

Shils then goes on to discuss the center's regard for those who are distant from the center. He note the center naturally "legitimates the smaller rewards received by those who live at various distances from the circles in which authority is exercised." The center, in his view, is inevitably disposed to look firstly after its own interests and only secondarily, if at all, after the interests of those who are distant from the center.

THE CONSOLIDATION OF CENTERS

Shils's generalizations refer to all societal units, regardless of scale, but in the development of his argument he observes a historical pattern of the consolidation of societal centers. At the height of the medieval period in Western Europe, there were as many as 500 societal centers. With advances in transportation and particularly in military technology, a process of consolidation began which ultimately culminated by the mid-nineteenth century in a much smaller group of powerful centers, known as nation-states, which are essentially the same national entities that have prevailed down to the present day. The major question since that time has been the relative preeminence within this small group. Paul Kennedy (1989), in *The Rise and Fall of the Great Powers*, traces a shift from Great Britain to Germany to the United States.

As these nation-states gained ascendency, their leaders sought by various means to strengthen their position of authority vis-à-vis constituencies both within and outside their national boundaries. The development of military strength was one means, but particularly for the consolidation of national power the leaders placed considerable reliance on mass education to instill a sense of loyalty and civil responsibility. National systems of education were established and supported by funds, curriculum, teachers, and instructional materials provided primarily by the center. These national systems, which have since come to be called modern educational systems, sought to build national unity through controlling the influence of familial, community, and religious values in the educational process—particularly where these traditional influences were perceived to be hostile to the new state. The centrally devised control procedures have inevitably led to systems that favor the center, no matter how egalitarian the rhetoric espoused by the educational leaders. However, there is variation in the degree of the central bias.

THE MAIN PATTERNS OF MODERN EDUCATION
Common to all of the emerging modern nation-states was the concern to promote education so as to provide the members of society with a common educational experience that would reinforce the center's authority. But the particular approaches that emerged varied according to national circumstances. It can be argued that six distinctive patterns of modern education emerged. The first four, to be discussed below, were administratively more centralized, while the last two were more decentralized.

French or Continental Model
The French case is perhaps the most celebrated example, because of the abruptness of the change. Up to the time of the French Revolution, the Catholic church had commanded a virtual monopoly in the field of education in France, and used this pulpit to reinforce the legitimacy of both the church and the monarchy. The founders of the First Republic sought to cleanse education of what it considered to be the traditional and superstitious influence of the church. Robespierre told the National Convention he was "convinced of the necessity of operating a total regeneration, and, if I may express myself in this way, of creating a new people." (Blum, 1986: 193).

Thus the First Republic declared an end to religious education, to be replaced by a new system of national schools. As Danton declared, "It is in national schools that children must suck republican milk. The Republic is one and indivisible; public instruction must also be related to this center of unity." (Pierre, 1881: 70.) But the Republic initially lacked the resources to establish a national system, and, moreover, many parents remained loyal to the church. Thus the progress of the new Republic in realizing these ambitious goals was staggered. It was not until the 1830s under Guizot that the Republic drafted a systematic plan for the delivery of republican education, and even then the major initiatives were in urban areas and at the secondary level. Only from the 1870s did the state fully assert its influence at the primary level by establishing a public school in every commune, regardless of whether it had a Catholic school or not. Jules Ferry, Minister of Public Instruction during this period, condemned Catholic schools as "establishments which are maintained as schools of counter-revolution, where one learns to detest and curse all of the ideas which are the honor and the purpose of modern France." (Legrand, 1961: 47.)

Thus we see in the French example a strong determination by the central state to impose a single pattern of education throughout the Republic. The central Ministry of Public Instruction established uniform guidelines on educational expenditures, which were to be jointly financed from local and central revenues. And it appointed officials in the administrative units of academies, departments and cantons to carry out its various policies on school construction, textbook utilization, teacher assignment and training, and instruction. Local participation in the educational process was limited, and little attempt was made to adjust educational approaches to take into account variations in local conditions.

The French approach led to universal primary education by the turn of the twentieth century—but there is much controversy concerning the uniformity of provision. A myth prevails that the system provided identical education throughout the nation and indeed throughout the French empire. But recent empirical research indicates a clear bias in this system to serve urban areas and particularly Paris. For example, the major *lycée* were located in the towns and cities, and most of the elite *grande école* were located in or around Paris. There was, and continues to be, a strong urban and upper class bias in the composition of students admitted to these elite institutions. Thus the centralized French system was more favorable to those at the center than those in the periphery.

Prussia

While the French pattern, by virtue of France's imperial domination, has had an extensive global impact, it is important to recognize that many of its features were inspired by the nearby example of Prussia. Through much of the nineteenth century, France and Prussia were joined in intermittent conflict. The Prussians, after suffering defeat under Napoleon in 1807, concluded that education was the vehicle of future strength. And thus Prussia took even more vigorous steps than France to develop a national educational system. But in the case of Prussia, the King enjoyed a relatively harmonious relation with the Lutheran church and with other local religious groups; thus Prussia devised an educational approach where the central state incorporated rather than rejected religious education.

Prussia's educational successes were widely admired throughout the Continent as well as in the New World. Especially notable was the systematic approach in teacher education and the promotion of strong research-oriented universities. The speed of Prussia's industrial revolution as well as the impressive strength of its armed forces were attributed to the rapid progress in educational expansion.

Prussia also relied more on local participation in the finance and governance of schools than did France. Of particular interest in the Prussian case was an equalizing provision in the central funding formula to insure that local areas which had difficulty in generating their own funds would receive additional support from the center. However, in most particulars the two systems had strong similarities and can be thought of as exemplars of the Continental Pattern.

The main features of this pattern can be summarized as follows: The central government played a leading role, while requiring local governments to provide at least partial support for the schools in their areas. Principles of control varied from nation to nation, though the most common approach was a line bureaucracy setting the major guidelines on curriculum and exams, textbooks, teacher training and assignments. Public participation in the control of education was relatively limited.

Lowlands Pattern

The Lowlands (now extending to Scandinavia) provide an interesting exception to the Continental Pattern. The nations now known as the Netherlands, Belgium, and

Denmark were not as distinct in the early nineteenth century as they are today; and when the French Republican government proposed a centralized secular educational system, the leaders in these areas were inclined to follow the French example, but for a different reason. In these areas, the religious commitments of the people were quite diverse, preventing the state from favoring a particular religion; might it not be preferable for the state to divorce itself from all religions?

The National Assembly of the Batavian Republic (later the Kingdom of the Netherlands) in 1796 issued *General Reflections on National Education*, in which the advantages of a secular approach were outlined:

> Through education and propagation of (Liberal) "culture" among all classes the circle of citizens could be broadened and the basis of the state as well. On this course a homogeneous Dutch nation would come into being, and would naturally take on a liberal coloration. This is the political core of the liberal school policies. The school as *nation-forming* must not be divided among competing "sectarian schools" or left in the hands of an exclusive political or church party. The Liberals considered themselves *algemeen* (that is, common, nonsectarian, nonpartisan). (Glenn, 1988 : 46.)

This secular approach was attempted for a number of years, but it did not lead to acceptable results. So by the second decade of the nineteenth century, educational leaders proposed a shift to a religiously oriented school assisted by state subsidies. The eventual outcome was a system of independently managed schools, subsidized and loosely regulated by the central government to insure common coverage of certain subject matter. State regulation became relatively more rigorous at the upper grade levels. Thus individual schools enjoyed considerable autonomy while receiving substantial state support.

Japanese

Distinctive approaches have also been set up in the socialist countries and in Japan, both drawing heavily on the centralized tradition of the European continent. However, particularly in the Japanese case, the social origins of the central leaders led them to develop special concern for the educational fortunes of children in peripheral areas. While the modern European states had gained ascendency on the wave of a bourgeoisie revolution, the modern Japanese state was formed by what is sometimes called an aristocratic coup. Lower- and middle-rank samurai from somewhat peripheral areas, fearful of the consequences of Japan's technological backwardness relative to the West, overthrew the tradition-focused center and replaced it with a new government that was committed to modernizing Japan. The new government was also more mindful of peripheral areas than had been its predecessor.

As in the continental case, the Japanese leaders promoted a centralized system and stressed a common curriculum that reinforced the legitimacy of the new government. But relative to the continental pattern, the Japanese system was exceptionally thorough in providing equal opportunities to children of the peripheral areas. For example, equalizing formulas were used to insure sufficient funds in impoverished local areas; and special incentives were developed to reward teachers who took up jobs in difficult settings. Also compared to the standard European model, the Japanese approach was more tolerant of private schools.

The Japanese system expanded much more rapidly than its European predecessors. It is generally regarded that the system achieved universal enrollment in basic education during the first decade of the twentieth century, or within four decades of the official commitment to compulsory education. In recent years, with increases in Japanese affluence and experience with democracy as well as a concern to foster national creativity, the Japanese system has encouraged more local control of education.

Socialist

The socialist approach was the last major system to emerge on the world scene. The first socialist system was developed in the former Soviet Union, while important variants were later developed in China and Yugoslavia. Drawing heavily on the Continental model, it is perhaps the most centralized of all the extant models, with central prescription in virtually all policy areas and no tolerance for a private sector.

The egalitarian rhetoric is prominent in socialist education, and most socialist educational systems have an exceptional role in providing basic education to all citizens. However, the systems vary in their provision at the secondary and tertiary level. Some critics suggest the socialist system, at least as developed in the former Soviet Union, has a strong urban bias. In socialist systems that have been instituted in large nations such as China, provincial governments are accorded a role in educational finance and are also allowed to conduct some of the education in their local languages.

Anglo and American Patterns

In contrast to the prominent role of the central state on the Continent, in England and later the United States local governments assumed a more prominent role, providing the great proportion of funding and enjoying considerable autonomy to develop distinctive local policies. In England, the state chose to subsidize worthy private schools whereas in the U.S. the state required private schools to be self-supporting.

In both of these decentralized approaches, local boards of education were established to assume responsibility for most educational policies in the local area. Individual schools and their executive officers were subordinate to district-level school superintendents who were in turn subordinate to these local boards. School-level discretion varied between localities.

However, the geographical scope of local boards as well as the funds they can access differ. In the U.K., which currently has a population of 55 million, there are approximately 106 local education authorities; whereas in the U.S., with a population of 240 million, there are approximately 15,000 school boards. The U.S. school boards are typically responsible for a smaller geographical area, and also draw the majority of their funds from this small area; if the area is poor, the schools tend to be poor, for the subsidies coming from other government levels are modest. Thus, particularly in the American system, there are enormous disparities between school districts. The best-funded are not in the "center" but rather in the suburban areas that encircle a major urban center. In the U.K., because of the larger districts, disparities between districts are not as marked.

While private schools are allowed in both systems, they occupy a more prominent place in the English system. In fact, a subset of the English private schools known as "public schools" are generally viewed as the appropriate vehicles for elite education. These schools do not receive much state funding, but they are generously funded through tuition and endowment. The success of these independent schools disposes U.K. (and, to a lesser degree, American) educational leaders to consider the merits of an educational system where the central government's role is sharply curtailed. Thus, in recent years in virtually all countries that have one or the other of these decentralized patterns, consideration is being given to a further devolution of control to the "self-managed school."

The development of new information technologies and the increasing professionalization of educational personnel has led educational policy makers to propose a reduction in district-level controls and an increase in the discretion of the heads of individual schools. This shift to increased school-level discretion is associated with new systems of accountability, both to the parents of children and to the system of public finance. In the United Kingdom the approach is to directly empower individual schools, whereas in the U.S. the current preference is for fostering local school markets through offering parents the means to choose among diverse school options. These market reforms promise to stimulate much innovation at the school level, but they also are likely to further the inequalities that are already inherent in these decentralized systems.

In sum, while the modern educational revolution has generated several distinctive models or patterns for the delivery of mass education, all of the models tend to be biased towards the respective centers of these societies, and to be deficient in reaching for the periphery.

MODERN EDUCATION AND INEQUALITY

The central bias of the modern system was the focus of extensive research and policy reform in the sixties. In the early stages of the modern era, reformers focused on equality of educational opportunity. Every child should have a right to attend a school that had "inputs" of equal quality. One finding from the research of this period was that the quality of inputs varied widely between schools. In the United States, for example, suburban schools generally had superior inputs to both rural and urban schools. And the differences in inputs were tied to differences in outputs such as student achievement or school completion. So one reform objective was a leveling of inequalities in inputs.

However, the research made an additional finding of critical importance. Even when the inputs of schools in different areas were similar, children in more "central" schools did better than those in more "peripheral" schools. Indeed in some cases, even where the central schools had higher student-teacher ratios, older buildings, or poorer laboratory equipment, the children did better. Factors associated with the central setting such as parental support, peer group interaction, and opportunity to learn from the environment were associated with the superior performance of the central schools. This finding of the relatively low salience of school factors relative to environmental factors led to a new policy focus, striving for equal outcomes. Thus reforms such as the preschool Head Start, enrichment programs, busing, and other equalizing changes were initiated. But within a few years, many of these reforms were abandoned. The modern system was not really committed to equality of outcomes. Thus studies conducted twenty years later show little change in the level of center-periphery inequality.

THE GLOBAL DIFFUSION OF MODERN EDUCATION

Following World War II, a large number of new states were established as the great powers liberated their former colonies; most of these new states affirmed a commitment to compulsory education in their constitutions. Perhaps of greater significance for the educational expansion of the new states was the emergence of powerful international organizations to perform coordinating roles in the evolving world system. Thus parallel to the central role of the great powers is the centralizing impact of the services provided by the United Nations and its technical agencies, that of the World Bank, and various bilateral actors.

The emergence of new states has not, by and large, been accompanied by the emergence of new educational approaches. Rather the new states have tended to adapt the administrative models of the early modernizers. Cultural ties have played a major role in the process of replication. For example, countries in the Commonwealth tend to follow the English model, those once under French control, the French model. Most Latin American nations threw off the yoke of Spanish or Portuguese colonialism at the time the French Revolution was inspiring liberation movements, and thus most of the Latin American nations adopted the French model.

IMPLEMENTING THE MODERN MODEL: THE CASE OF INDIA

The record of the new states in developing modern educational systems and especially in extending these educational services to the periphery has been checkered. Weiner's research on India, a nation where enrollment rates are pitifully low, reveals an interesting contrast between India's firm legal commitment to compulsory education (16 of the 22 states in India have laws on compulsory education) and a weak commitment to implementing these laws. Quotes from interviews with key political officials and policy analysts illustrate this reality:

A key senior official working on the National Policy on Education:
I think that by and large the people of India want their children to be educated, so we do not need coercive power to send their children to school. Besides, what right do we have to compel parents to send children to schools that are not worth much? The teachers aren't any good. Often they don't even appear at the school. We must first provide the country with schools that are worth something. Right now our schools are trash. (Weiner, 1991: 57.)

The Director of the National Institute of Public Cooperation and Child Development:
Look at the tribal children, for example. They have a tradition of learning crafts at home, but once we put them into school they won't go back to their own culture to

learn their crafts. This new culture we teach in the schools has given them nothing. They can't even get a job as a peon. The problem is that the schools pull the children out of their own culture. . . . If these low-income people had a chance, they would send their children to school to get degrees rather than learn the family craft. But that would be a mistake because then we would have more educated unemployed. Schools just add to the ranks of the unemployed. (Weiner, 1991: 76.)

Chitra Naik, a leading educational researcher:
The majority of these children (children from tribal and poor, rural families) evade the compulsion laws simply by enrolling in a nearby primary school, with hardly any intention to attend. The teachers usually connive at this stratagem since it is convenient for them to show large enrollments on paper and actually have a small attendance in class. This enables them to send to the "higher authorities" good reports on the spread of primary education, while their routine teaching load remains light. Such an arrangement is mutually convenient for everyone concerned, i.e., the children, parents, teachers, and even education offices where the "coverage" shown by enrollment statistics matters for the preparation of progress reports. The names of a few non-attending children are struck off the attendance register every now and then, thus satisfying the given regulation by token. The inadequate communication facilities in the tribal and rural areas prevent adequate personal supervision and lead to dependence on reports which cannot be easily verified. (Weiner, 1991, 77.)

THE CORRELATES OF EDUCATIONAL EXPANSION
Clearly, at least in the case of India, there are major constraints that stand in the way of realizing education for all. Cross-national studies have identified several dimensions of modern societies that tend to complicate the efforts of national governments in providing social services such as education.

Class
Modern states were typically formed through the realignment of class relations. In Europe, modern states were formed though the urban bourgeoisie displacing rural landed elites, and the policies of these states thus came to favor the city over the country. In Japan, it can be argued that a rural and peripheral aristocratic subclass displaced an urban and central elite; thus, the modern Japanese state has evidenced exceptional sensitivity in reaching out to the periphery. Nevertheless, even in Japan we find that the great universities are located in the leading cities, as are the most prestigious jobs. In Russia, urban workers were at the forefront and in China it was the peasant class. Hence, Soviet education is relatively well developed in urban areas, whereas in China there is a periodic rejection of the urban intellectual class— better red than expert. In sum, modern education favors the class that is preeminent in the modern state.

Affluence
While class dominance influences the pattern of distribution of social services, with increasing economic development it becomes possible for social services to be more equitably distributed, without sacrificing the interests of the dominant class.

Ethnicity
It is often the case that a particular national group is the primary force in national government; after all, the founding principle behind the current international order is the formation of states around particular nations. In a few nations, there is relatively little ethnic diversity. Cultural and religious barriers do not complicate the delivery of social services nor do they affect the government's will to provide these services to all. But mono-ethnic modern nations are a rarity. Where a nation is composed of multiple ethnic groups, there are a variety of options for structuring relations that can be more or less inclusive. But in most instances, it will be the case that one ethnic group is in the center of power, while others are likely to be neglected or even worse.

Language
Even where there is ethnic diversity, the delivery of social services can be eased by the command of a common language, as has come to be the case in many of the industrialized societies or in Indonesia or China. But in other contexts, the respective groups command different languages. Social services can either recognize this difference and be accommodative, or ignore it.

Geography
Possibly the most powerful force leading to peripheralization is national scale. The larger the scale, the more effort that is required in terms of serial communication and transportation to link the center with the periphery. Administrative modifications such as decentralization can ameliorate this condition, but it still remains the case that large nations tend to do the poorest job in providing social services to their entire population. In large nations, those in rural areas particularly remote from the capital are most likely to be peripheralized. The Indian subcontinent is somewhat of an extreme case; in India in 1981, 67.3 percent of rural young people aged 15-19 were illiterate compared to 34.9 percent of urban young people; in nearby Pakistan, the difference was even more extreme, 82.6 percent versus 53.1 percent. In rural Pakistan, 92.7 percent of rural females 15-19 years old were illiterate! (Carceles, 1990: 17.) While physical distance from the center is a critical determinant of peripherilization, it is also often the case that large numbers of peripherilized can be found near the center, in shanty towns, townships, or as in the U.S., in urban ghettos.

Difficult Terrain
Aggravating national scale are such factors as low population density, which makes it difficult to reach sufficient numbers of people with standard approaches for the delivery of social services. Similarly, where a population is located in difficult terrain such as on islands or in mountains or jungles that lack roads, these difficulties are compounded.

GOVERNMENT STRUCTURE AND POLICY

The actual resolution of these different interests is shaped through the political-administrative process. Governments tend to reflect these other factors to some degree, but also it can be argued they have a life of their own. Our historical work has identified six different political-administrative patterns, that vary in terms of degree of centralization, inclusiveness of representation at the policy level, local control of revenues and services, and openness to private initiative. These are the Continental, Lowland, Japanese, Socialist, English, and American variants.

In our judgement, these structures vary in their attentiveness to peripheral areas in somewhat the following manner: The Japanese polity may be the most responsive to the periphery, simply because it does not acknowledge class, ethnic, or geographic differences. The socialist structures rank second in terms of attentiveness. The decentralized structures, while having the potential for incorporating various social and ethnic interests, often are dominated by a single ruling group, and thus seem to be least attentive.

Relative attentiveness is expressed through the various policies devised by the respective polities. One simple indicator is the relative equity in government expenditures by region and subregion down to the operational units for the delivery of social services. While the Japanese and socialist governments are relatively more attentive in reaching out to the periphery, we would argue that even they are deficient. The modern state, whatever the pattern, is ultimately committed to serving the center.

THE DIFFUSION OF MODERNISM AND PERIPHERALISM

While the modern century has focused on realizing the ideal of equality, it is remarkable that few official statistics have been devised to measure its progress in realizing this ideal. Indeed, only in recent years have scholars begun to probe this issue, and most of the indicators they have proposed (e.g. Gini indices of regional equality, of income distribution, of the distribution of social services) have yet to be adapted by national governments or international agencies. It is as if the modern state was committed to the rhetoric of equality but not the reality.

Turning to the scholarly work on equality and peripheralism, two patterns of analysis are evident. The first pattern relies on a straight count of the proportion of the target population that receives a particular service. In the field of education, this research often focuses on enrollment ratios, the proportion of the primary age group in a nation who attend primary schools or the proportion of the secondary age group who attend secondary schools. Data on these indicators tend to be widely available, and thus are more amenable to comparative analysis. Table 1.1., below, which relates national differences in these proportions to various national characteristics, again shows that equality of provision is affected by national income level, degree of urbanism, extent of population concentration, national scale, ethnic homogeneity, government centralism, and even government tradition.

The second research tradition attempts to establish measures of the spread of services between geographical units of societies, that can then be compared across societies. Statistics such as Gini coefficients and coefficients of variation are typically employed.

The most extensive work has focused on income distribution, and generally finds a curvilinear pattern with relative equal income distribution in the least and most developed countries and greater inequality in the intermediate stages. However, while income is somewhat evenly distributed in advanced societies, between these societies there are wide variations that seem to be related to several of the factors we have noted above: greater ethnic and linguistic diversity, geographic dispersion, and political decentralization are all correlated with greater income inequality. Other studies which focus on the equality of government expenditures or equality in the provision of services tend to find a similar pattern.

Table 1.1. Cross-National Correlates of Enrollment Ratios, 1985

Correlate	Primary Enrollment Ratio	Secondary Enrollment Ratio
GNP Per Capita	.29	.67
Population	.16	.04
Population Density	.10	.20
Urbanization	.52	.81
Ethnic Complexity	-.36	-.45
Centralized Govt.	-.37	-.53
Centralized Finance	-.20	-.40
English Tradition	-.09	-.04
French Tradition	-.30	-.46

Source: PIE Data Bank

In the field of education, research studies carried out largely in the more advanced societies suggest a consistent urban (central) bias in academic achievement, with elite (and often) private schools performing well above national norms. Regional and ethnic differences are also substantial. Some efforts have been made to compute indicators of degree of spread (typically the coefficient of variation in national scores, or ratios of urban to rural scores) and relate these indicators to national characteristics. Again, there is evidence suggesting that the more centralized and ethnically more homogeneous societies achieve greater equality.

In poorer countries, an even more fundamental concern than academic achievement is school enrollments. As noted above, the enrollment rates are comparatively low in India. However, in the state of Kerala, nearly all children enroll in the primary grades and 88 percent of the age cohort are enrolled in secondary schools. Thus Kerala has a literacy rate of 70.4 percent, or twice the national average. (Weiner, 1991: 175.) So within nations, not only are there rural-urban but also important regional differences that require examination.

THE UPPER LIMIT OF MODERN EDUCATION

The biases of the modern state are less evident in good times when the economy is thriving, and the government can spare resources to accommodate various interests. But when the modern state faces hard times, it is liable to turn inwards and focus on its core interests and clients; the periphery becomes neglected.

For much of the period since World War II through the early seventies, most national economies enjoyed relatively stable growth and government enjoyed a steady expansion of revenues. Education benefited from this growth. Expanding government budgets resulted in an expansion of educational facilities, and in most nations in an increase in pupil enrollment ratios. Figure 1.1 provides a comparison of historical trends in primary-level pupil enrollment ratios by geographic region. In all of the major regions of the world, the ratios steadily increased through at least the early seventies. But African levels were initially lower and thus did not climb to the same level as the other regions. Latin America, Asia, Europe, North America (the latter two plotted together with the Middle East as EMENA) had relatively high levels from the beginning, and thus did not experience much change.

Figure 1.1. Growth in Educational Participation Since 1960

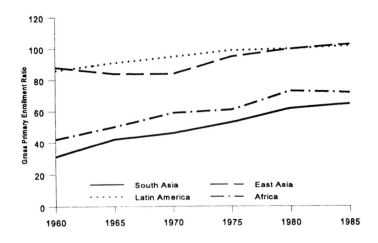

Source: Crouch, Spratt, and Cubeddu, 1992.

But the events surrounding the "oil shock" led to a major interruption of the upward trend. As governments faced a leveling of revenues, they had to make hard choices on priorities. According to one study, these choices more often than not involved a reduction in real expenditures for education (Lewin and Little, 1982). With leveling or declining educational expenditures and, due to population grown, an expanding number of school-aged youth, enrollment ratios tended to stabilize or even, in several cases, to decline. A recent UNESCO study indicates over the eighties that enrollment ratios for the primary level have decreased in 26 nations and have shown no advance in another 23. (Carceles, 1990: 18.) This pattern of stabilization has continued into the nineties, even as the world economy has begun to improve. Thus the cross-national educational gaps, which once seemed to be narrowing, became a new area of concern.

Aggregate national statistics are based on summations of local statistics. When national totals go down, it is often the case that some areas go down faster than others. In the recent downward shift in enrollment ratios, it turns out at least for some countries that the peripheral or rural areas have suffered sharper declines than the central or urban areas.

LESSONS FROM THE PRIVATE SECTOR

The strategies of nations may gain some insights from the experience of large business corporations, which also traditionally have attempted to reach diverse markets in dispersed localities with centralized management structures. For a time, large multinational corporations such as General Motors, Caterpillar, IBM, and Sony achieved considerable success with their centralized structures. But in recent years there have been major changes. Peters's and Waterman's *In Search of Excellence* (1982) tells how the most successful among these corporations have placed a new emphasis on "Getting Close to the Customer" and "Nichemanship."

This change can be illustrated by focusing on a common product such as a wristwatch. In the early stages of the new quartz watches, most of the multinational watchmakers concentrated on a small number of models which they mass-produced in large quantities and marketed throughout their national and even international markets. Low prices made these watches competitive, and, at least for the first few years, sales were impressive. But at a certain point, sales slacked off. Yet there were large numbers of potential clients who had not bought the new watches. The companies realized they had to get closer to the customer. And to do so they radically decentralized both marketing and production. Separate and largely independent units were established with the companies to focus on distinctive markets—young people, sports people, swimmers, joggers, musicians, classy dressers, casual dressers. The once uniform market was divided up into dozens of smaller niches, and unique approaches were developed that conformed to the needs of each of these niches. The considerable interest of employees in the small independent units in developing unique products resulted in continuing high-quality production, but with much greater diversity than had previously been possible. In this way, sales were once again invigorated and a near saturation of many markets was realized.

PUTTING THE PERIPHERY FIRST

In the production of watches, a fundamental realignment of corporate strategy was required. The corporate centers came to realize they did not or could not have all the answers; they thus streamlined the role of the center to the formulation of broad goals, and the development of standards of accountability for the various quasi-autonomous production/marketing units. Within the limits of this framework, the diverse units were granted the freedom to work close to their clients. The successful corporation made a clear distinction between the center and the field—or what we call here the periphery.

In education, we think such a distinction is also required. We think it is important to recognize that the established programs favor those at the center, and slight those distant from the center, those in the periphery. A new approach is needed which will give more attention to the periphery.

The introduction of the concept of "Periphery" into the strategic vocabulary of educators can provide a point of departure for reappraising the limitations of established approaches and legitimizing the development of new strategies. Thus we believe that the recognition of the periphery is a critical first step towards starting the second half of the journey towards EFA. Our conclusions are not especially new, for there already is in the lore of education considerable recognition of nontraditional approaches, of nonformal education and so on. But it may be that these approaches do not have a forceful rationale, and for that reason were relegated to a secondary status in government strategies.

RATIONALE FOR A NEW STRATEGY

In earlier times governments may have been able to ignore the periphery or give it short shrift. But we would argue that those days are past. In part, yes, the argument is moral—governments should keep their promises. But there are also practical reasons. On the political front, it is now apparent that governments who fail to relate effectively to their peripheries fall apart—e.g., the former Soviet Union and possibly India.

And there is also a strong economic rationale as well. Whereas in the past, most individuals could make a reasonable livelihood through hard physical work or personal charm, this is no longer the case. As the world economy moves into a new stage where the processing of codified knowledge is the key to success, it is no longer justifiable on economic grounds to leave people unprepared.

THE ELEMENTS OF A NEW STRATEGY

While governments and international agencies have repeatedly issued calls to eradicate illiteracy and spread enlightenment, and in most instances have set up elaborate programs of public education, there are today far more people who cannot read than there were in 1789 or 1945. Clearly the established educational programs miss large proportions of the world's citizenry.

In thinking about what has gone wrong, we have reached the conclusion that the established programs may be incapable of making much further progress. They may have reached an upper limit. And the EFA initiative, channeled through international donors and central governments, offers little that is new. What are the limits of modern education, and what needs to be changed?

1. The established programs tend to be tailored to the standard situation, that found in the large cities and places of population concentration. To be specific, the established programs are based on:

- A system of centrally funded instructional and infrastructure support that considers schools as the major unit for planning rather than the communities which they serve, and treats all schools as equal, independent of the school's resource base or the challenge it confronts;
- A centrally devised curriculum, typically authorizing instruction in the metropolitan language; centrally produced textbooks;
- A school premised on separate classes for separate grades;
- Teachers trained for standard settings, and rewarded by a salary schedule and a promotion ladder that culminates in a central bureaucratic office;
- Principals appointed from the center who have authority to operate independent of community will.

Modifications of these programs are often introduced to accommodate settings that differ from the standard. But these modifications on the "One Best System" are not enough.

2. Rather than seek modifications to central formulas, if the concern is to reach to the periphery, it will be necessary to encourage unique approaches for a diversity of unique local settings. These unique approaches may include multigrade classrooms, locally tailored curricula and learning materials, community involvement in decision making and instruction, locally recruited and specially trained teachers, and instruction in the local language.

3. While the focus of central educational systems is on the schools established by the center, it should be on communities and their educational needs. Communities have legitimate leaders who can become partners in education, helping to identify priorities, mobilize local resources, propose approaches that fit local circumstances, and provide continuity.

4. Central support for schools tends to provide equal support for each educational administrative unit, based on the number of pupils that unit serves:

- But these formulas provide equal funding for unequal conditions. Some areas are more challenging, because of difficult terrain, dispersed populations, and lack of pupil preparedness; these are the peripheral areas. A truly equal funding formula would provide support in direct ratio to the challenge.
- These formulas do not take into account the differential ability of the pupils within the administrative units to support education. An equalizing formula

favorable to the periphery would provide central support in inverse ratio to a local area's ability to support education.

5. Central funding, when channeled through local administrative units, can often lead to waste and excessive regulation. New approaches to funding need to be considered that are more equitable and that reward performance:

- Central support to administrative units enables these units to allocate funds and other resources between schools, according to criteria decided by the administrators often with little concern for the differential need of schools. A more equitable approach would be to channel funds and resources directly to the schools.
- Funding directed to schools might be provided in response to budget requests by schools, and allocated in such a manner as to provide incentives for those schools that are most prepared to help themselves. Alternately, funding might be provided in proportion to school improvement in academic or other areas of performance.

CONCLUSION

In this first chapter, we have explored the concept of periphery and outlined some of the forces behind peripheralization. This seems important, because without understanding what is behind peripheralization, we will not know where to start in altering the situation.

But we see little diminution in the strength of these factors. Thus we reach the somewhat pessimistic conclusion that there is little objective evidence to suggest that the prevailing governments of the contemporary world are likely to improve on their record of promoting enlightenment until they face up to their limitations. However, as nations come to recognize the need to serve their peripheries, our analytical work suggests some handles on which to attach their efforts. The next chapter will present a variety of real examples of the *miseducation* of children in peripheral areas, reinforcing the need for the reconceptualization of schooling for peripheral groups. The chapters that follow will develop in greater detail strategies that will enable educators to reach the periphery.

Bibliography

Benavot, Aron, and Phyllis Riddle. "The Expansion of Primary Education: 1870-1940. Trends and Issues." *Sociology of Education* 61 (July 1988): 191-200.

Blum, Carol. *Rousseau and the Republic of Virtue: The Language of Politics in the French Revolution.* Ithaca, NY: Cornell University Press, 1986.

Carceles, Gabriel. "World Literacy Prospects at the Turn of the Century: Is the Objective of Literacy for All by the Year 2000 Statistically Plausible?" *Comparative Education Review* v 34, n 1 (Feb. 1990): 4-20.

Carnoy, Martin, and Joel Samoff. *Education and Social Transition in the Third World.* Princeton: Princeton University Press, 1989.

Crouch, Luis A., Jennifer Spratt, and Luis M. Cubeddu. "Examining Social and Economic Impacts of Educational Investment and Participation in Developing Countries: the Educational Impacts Model (EIM) Approach." *BRIDGES Research Report Series* No. 12 (April 1992).

Cummings, William K. *Education and Equality in Japan.* Princeton: Princeton University Press, 1980.

Cummings, William K., and Abbey Riddell. "Alternative Policies for the Finance, Control, and Delivery of Basic Education." HIID Occasional Papers, 1992.

Fuller, Wayne. *The Old Country School: The Story of Rural Education in the Middle West.* Chicago: The University of Chicago Press, 1982.

Gildea, Robert. *Education in Provincial France 1800-1914.* Oxford: Clarendon Press, 1983.

Glenn, Charles Leslie, Jr. *The Myth of the Common School.* Amherst: The University of Massachusetts Press, 1988.

Kennedy, Paul. *The Rise and Fall of the Great Powers.* New York: Random House, 1989.

Legrand, Lois. *L'influence du positivisme dan l'oeuvre scolaire de Jules Ferry: Les origines de la laïcité.* Paris: Marcel Riviere, 1961.

Lewin, Keith, Angela Little, and Chrisotopher Colclough. "Adjusting to the 1980s: Taking Stock of Educational Expenditure." In International Development

Research Centre (Canada), *Financing Education Development: Proceedings of an International Seminar.* Mont Sainte Marie, Canada, May 19-21, 1982.

Ministry of Education, Science, and Culture. *Japan's Modern Educational System: A History of the First Hundred Years.* Tokyo: 1980.

Passin, Herbert. *Society and Education in Japan.* New York: Teachers College Press, 1965.

Peters, Thomas J., and Robert H. Waterman. *In Search of Excellence.* New York: Warner Books, 1982.

Pierre, Victor. *L'Ecole sous la Revolution francaise.* Paris: Librairie de la Société Bibliographique, 1881.

Ringer, Fritz K. *Education and Society in Modern Europe.* Bloomington: Indiana University Press, 1979.

Shils, Edward. *Center and Periphery: Essays in Macrosociology.* Chicago: University of Chicago Press, 1975.

Tyack, David B. *The One Best System: A History of American Urban Education.* Cambridge, MA: Harvard University Press, 1974.

UNDP, UNESCO, UNICEF, and World Bank. *World Declaration on Education for All and Framework for Action to Meet Basic Learning Needs.* Jomtien, Thailand, March 5-9, 1990.

Weiner, Myron. *The Child and the State in India.* Princeton: Princeton University Press, 1991.

CHAPTER 2

The Last Frontiers of Education for All
A Close-Up of Schools in the Periphery

H. Dean Nielsen

SCHOOL LIFE IN THE PERIPHERY

In the middle of Guizhou Province, a mountainous state in the southwest of China, lies the county of Leigong Shan or Thunder God Mountain. The county is part of the region of Kaili, classified by the People's Republic of China as politically autonomous, because its population consists mostly of ethnic minorities (predominantly Miao). The Miaos of Kaili are cousins to those in Thailand, Laos, and Cambodia, sharing much with them in the way of language and culture.

Three local researchers and I visited schools in a series of small, isolated Miao villages in Leigong County, including one perched on a steep bank above Peach River. We find Peach River School, housed in a small, two-room building, in session. In one room, 19 first graders (10 girls and 9 boys) are being led in a Civics lesson by an older first grader—older because he had already repeated the grade twice. With a stick he points to a series of Chinese characters, one by one, as the children recite "My Fatherland Is the People's Republic of China." One of my companions stops the chant and points to a character in the middle of the sequence. None of the children can read it.

Most instruction and all textbooks in this village school are in Mandarin or standard Chinese, a tongue which most of the children in Peach River have never used prior to entering school. And, although some teaching in the first two grades is in the Miao language, all *language* learning and all *reading* and *writing* are in standard Chinese. Most pupils will leave this first-grade class without knowing how to do either.

In the other room, four second graders are clustered in a dark corner, gazing at open textbooks, while the teacher, a white-haired male, reads to them. Their field implements lay on the nearby table. All four are boys.

Since the village and the school are very small, only two grades are taught in Peach River. Any child wishing to go beyond the second grade has to enroll in the full-size school in the township center. Since this school is several hours away by foot, Peach River children who attend it generally stay in small but crowded hostels, where they cook for themselves. Girls from Peach River almost never make it to the Township school; in fact, very few make it past the first grade. Their contribution to family subsistence, daily tasks such as fetching water and firewood and/or tending infants, keeps them more tied to the household than boys, whose work is more seasonal. Moreover, while Miao boys and girls, like minority group children anywhere, both have difficulty learning in the dominant (national) language, girls generally receive less encouragement and support from home and school, and thus drop out more readily.

In Leigong County as a whole the participation of girls in primary education is only between 20 and 30 percent; for boys, around 80. Female teachers in the region are even rarer than female pupils. An exception is the mother of one of my co-researchers. For years she taught at a village school. Her daughter (my colleague) followed her into teaching and now is a lecturer at a provincial university. Her grandson at four years can already read and write full sentences in Chinese characters. It is clear that this teacher has had a profound effect on her family as well as on generations of children (particularly the girls) from other Miao families.

Far to the south on the Indonesian island of Borneo is the equatorial province of Central Kalimantan. This province, a large tropical rain forest, has eleven major river systems. Near the headwaters of one of the largest systems is the remote subdistrict of Sanaman Mantikei. Since the attempt to visit the remotest village in this system was frustrated by shallow water and treacherous rapids, my companion and I visit a cluster of small Dayak villages near a lumber camp. The first village, called Kuluk Habuhus (Bald Head), has, to our surprise, two primary schools. The first was organized years ago and originally housed in a building provided by the community. The second was established a decade or so ago during the height of Indonesia's massive *INPRES* (Presidential Instruction) school-building program. The new school's two buildings were placed near the old school, and when the old building decayed beyond use, the two decided to share the same premises. Now there are two schools using the same buildings, one having 25 students in two grades (1 and 2), and the other 80 students in five grades (2-6). Both schools have only one teacher (the second school having lost two to transfers recently). The teacher who oversees five classes keeps the 15-20 pupils in each in separate classrooms, and visits each in turn, giving traditional teacher-centered lessons. Thus, each of his classes gets only one-fifth of a full day's instruction. And although each school on the premises has a small second-grade class (10 and 15 students, respectively), the two groups of second graders are kept separate, since they belong to different schools.

The next village upstream is very near. Its small, one-room school is only six minutes away by trail. It has only 33 pupils in four grades, yet has four teachers. Thus, within a six-minute radius, there are three schools where there could easily be one, since the villages' households are closely clustered and the total number of pupils is only 138. With a total teaching staff of six, such a school could have one teacher per class, with an average pupil-teacher ratio of 23:1, just under the national average. Instead the pupil-teacher ratios of the three schools are 8:1, 25:1, and 80:1.

Hundreds of miles to the east on the Indonesian half of the island of New Guinea is the province of Irian Jaya. In its upland Baliem River Valley near the highest mountains in the country is the district of Wamena. In a junior secondary school in one of its remote subdistricts the principal has been working for more than a decade to add local color to the school's curriculum. He has created a small oasis of local and nonlocal plants, which have been found, through experiments conducted by him and his students, to thrive in the local environment. Through such activities he has taught the students how to raise flowers, vegetables, and trees, and has helped them to plant these at home and throughout the surrounding countryside. In addition, he has helped the students make fish ponds and care for livestock, using sustainable ecosystems which provide natural fertilizer and pest control for the plants.

Frustrated by his inability to convey to his classes the idea of their living on an island, he has dug a large pond in the middle of which he has fashioned a small island in the shape of their province, New Guinea. He has also built several small dormitories on school property with the help of the students, temporary residences for those who live beyond walking distance of the school. The building design is indigenous and materials are local. The principal uses their construction as a context for teaching students building skills and local crafts.

The aim of this dedicated rural educator has been to equip students with knowledge and skills that they can use to improve their livelihood in the village. Ironically, over the past few years enrollments in his school have been falling. A paved road has recently been built which links the village with the district capital, a town with an airport and a growing tourist trade. Village youth have begun to seek schooling in the town where they can also earn a few tourist dollars. Many will drop out of school; those who graduate will find that the town's urbanized curriculum has provided them little help or incentive for returning and contributing to their villages.

These landscapes reveal what could be called the "unfinished business" of the Education for All movement. In these frontier areas, at the end of the road or waterway, schools have been built and teachers provided, much to the credit of the respective governments, but access and quality are still far below national standards. The 1990 World Conference on Education for All in Jomtien, Thailand, affirmed two basic ideals: first, that there should be equal access to basic education for boys and girls, and second, "Education for All" means access to quality—at least sufficient to lay the foundations for better life opportunities for graduates. (UNDP, UNESCO, UNICEF, World Bank, 1990.)

What makes this business urgent is the fact that the frontiers of Education for All are often found at the frontiers of nations, in the sense that a) they exist in marginal, sparsely populated areas along national borders (the case with almost every Asian country), and b) they represent major future growth centers of untold opportunities and natural resources. Globalization trends in the form of breakthroughs in communications, transportation, and trade in these frontier areas have drawn people on national borders into closer contact with one another, creating prospects of either conflict or peaceful coexistence. Basic education of sufficient depth, breadth, and quality is needed in these frontier areas to prepare people to deal peacefully and reasonably with one another. On the other hand, global economic development will inevitably bring powerful national and multinational enterprises into these promising frontier areas. The human resources in these areas will need sufficient basic education and skills so that they will be able to participate in and benefit from this development, and so that they can understand and be able to stand up for their rights in case, for example, socially or environmentally unsound practices are introduced (as has already been done by the logging industry in Borneo). In short, at the frontiers of nations (and the Education for All movement), basic education of sufficient quality is needed to allow marginal populations to participate in and enjoy the fruits of global economic development, while at the same time to safeguard the integrity of their communities and natural environment.

But what is it that has until now stood in the way of quality education for all in these frontier areas near the outer limits of government service delivery?

Analysts of core-periphery disparities (Chambers, 1983; Myrdal, 1968) have described the strong centripetal forces which have drawn resources and educated people away from the peripheries and in towards the cores. "In the cores," states Chambers, "there is a mutual attraction and reinforcement of power, prestige, resources, professionals, professional training, and the capacity to generate and disseminate knowledge." (Chambers, 1983: 4.) In contrast, those in the periphery are caught in pernicious webs of poverty, isolation, powerlessness, vulnerability, and physical weakness, often caused by those in the core by design or simple neglect. Given the obvious disparities of wealth and power between the core and the periphery, it is not surprising that resources for education in the core almost always exceed those in the periphery.

Less obvious, even to school managers, are the conditions in the periphery which typically make standard models of schooling so ineffective there. Thus, all too often governments respond to the call for more equity in educational access by implanting the urban school into the peripheral area; by making the final linear extension of the conventional school system. Behind this is the fact that most educational planners have never visited the communities at the outer limits of their systems; they, like the "rural development tourists" of the above Chambers book, simply have no concept of life and conditions there.

Their folly is illustrated by a simple principle of Einsteinian physics: objects traveling near the speed of light will experience changes or distortions in mass, shape, and even time. By analogy, when education systems are extended to the outer limits of the national population , distortions occur in the shape of schools and the way in which they operate. Let's go back to Peach River and Bald Head (Kuluk Habuhus) for examples. In Peach River, conventional concepts of schooling were being applied: namely students were segregated by grade and taught by a trained teacher in the dominant national language. Since the school only had two classrooms and one trained teacher, it was limited to teaching two grades. Requiring the rest to seek schooling in a faraway town presented a barrier which virtually none of the girls—tied to their households by work obligations—could overcome. The use of the national language became a barrier to the acquisition of reading and writing skills for both boys and girls, but lack of support at home and school put the girls especially at risk for dropping out.

In Kuluk Habuhus, the concepts that every hamlet should have a school and every class a teacher has led to some maldistribution of resources: for example the establishment of a four-classroom school with four teachers catering to 33 pupils within easy walking distance of two other small schools. In addition, a teacher's concept that each class, however small, should be taught separately in their own classrooms has meant that students in one school are on task for only about 20 percent of the day. Similar distortions in school time (time on task) were found in other places. For example, on a tiny Indonesian island near Singapore two teachers were sharing the teaching of 77 pupils, distributed across all six grades. Although the classes were small they were kept separate, and taught in two shifts: one in the early morning and one in the late morning. Thus the teachers had a regular work load, but the students were getting only about two and a half hours of instruction each day, hardly enough time to cover the curriculum and thus to acquire basic skills.

With this extension of the conventional school also comes the conventional curriculum. Centrally controlled systems like those in China and Indonesia have very little room for local content and activities. Consequently, children of the Miao community of Peach River, although technically members of an "autonomous" region, are still taught to recite "My Fatherland is the People's Republic of China," and an innovative, locally oriented school in New Guinea's Baliem River Valley is losing students. Parents might support the idea of local content in schools, but until official textbooks and leaving/entrance examinations reflect diversity, they are not likely to run the risk of their children being left behind.

I conclude that working on the frontiers of Education for All—now and into the twenty-first century—requires us to abandon the concept of conventional schooling for all. The vain attempts to push the conventional school to the outer limits only leads to distortions in school shape and learning time, and ultimately, educational quality and student learning outcomes. What we need is a set of new concepts for working on the frontier. Most importantly, we need new concepts of the school, the curriculum, the teacher, and school management.

THE SCHOOL

The prevailing concept of the school today, in developed as well as developing countries, is based on the industrial model. We even use an input-process-output framework to explain what happens in them. Pupils, the input, are strictly age-graded and then processed in batches, being moved from one level to the next, until they come to the end of the assembly line, where they are tested, certified, and released into the market place. Everyone knows that children of the same age group vary enormously in their rate of development and their intellectual capacity, but management efficiency requires that they be processed in batches anyway. Also, a single teacher can comfortably handle a student load of 25 to 40 pupils, although the age-grading model keeps classes separate even if there is only a handful of pupils at each level.

One new concept of the school for the frontier is actually an old concept, a notion compatible with the "time-travel" option available to those working at the outer limits. The old concept is that of the "one-room school," a celebrated institution in frontier America (Fuller, 1982). This kind of school is built more on the "family model" of education than the current industrial model. In it children are not strictly segregated according to age and grade, but grouped in multigrade classrooms. An entire school can thus be managed by one or two teachers. The Indonesian "small school," which is already being used in many remote areas throughout the country, employs some forms of multigrade teaching, especially self- and small-group instruction using self-instructional modules and worksheets. In addition, pioneer teachers in remote areas in Indonesia and elsewhere have often invented their own one-room school routines, which are well adapted to local conditions but rarely recognized and validated.

Multigrade teaching is, to be sure, a more complex model than the conventional age-graded model, but in the context of small frontier schools (where an entire school may have no more than 35 students), it generally presents the teacher no heavier student load than that of her urban counterpart. Such a model would solve Peach River's problem of having to send its few third through sixth graders off to a boarding school; it would also solve the 20 percent time-on-task problem at Bald Head, and the double-shifting mentioned above.

Educators throughout the world are beginning to recognize that multigrade teaching situations already exist in their countries—either because schools are just now being pushed into frontier areas or they are shrinking due to family planning and urban migration trends. Sometimes multigrade teaching has existed for years but in a sort of invisible, unacknowledged way—a "temporary" problem to be solved once more teachers are available.

New interest in multigrade teaching, perhaps spurred by the Education for All movement, has led to a growing body of research in this field (also described in chapter 7 of this volume). A recent *Handbook on the Multigrade Classroom* (Miller, 1989) presented a review of 23 studies of multigrade teaching in different parts of the world (mostly the industrialized North and Australia). The research results were encouraging: in terms of cognitive achievement, students from schools which used multigrade teaching fared just as well as their single-grade counterparts; with respect to affective measures, most studies showed more positive developments on the part of multigrade-classroom students, in terms of learning self-concept, attitude towards school, cooperation, and feelings towards their fellow students and teachers. Multigrade were compared to single-grade classrooms in nine studies, using 23 separate measures of student attitudes. "Sixty-five percent of the measures favored the multigrade classroom at a significant level, 13 percent indicated a trend toward multigrade students out-performing their single-grade counterparts, and 22 percent revealed no difference between the classroom types. Only one measure favored the single-grade classroom." (Miller, 1989: 9.)

These studies were all conducted in developed countries; to date there have been very few studies conducted in the developing world. One of the few was recently conducted in the tiny Central American country of Belize, set up under the Learning Technologies Project sponsored by USAID. One component of the study included identification and observation of schools which had established—on their own—particularly effective forms of multigrade teaching, so that there experiences and methods could be documented, legitimized, and made available to others. I had the chance to observe one such school in operation: a one-room school at Willow's Bank, a few hours' drive from the district capital. The school has 77 students distributed across two levels of kindergarten and six primary grades. It has two teachers, who have been there for 16 years and 12 years, respectively. The two kindergarten levels and grades one and two are clustered around the teacher at one end of the long room; grades three through six are clustered around the second teacher at the other end. In one corner of the building is a small library and activity center. During one hour the teacher set things up so that the preschoolers were helping each other with word recognition, while the first graders were working at their seats on math problems which had been written on the blackboard. The second graders were playing a spelling game led by one of their group members. At the other end of the room, the teacher had the third graders solving math problems on the blackboard, the fourth graders reading a story, and the fifth and sixth graders working together on a geography assignment. He moved smoothly and continuously from one group to another, giving encouragement, correcting mistakes, and answering questions. The amazing thing about this classroom was that 100 percent of the students were engaged in their tasks, and that six different lessons were going on at the same time. The teachers had, on their own, developed some extraordinary classroom management skills over the years.

It is research findings and examples like those which have begun to give multigrade teaching the aura of *respectability*. In fact, in some places (such as British Columbia in Canada) it is seen as not just an alternate way of organizing instruction, but the *preferred way* for all schools. Whether the one-room school will make a comeback in the industrialized countries during the twenty-first century is anybody's guess, but clearly such a school is a fitting substitute for the conventional school in new frontier areas.

THE CURRICULUM
It has been done so many times that it is almost trite to assert that a reconceptualized curriculum for the periphery should be relevant to the community and its needs, values, and aspirations. Indeed the *World Declaration on Education for All* (UNDP, et al., 1990: Article 5) maintains that "primary education must be universal, ensure that the basic learning needs of all children are satisfied, and *take into consideration the culture, needs and opportunities of the community*" (italics added for emphasis). Nevertheless, instances of successful local involvement in curricular planning and decision making are rare. As suggested above, there is still an ambivalence among both the producers and consumers of education about locally constructed curricula. The producers worry about a loss of control and a possible erosion of standards; consumers worry about the missing material that would help them compete for high-level schooling and jobs.

In fact there are some trade-offs in moving towards a more locally controlled curriculum, and some possible extremes to look out for. At one extreme is the isolationist curriculum which focuses only on local topics and opportunities; at the other is the metropolitan curriculum, which is geared towards the urban, industrialized world. The appropriate curriculum for peripheral areas would be an accommodation between the two extremes: a curriculum which adequately addresses local problems and needs, but which also maintains an opening towards the national and international communities and their opportunities.

Creating a balanced curriculum of this sort is not simply a matter of developing new curricular guidelines, objectives, and topics. In order for such a curriculum to work, attention will also need to be paid to textbooks (providing those with both local and "metropolitan content"), and examinations (de-emphasizing standardized completion and selection examinations). For example, the Miaos of Southwest China may do well to cover social studies or language arts in their own language, but unless they have learning materials to match those objectives they will not go very far.

Similarly, an innovative, locally oriented principal in Indonesia will quickly lose ground if his/her graduates find they cannot pass the admission examinations for the next level of schooling.

Another crucial issue in working through this model is, *How local is local?* Clearly it is not practical for each community to have its own unique curriculum, nor is it reasonable to expect that planning at the provincial level will adequately address the diversity that is likely to exist within it. In this discussion of the periphery a reasonable concept of "local" for purposes of curricular planning may be cultural and linguistic communities. In the relatively rare cases in periphery where cultural groups are intermingled, "local" may need to be defined in more geographical terms.

Ultimately, the ideal would be for each teacher to have a strong hand in creating curriculum for his/her own students, according to individual and group needs and interests. The most active and creative teachers already do this, but such local initiative is rarely encouraged, except in private schools or school-based management systems. Working on the frontiers of the educational system, where multigrade teaching is often required, will demand more creativity and decision making by the individual teachers. This in turn will require bold new ideas concerning the selection, training, and professional support of teachers for the periphery, a topic to which we turn next.

THE TEACHER

Like the school and curriculum, the concept of the frontier teacher will also need to be changed. In the current industrial system, teachers are essentially assembly-line workers, adding value to students who are passed up to their levels. A teacher in a small village school will need to operate more like a professional chef in a crowded restaurant, creating many fine dishes at the same time, each with its own ingredients, flavoring, cooking temperature, and time. Working like this is clearly more demanding and it requires special training, but, as the example of Willows Bank shows, it is within the reach of rural teachers. The fact that it is more demanding makes a special case for providing incentive pay to multigrade teachers, at least equivalent to the amount that they forego in extra income because of the need for extra lesson-preparation time.

The concept of teacher selection for these frontier areas also needs serious re-examination. The general teacher-selection method is for teacher trainees to be selected on the basis of competitive testing. Since in places like Indonesia there is now a surplus of trained teachers, those successful in obtaining teaching appointments are generally from the better schools in the urban areas. These new appointees may initially accept teaching appointments in remote areas as a way into the profession, but will soon find the means to be transferred out. The teacher trainees who come from the remote regions and who would stay there if assigned— generally the best and brightest from their villages—are generally screened out of the profession because of their inability to compete with their urban counterparts. A related problem is that noted in Guizhou Province. Since girls rarely make it through primary school, there are very few female teaching candidates, and thus village girls rarely see an educated female role model. What these conditions seem to call for are new mechanisms of teacher selection, methods which would allow the best and brightest among village boys *and girls* to be identified, trained, and placed as remote village teachers.

One example of the above is a new program recently launched in Indonesia by the Ministry of Education and the Social Welfare Ministry for selectively recruiting those education-school graduates from remote areas for new jobs in select isolated villages. Another encouraging sign is that Indonesia's new program for training primary-school teachers at the post-secondary level also will encourage colleges to obtain some of their candidates from rural areas by "talent scouting." For such programs to work they will need to include scholarship support for the candidates selected as well as assurances that they will get a teacher appointment. In exchange, there should be some assurance from the trainees that they will accept and remain in appointments in or near their villages. In addition, teachers who are to be assigned to work in such villages need to be trained in multigrade management. This is not as straightforward as one may think. Although most countries in the world have at least a few multigrade classrooms, teachers are almost never trained to work in them. Often this is because there are no small village schools close enough to the college to serve as sites for student teaching. In addition, teachers in remote areas often miss out on in-service training opportunities available in more populous areas. Innovative ways need to be developed to allow teachers in frontier areas to upgrade and modify their skills, perhaps through the use of teacher study groups, or, where teachers are too dispersed, through innovative use of electronic media (interactive radio programs or single-side band two-way radio communications). In fact, plans have been set into motion in Indonesia to experiment this year with different media packages in the delivery of a national teacher upgrading course (with a special module on multigrade teaching) to teachers in three remote area provinces.

SCHOOL MANAGEMENT

Finally, changes are needed in the concepts of school management. First is the concept of financial allocations. School systems generally allocate funds to schools on the basis of a standard per-student formula. The fact is, education in frontier areas is more expensive than that in the more populated regions. This is not only because of added transportation and communication costs; it is also because the cost of living in these areas is higher, often twice as high as in the provincial capitals. Supervision is also a big problems in such areas. Many remote areas I have visited do not have primary school supervisors. Where supervisors are available they often have impossible assignments: too many schools to visit over too large an area, at too high an expense. Rigid models are also applied to this aspect of education. School supervisors in Indonesia receive a standard transportation allocation of Rp 600 (about 30 cents U.S.) per school visit, whereas in some small island or remote river districts transportation to a single school may cost as much as Rp 10,000 (about $5).

What this reveals is once again the general principle that I have been developing: the application of bureaucratic formulas at the outer limits of the government's educational network leading to distortions. Working at the frontiers of Education for All requires a new approach to management problems: not bureaucratic, but problem solving in orientation. This applies both at the school level and at the district level.

Many primary-school curricula in Asia are now designed to promote problem-solving skills among children. Yet we educational managers and developers are among the worst problem solvers of all. Children learn by both direct instruction and by modeling the attitudes and behaviors of others. It is time for our educational systems and their personnel to model to the children the kinds of problem-solving skills that we are trying to teach them. In the management of the educational system, as in the classroom, this requires more latitude or authority for local or grass-roots decision making. In addition, it requires the development of simple tools for identifying and understanding problems. Most remote districts that I visit have the raw data for identifying and understanding serious systemic problems: but local administrators have neither the training nor the authority to use them in local problem solving. Part of the unfinished business of providing quality education for all in remote areas is to give administrators the training and the authority they need to engage in local problem solving.

CONCLUSION

Robert Chambers's influential book on rural development (1983) draws upon a biblical phase for its subtitle, "Putting the last first." Those who live in the remote areas, the ethnic and linguistic minorities, the marginal or nomadic populations, have indeed been last in terms of the quality of the educational services provided to them. If we are at all serious about reaching the last frontiers of education for all in this century, they will need to be put first.

Bibliography

Chambers, Robert. *Rural Development: Putting the Last First*. London: Longman, 1983.

Fuller, Wayne E. *The Old Country School: The Story of Rural Education in the Middle West*. Chicago: The University of Chicago Press, 1982.

Miller, Bruce. *The Multigrade Classroom: A Resource Handbook for Small, Rural Schools*. Portland, OR: Northwest Regional Educational Laboratory, 1989.

Myrdal, Gunnar. *Asian Drama; an Inquiry into the Poverty of Nations*. New York: Pantheon, 1968.

UNDP, UNESCO, UNICEF, and World Bank. *World Declaration on Education for All and Framework for Action to Meet Basic Learning Needs*. Jomtien, Thailand, March 5-9, 1990.

Strategies

CHAPTER 3

Improving School-Community Relations in the Periphery

James H. Williams

A PERSPECTIVE ON THE ROLE OF THE COMMUNITY IN THE PROVISION OF EDUCATION

The roles of the community and the state vis-à-vis education have changed, first, with the development of mass schooling, and second and more recently with the growing awareness of the limitations of government. Mass education, as currently organized, places relatively little value on the community, whether as a participant in the education of children, as a legitimate source of knowledge, or as a partner in the management of educational change. This may be changing. Conditions are ripe for a reconsideration of the contribution of the community, especially in the periphery, where the reach of the system usually falters.

Three Models of Education and Community

The community has not always played a passive role in children's education. Table 3.1 summarizes salient characteristics of three models of education, two historical and one currently emerging. Until the middle of the last century, responsibility for educating children rested with the community. (LeVine and White, 1986.) In a model we have called the traditional community-based education model, communities provided new generations of young people with the education necessary for transmitting local norms and economic skills. Education was deeply embedded in local social relations, and as such school and community were very closely linked. The government played a minor role. This model of education, while fostering social continuity and cohesion in the community, provided little basis for political integration at the national level and was of little use in meeting the specialized training needs of an industrial economy.

This community-based model has largely been replaced with government-provided education. First in the industrializing nations of the West, then in colonies ruled by Western countries, and finally in the newly independent nations themselves, governments have assumed responsibility for providing or regulating education. Initially, education was designed for the elite classes. Later it came to be viewed as

Table 3.1. Models of School and Community in the Provision of Education

	TRADITIONAL COMMUNITY-BASED EDUCATION	GOVERNMENT-PROVIDED EDUCATION	COLLABORATIVE GOVERNMENT-COMMUNITY EDUCATION
PURPOSE OF EDUCATION	Socialization into community; survival of community	Socialization into national culture; political, economic development of state	Socialization into national and local cultures; serves local and national "improvement"
NATURE OF KNOWLEDGE TO BE ACQUIRED	Transmission of local economic skills and community norms	Transmission of state-approved knowledge	Negotiable: usually state-approved knowledge adapted to local needs
EMPHASIS	On community	On individual and state	On individual as member of both community and state
VISION OF COMMUNITY'S ROLE	All-encompassing	Passive recipient; potentially disruptive of government's project	Negotiable: ranging from community as focal point of development effort to community as important arm of the government
ROLE OF GOVERNMENT	None to the extent that government does not interfere	Assumes complete responsibility for provision of education	Negotiable: ranging from source of support for education defined by community to virtually complete control

appropriate and necessary for everyone and as such was the proper business of government. Through government provision, education is delivered through formal school systems, coordinated by bureaucracies placed above the community. To a great extent the content of education has been standardized within and across countries (Ramirez and Rubinson, 1982; Ramirez and Boli, 1987; Meyer, Ramirez, Rubinson, and Boli-Bennett, 1977). In attempting to equalize access and promote political integration and economic development, governments diminished the role of the community. The community, if considered at all, has been viewed as backward, or at least in need of transformation.

The Limitations of Government Provision
While government-provided education has led to the greatest expansion of formal educational opportunities that the world has ever known, its limitations are becoming increasingly apparent. Most obviously, financial constraints have made it difficult for governments to provide metropolitan models of education to all who aspire to schooling. Many governments simply lack the funds to provide every community with a fully equipped school building and a full range of grades, teachers, and instructional materials.

Even when governments are able to provide all communities with schools, the schools often fail to provide all children with adequate education. In some places, children remain outside the schools, because of distance, demands at home, or cultural norms hostile to formal schooling. (Anderson, 1988.) In other areas, retention is the greater problem. Children enroll in school but drop out before reaching their educational potential. In still other areas, the greatest problem is the quality of learning. Whether through lack of inputs on the part of the school system or lack of motivation on the part of learners, students fail to learn what they might.

Whereas part of the problem is finance, another is management. Most developing education systems are administered with greatly expanded versions of arrangements set in place by colonial governments. Colonial education systems were designed to achieve elite goals, with much smaller systems serving more homogeneous and less dispersed populations. Many developing systems have expanded very rapidly, under conditions of relative austerity, but with little change in structure and little development of management capacity. As a result, many systems lack the personnel or capacity to provide all schools with adequate levels of administrative support.

Finally, even when a system is adequately managed, there are some aspects of the educational process that a government simply cannot attend to. Governments cannot, for example, provide a home environment that is supportive of student homework. Yet a number of studies suggest the importance of such support. Parents and community members can reinforce the work of the school, *if they believe in what the school is doing*. What governments can do is work to establish conditions that will foster such parental and community support.

The role of the community is being reevaluated. Various countries around the world, including some very poor ones, have initiated imaginative projects that provide a more important role for the community. While this "collaborative" model is still being defined, one common characteristic is clear. The collaborative model recognizes both government and community as important actors in education. For example, most communities lack the resources to provide children with an adequate education on their own and thus need the additional resources governments can provide. However, if governments exercise so much control over education that they begin to ignore community needs and values, then other problems arise. The collaborative model sees the school as supporting the community and its values, and the community supporting the school. In difficult areas, such as remote, rural villages, where resources are scarce and school- community relations tenuous, school-community collaboration may be the only possible strategy for realizing the goal of full access to quality education.

The Community and the Periphery
Peripheral groups do not participate in the mainstream of social, political, and economic life of the countries in which they live. They have relatively little economic or political power and thus tend to be underserved by education, health, and other public services. Although remote, rural populations are generally peripheral in this sense, poor urban dwellers may also lack access to power and services that characterize the periphery.

In the periphery, changes in the roles of school and community are particularly important for several reasons. First, any problem in the center, whether of access, quality, or finance and management, is typically more severe in the periphery. Thus, barring extraordinary government commitment, financial setbacks in the center will be manifested as more dramatic cutbacks in peripheral schools. (Jolly and Cornia, 1984.) Second, communities in peripheral areas tend to play a more important role in children's lives than do communities in the center. If, for example, local values are hostile to school attendance, the community's perspective will often prevail over the school's, and many children will remain outside the school. At the same time, the government's hand is usually weaker, so compulsory school attendance laws, for example, may be difficult or impossible to enforce. Third, given the general lack of services and government institutions in peripheral areas, schools are more visible. Thus, where there is demand for education, peripheral communities may take a more active interest in their schools than do communities in the center. By the same token, government interventions may have more effect.

Thus the issue of community demand or interest in education is particularly important in the periphery. Peripheral demand for education is typically characterized by one of two patterns. On the one hand, demand for education may be high and largely unmet. In such cases, evidence suggests that communities are willing to do a great deal to improve the quality of education with a minimum of government support. On the other hand, demand for education may be low due to cultural, ethnic, or other differences with the center; lack of felt need for schooling; or other reasons. In such cases, an appropriate initial response by governments would be to adapt schooling to better meet community values and needs. In either case, the community plays an important role in schooling, whether acknowledged, planned for, or not. Implications for the periphery are outlined in Table 3.2.

Table 3.2. Local Demand and the Role of the Community

DIMENSION	HIGH LOCAL DEMAND	LOW LOCAL DEMAND
INITIAL ATTITUDE OF COMMUNITY TOWARD SCHOOL	Positive	Indifferent/Resistant
ROLE OF COMMUNITY	Potential support to supplement and reinforce government action; Can support schools in ways government cannot	Can block/undermine educational efforts
KEY VARIABLES DETERMINING COMMUNITY ROLE	Community lacks way to provide support	Match between content/delivery of schooling and local values, needs, economic constraints
GOAL OF GOVERNMENT INTERVENTION	Provide useful ways community can support schools	Adapt content/ delivery of schooling to local context; Provide education useful to community

ORGANIZATION OF THE PAPER

A number of projects have attempted to link school and community more closely. Review of these projects shows that there are a number of low-cost options for improving education through better ties between school and community. This paper reports on these options. The idea is not to prescribe a set of approaches that should work in all contexts but to focus attention on a range of strategies and ways of thinking about problems in the periphery that can address different contexts. Given its resources and responsibility for education, we first focus on what the government can do to improve school-community relations.

If education is for all, then the first task of educators is to get children in school and keep them there. We assume that all children want to learn, though they may not want to attend school as it is structured. Thus the next section describes strategies to increase educational participation in areas of low demand by tailoring educational programs to better meet community needs and values. Strategies described in this section depend, in large part, on government action, often opening up the regulations governing schools to more flexible programmatic options. The subsequent sections look at school-community relations in communities where there is both access to and demand for education. The focus in these sections is on ways of increasing the quality of what children learn through greater and better community participation in schools and through school involvement in the community. Strategies discussed in these sections focus primarily on school- and community-level action. We propose the idea of school-community exchange, in which schools and communities collaborate in development projects of mutual benefit. Though the literature provides few examples of programs in which educational policymakers consider direct school contributions to the community an important issue, our review suggests that school action on behalf of the community improves both the demand for education and community participation. The last section summarizes previous discussions with a series of recommendations for reaching the periphery through improved school-community ties.

APPROACHES TO IMPROVING SCHOOL-COMMUNITY RELATIONS

Adapt Educational Programs to Local Values and Needs

Community attitudes toward education are an important determinant of the effectiveness of schooling, especially in the periphery. Our survey of the literature suggests that community attitudes toward the school range from outright hostility to apathy to enthusiastic support, and that these attitudes can either retard or block government efforts to expand schooling or can serve as an important base of support. Government strategies should vary accordingly, depending on the extent of community demand. In contexts where schooling is valued, the basic problem facing government is to devise helpful and realistic ways for the community to provide support. In contexts where schooling encounters indifference or resistance, the government must adopt a different approach, one of engaging community interest in schooling. This latter strategy implies: 1) a search for the reasons for lack of interest in education, and 2) a willingness to adapt the content and delivery of educational programs to fit the needs and values of diverse communities.

This section looks at ways to enroll and retain children who, despite the existence of a nearby school, do not participate. Thus, we do not consider here the provision of schools where there are none. A review of the literature shows that in many cases, low levels of demand for education are not immutable but can be changed through appropriate government and community action.

Identify Reasons for Low Enrollment

In many cases educational participation is low because the government has lacked the resources to provide education to the more-difficult-to-reach periphery. In other areas, however, children remain out of school despite the government's provision of nearby schools. The first step in addressing problems of low educational participation is to determine the specific reasons for lack of local demand.

Research has identified a number of possible reasons. (Anderson, 1988; Kelly, 1987; Wan, 1975; National Council of Educational Research and Training, 1970.) Communities may resist schooling when delivered in ways that are incompatible with local values, such as in Pakistan and Bangladesh, where religious norms proscribe public interactions between girls and boys. (Bellew and King, 1991.) Parents may also hesitate to enroll their children in school when school schedules prevent children from attending to household tasks, or when travel time to school is excessive. Rigid age and attendance requirements may prevent children from acquiring an education they would want if it were timed more flexibly. Parents are unlikely to educate their children when direct costs, such as school fees and uniforms, are perceived as being too high, or when the benefits of education are low. (Nkinyangi, 1982; World Bank, 1987a.) Moreover, the relative values of such costs and benefits may differ at the periphery from those of the center.

The content and quality of schooling are other issues. Parents may feel that the school teaches their children little that is useful in village life. They may be critical of teachers who are poorly trained, frequently absent, or prone to use physical punishment. As discussed in the chapter on language policy, further alienation may occur if schooling is provided in a non-native language, which is often the case in the periphery. Finally, there may be a generalized resistance to education where schools are viewed as attempts by the government to weaken or destroy a community's cultural or ethnic identity.

Again, consequences of these problems may be more severe in the periphery than in the mainstream (UNESCO, 1984c), and some groups, such as girls, may be more adversely affected than others. (Anderson, 1988; Kelly, 1987.)

The following discussion highlights strategies that have been used to address each of these problems. Key points are summarized in Tables 3.3-3.6.

Work Around Community Values
Schooling often represents a challenge to the traditional norms and allegiances of the community. Of course, one of the primary purposes of schooling is the inculcation of "modern" values and national allegiance. In many cases, however, the organization and delivery of schooling challenge community values in ways that are neither intended nor necessary to realizing the stated goals of education.

Not surprisingly, in many parts of the world such value conflicts center around gender roles. If, for example, a coeducational school is established in a community whose culture proscribes public interactions between female and male students, parents are faced with a choice between their values and those of the school. If the parents' values win out, girls lose the opportunity to get an education. Even if girls are enrolled, their participation is likely to be short-lived. In cases such as these, steps taken to adapt the delivery of educational programs to bring it into greater harmony with local values are likely to pay off in terms of increased participation and achievement.

Some problems are rather easy to remedy; when parents and community members have specific and identifiable objections to the way education is provided, it may be possible to increase participation simply by fixing the problem. This appears to have been the case in Pakistan, where building boundary walls around schools eased parents' concerns over their daughters' safety (World Bank, 1987a, 1987b), and in Bangladesh, where the provision of enclosed latrines overcame an important community objection to schooling for girls. (World Bank, 1985.)

Single-sex schools may provide an important way for governments to provide a "safe" learning environment for girls. A study of girls' mathematics achievement in single-sex and coeducational schools in Nigeria found that girls learned more and exhibited more positive attitudes toward mathematics in single-sex schools than in coeducational settings. (Lee and Lockheed, 1990.)

Table 3.3. Adapting Delivery of Education to Local Values

REASON FOR LOW PARTICIPATION	MEASURES TO ADDRESS PROBLEM
Method of Delivery Conflicts with Local Values Related to Gender Roles	Correct specific problems (Build walls, latrines, etc.); establish single-sex schools
Generalized Mismatch between Values of Schooling and Local Values	Link schools with important local institutions such as religious bodies; upgrade quality of such programs
Lack of Appropriate Role Models as Teachers; Lack of Sufficient Numbers of Teachers for Peripheral Schools	Recruit and deploy more female and/or local teachers: recruit and train locally, modify entrance requirements, subsidize teacher- training, provide room and board, set up flexible posting policies; recruit and train educated community members as teachers

Sometimes however, low community demand for education is associated with a more generalized mismatch between local values and those implicitly espoused by modern schooling. One potential solution is to link educational programs with important local institutions such as religious bodies. Pakistan, Kenya, Bangladesh, the Gambia, and other countries have accredited Koranic schools by training teachers to add general primary school content to the school's religious curriculum. Such schools enjoy the respect of local people and form a continuity with traditional community-based education, but often suffer from poor quality. (Warwick, Reimers, and McGinn, 1989; World Bank, 1987b; Eisemon and Wasi, 1987; UNESCO, 1984a; Bellew and King, 1991.) In such cases, it may be necessary to take steps to improve the quality of Koranic schools, as has been done in the Gambia, by working with religious organizations to broaden the curriculum and provide better trained teachers. (Bellew and King, 1991; World Bank, 1990a.)

Greater recruitment and deployment of female teachers is often suggested as a way of increasing girls' enrollments. (Anderson, 1988; Kelly, 1987; National Council of Educational Research and Training, 1970.) Female teachers serve as important role models and can make girls feel comfortable in the possibly "foreign" atmosphere of the school. For similar reasons, deployment of teachers from peripheral communities may increase enrollment and retention. Recruitment and training of local teachers may solve some of the problems faced by teachers from the outside, such as isolation and difficulty fitting in. (Dove, 1982). However, deploying greater numbers of peripheral and female teachers is difficult, for many of the same reasons that their enrollment is low in the first place. (See chapter 6 in this volume.)

A combination of strategies seems to be most effective in increasing the number of female teachers (and by extension, teachers from peripheral groups): recruiting *and training* in local areas (rather than urban centers); reducing requirements for entrance into teacher-training programs where appropriate; subsidizing teacher education; providing room and board to those in teacher training; and designing flexible posting arrangements so that teachers can obtain postings near their homes. (Bellew and King, 1991.) Nepal successfully implemented a program combining these characteristics, contributing to a three-fold increase in the proportion of female teachers in primary schools over an eight-year period (UNDP, 1982).

Another option is recruiting relatively well-educated members of local communities and training them. Nonformal programs in Bangladesh and Maharashtra, India, that have recruited and trained educated community residents have been very successful. (Lovell and Fatema, 1989; Mallon, 1989; UNESCO, 1984a.) Part of the Bangladesh Rural Advancement Committee's (BRAC) success in attracting girls to its schools appears to have been the fact that two-thirds of its teaching staff are women (see Box 3.1).

Box 3.1. Bangladesh Rural Advancement Committee (BRAC)

The Bangladesh Rural Advancement Committee (BRAC) set up schools to reach the unreachable in a context where being poor, rural, and/or female in Bangladesh meant getting a low-quality education, if any at all. BRAC's schools arrange instruction around the needs of students and families. Schools operate before or after the main workday, thus providing children who must work with an opportunity to learn. BRAC's schools are free from many of the regulations characterizing the formal school system. Students may enter at nonstandard ages and progress at their own rate. Examinations are infrequent and tied to the material that has been taught. Local communities are required to provide school facilities according to BRAC guidelines. Teachers are recruited from local communities and provided with training and a small stipend. Special efforts are made to hire women as teachers. The curriculum is geared toward local concerns but coordinated with the formal school curriculum so that students can continue their studies if they so wish.

The success of projects such as BRAC's suggest that when education is provided in ways that make it truly accessible, children will attend school. BRAC's schools, established in rural areas where educational participation has traditionally been very low, have a dropout rate of one percent. Eighty-three percent of BRAC's students continue their studies in regular schools, whereas few previously would have gotten any schooling at all.

Modify the Timing and Structure of Learning
The delivery of education may also conflict with a family's economic needs, again in ways neither intended nor relevant to the content of education. (Kelly, 1987; National Council of Educational Research and Training, 1970; UNESCO, 1984c;

Wan, 1975.) Family well-being may depend on children's help in caring for siblings (Coletta and Sutton, 1989), preparing food, gathering fuel and water, or working on the farm. Parents may choose not to enroll their children in school when school schedules prevent the youngsters from attending to such tasks.

The school year is generally scheduled in ways that make it difficult for children to play an economic role in their homes (Kelly, 1987). Most school curricula require: that children enter school at a certain age; that they spend most of their day at school; that they attend school most days the school is open; and that they progress from one grade to the next without interruption. Failing to abide by these requirements means failure at school and failure to get an education. It is a difficult system to combine with work, an easy system to fail at, and a system permitting few second chances. Each of these requirements results in the loss of potential students, and none have anything to do with the content of what is learned. Children who do not enter school at the appointed age become self-conscious about studying with younger students and are more likely to drop out. (National Council of Educational Research and Training, 1970.) Children who miss part of the school year often have to repeat the entire year; many drop out instead. The result is often a vicious cycle of failure.

A UNESCO study of the dropout problem in Asia, for example, found that two-thirds of Thailand's dropouts had previously repeated a grade. The report went on to propose that automatic promotion be established as a matter of policy, as has been done in Malaysia and Korea, and that exams be abolished in early grades. (UNESCO, 1984c.) Other research supports the educational value of automatic promotion (Haddad, 1979) and the detrimental effect of too many exams too early.

Several education programs have addressed these problems by structuring their programs around the demands facing target students (refer to Table 3.4). Special child care arrangements have permitted many girls, who otherwise would have stayed home to babysit younger siblings, to attend school in China, Colombia, and India. (Coletta and Sutton, 1989; Lockheed and Verspoor, 1990; UNESCO, 1984c.) For example, new regulations permitting girls to bring their siblings to school have been piloted in Ghansu, China. Site-based child care has permitted women workers to care for their children, thus freeing their daughters to attend school. In Colombia, the *Hogares de Bienestar Infantil* program provides community-based child care in poor areas, again permitting girls who would otherwise have had to take care of younger siblings to attend school. The *Vakaswadi* project in India identified the need to care for younger children as an important constraint on girls' attendance at school. By providing nurseries at school, enrollments increased and dropout rates fell.

Several programs have the structural flexibility to meet the scheduling needs of target children. BRAC and *Escuela Nueva* permit students to enter at different ages. (Republic of Colombia, 1990; Lovell and Fatema, 1989.) The Maharashtra project targets pupils ages 9-14 who have passed the prescribed age for entry into the formal system. (Naik, 1982.) *Escuela Nueva* assumes that children will have to work much of the day and will be unable to attend school every day. Learning is structured with sequential, semiprogrammed teaching materials that children can put down and pick up again when they are ready. Repetition has been structured out of the program through "flexible promotion." (Republic of Colombia, 1990.) The Maharashtra program structures learning along principles of ungraded mastery learning. BRAC

Table 3.4. Adapting Delivery of Education to Constraints Children Face

REASON FOR LOW PARTICIPATION	MEASURES TO ADDRESS PROBLEM
School attendance prevents children from caring for siblings	Permit siblings to attend class; Set up day-care centers near school or at work sites
School attendance prevents children from attending to household tasks: preparation of food, planting and harvesting, etc.	Schedule school for morning or afternoon only; Schedule school year around growing seasons
Curriculum requires that students: enter at a particular age, attend school virtually every day, continue without interruption, complete an entire year or fail	Develop non-graded, unit-based curricula; Allow children to enter, progress at own pace
Children pass the prescribed age of entry	Develop second-chance programs; Provide ways for children to join formal schools later
Failure is easy	Automatic promotion; Elimination of exams in early grades

lets each community decide whether classes will be held in the morning or evening, so as to conflict least with children's household tasks. By targeting the delivery of educational programs to the needs of those bypassed by the rigid schedules of formal schooling, these programs have stimulated local interest in education and made it easier for students to succeed in learning.

The *Vakaswadi* project in India modified not only the scheduling of school but the location as well, literally taking the school to the meadows where children tended cattle. Children took turns watching the herds and studying. (UNESCO, 1984c.)

Other projects that have attempted to restructure learning illustrate that unanticipated outcomes and resistance to new ideas often accompany success in the implementation of new ideas. The IMPACT project in the Philippines replaced teachers with "instructional supervisors" who oversaw the learning of an average of one hundred students. Community members were involved as teacher aides, and upper-grade pupils tutored younger students in multigrade classes. Instruction was provided through self-instructional units for grades four through six. The pilot program was successful in terms of student outcomes and cost-effectiveness. IMPACT students scored as well as conventional students on standardized curriculum-based tests; a greater percentage went on to regular high schools; fewer were unemployed; and costs ran 50 percent less than for conventional schools. However, the program ran into administrative difficulties and stiff resistance from the vested interests of teachers during the process of expansion to the national scale.

Lack of commitment to the project at the national level led to difficulties in arranging the funding necessary for dissemination. When given an option of programs, parents opted for conventional schools. (Nielsen and Cummings, 1985; Stromquist, 1981.)

Several other countries attempted to adapt the IMPACT program to their own contexts. Again, while some objectives were achieved, certain problems were encountered. The PAMONG project attempted to replicate IMPACT in Indonesia but ran into resistance from the educational bureaucracy. The program was successful in reaching dropouts and meeting the needs of isolated schools where multigrade teaching was already widespread. The bureaucracy, however, was unwilling to make the changes necessary to realize potential cost savings from the project: Ministry officials failed to modify their formula for calculating the number of teachers needed in a particular school and to permit PAMONG-developed materials to be used instead of ministry-approved textbooks. The testing schedule was not changed to match the PAMONG instructional schedule. In addition, music and physical education, while included in standardized tests, were not taught in the PAMONG materials. (Nielsen and Cummings, 1985; Stromquist, 1981.)

IMPACT was brought to Malaysia in the form of Project InSPIRE and was used to provide remedial instruction in peninsular Malaysia and to reach outlying communities in Sabah. In the Malaysian context, teachers are reported as having welcomed the self-instructional materials, while Ministry officials objected. The project managed to survive by affiliating itself with a local university and obtaining press coverage. (Nielsen and Cummings,1985.) Bangladesh also attempted to replicate IMPACT with even less success. (World Bank, 1985; Nielsen and Cummings, 1985.) Enrollments did not increase, nor did dropout rates decrease. Parents apparently lacked confidence in a strategy where older children taught younger children. In addition, the self-instructional units required greater supervision and teacher attention than initially expected.

Liberia introduced programmed instructional materials to provide greater access to education in a context of too few teachers and instructional materials. (Boothroyd and Chapman, 1987; Improving the Efficiency of Educational Systems, 1986; Nielsen and Cummings, 1985; Windham, 1983.) The Improved Efficiency of Learning (IEL) was successful in terms of some objectives—access, achievement, and cost- effectiveness. Enrollments increased by 71 percent with no increase in the number of teachers. Dropout rates were lower than in comparison schools, and students scored significantly higher on English and mathematics tests. Costs compared favorably with those of conventional classroom instruction. The effects of the program on learning differentials by gender, however, were discouraging. Girls in IEL classes scored significantly lower than boys did in either IEL or comparison groups, and lower than girls in conventional schools. Evaluators suggested that the reasons for these discrepancies were the greater demands of the self-instructional materials in terms of independent study, which conflicted with the demands on girls' time at home. They cautioned that in communities where educational levels are low, instructional materials must be carefully adapted to the level of instructional support children are likely to find *at school*.

The programs outlined above operate at the early stages of education, their basic objective being to provide out-of-school and at-risk children with basic educational opportunities. An important consideration in the design of such programs is whether children enrolled in such alternative educational programs will be able to enter conventional schools should they decide to seek further education. Bangladesh seems to have been particularly sensitive to this problem. BRAC explicitly established linkages with the formal primary system so that graduates of the BRAC program could continue their studies. Bangladesh established some two hundred "feeder schools" organized by village workers and explicitly designed to provide out-of-school children with the basic skills necessary for enrollment in government primary schools. (Rasmussen, 1985.) Similarly, graduates of Bangladesh's Underprivileged Children's Program (UCEP) are entitled to enter public vocational schools. (UNESCO, 1984b.)

That BRAC, *Escuela Nueva*, and the Maharashtra programs were more broadly successful than the IMPACT programs may be understood as a function of community and governmental support. Problems with these programs arose as a result of either a mismatch between program design and community needs and values, or resistance from the educational bureaucracy. BRAC, *Escuela Nueva*, and the Maharashtra programs involved the community in planning, implementing, staffing, and managing their educational programs. Just as significant, perhaps, was the fact that the government did not interfere. By way of contrast, lack of community involvement was cited as a primary reason for problems with the IMPACT model in Malaysia and the Philippines. Parental objections to older students teaching younger students helped undermine successful replication of the IMPACT model in Bangladesh. Resistance from the educational bureaucracy and from teachers undermined the effectiveness of IMPACT in Indonesia, the Philippines, and Malaysia.

Adjust the Costs and Benefits of Education

Parents also make enrollment decisions on the basis of more direct economic concerns: How much does school cost? What economic benefits can children be expected to get from school? Do expected future benefits outweigh the current opportunity costs?

In some cases, parents may want to enroll their children in school but are prevented from doing so by the direct and indirect costs of education: school fees, clothes or uniforms, textbooks, and other materials. The school may be located too far from home for the child to commute, especially at the secondary level, and parents may be unable or unwilling to board children near the school. In other cases, the benefits of education may be unclear. Education may not, in the parents' estimation, be of much use in helping their children obtain future work. The school's curriculum may seem (or be) unrelated to community needs; it may not teach anything (seen to be) of practical value. The curriculum may be geared toward preparing students for continuing in the next level of education, an option that may not appear desirable or possible. Finally, the benefits of education may accrue differently to different groups. What is the use of seeking an education if one is effectively barred from participation in future schooling or work outside the area? If women, for example, have few opportunities in the work force, why, parents might ask, should they be educated for such jobs? These questions may be particularly important for the periphery, which is likely to be poor and outside the mainstream economy, less able to afford costs, and less likely to see benefits.

As with other aspects of parent and community demand for education, government policies can influence parental choices (refer to Table 3.5). Despite the fact that primary education is "free" in most countries, there are hidden costs that may prevent poor children from attending school. (National Council of Educational Research and Training, 1970.) Many countries require uniforms, charge fees of various kinds, or require payment for textbooks. In cases where costs such as these have been identified as barriers to school attendance, governments have tried several approaches to reducing the costs to families. In terms of uniforms, governments have experimented with providing uniforms free of charge in Bangladesh and eliminating the regulations requiring uniforms in rural areas of Sind, Pakistan. (Bellew and King, 1991.) Sri Lanka's free textbook program has formed part of the government's comprehensive strategy to enroll all children in school, regardless of socioeconomic status. (Enquist, 1982.) Such programs can be expensive, however, as can programs to eliminate fees entirely. They may also encounter unforeseen problems.

The Kenyan government announced in 1974 that it would eliminate primary-school tuition. A subsequent study found that the plan did not provide a way to replace the lost revenues to schools. To meet their expenses, schools had imposed other fees. The net result was that the poor ended up with even less access to schooling than before, thus pointing to the need to consider the broader ramifications of specific policies, however apparently benign. (Nkinyangi, 1982.)

Theoretically, it is possible to adopt a sliding-scale approach to tuition and fees, whereby students would pay what they could according to some objective scale. We were unable to find any examples of this approach, however, perhaps due to the administrative and political difficulties governments would face in implementing such a scheme. On the recommendation of the World Bank, Malawi did implement a scheme where students were charged user fees at the secondary level. The funds thus obtained were to be used to finance primary education and a scholarship program for poor secondary students. (Thobani, 1983.) It is unclear, however, whether the funds were actually used to make improvements in the primary system or whether the intended recipients actually received secondary scholarships.

However, despite expense and administrative difficulties, targeted scholarship programs have been successful in increasing girls' participation rates in Bangladesh and Guatemala and increasing the longevity of girls' attendance in Nepal (Bellew and King, 1991.) Presumably programs such as these might work with other disadvantaged populations. The Bangladesh program almost doubled the proportion of girls attending school in project areas; dropout fell from 15 percent to 4 percent. The program has had a multiplier effect. Girls are encouraging their sisters to attend school, are learning financial independence, and postponing marriage plans. Local schools have also improved with the guarantee of incoming funds from scholarship students. The Guatemala program links scholarships to requirements that the girls maintain a 75 percent attendance record and not get pregnant. The program was successful in keeping girls in school; more than 90 percent of scholarship recipients are reported as completing the school year.

Table 3.5. Adjusting the Costs and Benefits of Education

REASON FOR LOW PARTICIPATION	MEASURES TO ADDRESS PROBLEM
Direct costs are too high	• Reduce fees, cost of uniforms, materials, etc. across the board; • Establish sliding scale, to vary by community or student, for fees, uniforms, materials, etc. • Eliminate fees and/or uniform requirements; • Provide materials free; • Establish student loan programs
Differential costs/benefits for sub- groups	• Target scholarships to sub- groups; • Charge according to ability to pay, etc.
School too far from community to commute	• Establish boarding facilities; • Create small schools; • Use itinerary teacher
Opportunity costs too high	• Incorporate income-generating activities into curriculum; • Combine work with academics
Few future economic benefits seen to attending school	• Incorporate job training into curriculum with strong placement and counseling support; • Establish affirmative action programs in workplace
Little potential for further education	• Publicize education opportunities; • Provide support for further education and work

While student loans have been suggested as a way to assist low-income families in educating their children while limiting costs on the part of the government, few governments have attempted to implement loans for primary or secondary education. Provision of boarding facilities, sometimes targeted to specific populations, has been used to increase participation in school. For example, various Indian states established free ashram boarding schools for "scheduled" tribal children. Ashram schools emphasize practical skills and encourage children's self-reliance, with students growing their own food and "managing their own affairs." (UNESCO,

1984a.) Bhutan, in order to allay parental fears about the safety of their girls and to encourage girls to continue their schooling, provided boarding facilities for upper primary grades (Bellew and King, 1991). Boarding schools are expensive, however, and it is sometimes difficult to ensure that targeted populations will reap the benefits. Kenya, in an effort to encourage enrollment by students from peripheral tribes, set aside places in its boarding schools for such students. However, the school's requirement that students provide their own bedding and cutlery apparently prevented the intended beneficiaries from taking advantage of the places reserved for them. Instead, students from more advantaged regions were found to occupy the reserved beds (Nkinyangi, 1982), an important lesson in how costs reasonable to one population may be prohibitive to others.

Reducing the direct costs of education to students and families necessarily implies increased costs to the government and difficult choices among competing priorities. Obviously, the cheapest strategy is to do away with requirements for unnecessary items such as uniforms. The difficulties of targeting specific groups have been noted, along with the potential benefits. Another strategy is to decrease the current opportunity costs of school enrollment or increase the future benefits of education. As discussed earlier, schools can compensate for the current opportunity costs of schooling by adapting delivery to the household tasks facing children in particular contexts. There is evidence that children whose families depend on them to earn income will study when classes are scheduled before or after work or when they can combine work with school.

In some contexts, nonformal schooling can be combined with income-generating activities, as in two projects in India. An experimental program in Madhya Pradesh, India, paid children to produce mats and chalk for the Department of Education, and linked students' employment with a basic educational program. Program costs were 40 percent of conventional programs, and the Department of Education earned a 15 percent profit on its investment. Children who had dropped out or never enrolled in school were able to acquire a basic education; some children continued their education in the formal school system. (Singh, 1982.) A similar program in Maharashtra, India, set up woodworking shops and negotiated contracts with private firms. As part of their studies, children learned crafts while producing objects for sale. As a result, primary enrollments are reported to have increased while dropout rates have decreased. (UNESCO, 1984a.) Students at the Philippines' *barrio* high schools paid their own tuition through income-generating activities coordinated by the schools. (Orata, 1977.) In some contexts, extreme deprivation may prevent any education at all unless programs are accompanied by attention to income and other essential needs. A comprehensive program of vocational training centers targeted women in Bangladesh, integrating education with training in productive skills, day-care, food, and medical care. (Bellew and King, 1991.) Even when direct and opportunity costs are not a barrier to education, however, parents may decide not to enroll their children because they see little future use for education. Part of this may be a failure to ensure that parents understand the benefits of education. Three programs discussed earlier—BRAC, *Escuela Nueva*, and Maharashtra schools—were successful in areas where demand for education had once been low. All three paid special attention to communicating their objectives to parents and enlisting community support in planning and implementation. Evaluations of these programs noted parents' appreciation of the practical benefit of the skills taught by the programs. (Lovell and Fatema, 1989; Naik, 1982; Republic of Colombia, 1990.) At the same time, however, all three programs emphasized practical skills that could be put to immediate use in daily life. Thus in planning education for low-demand areas, school officials need to make certain that the benefits of their educational programs are real, given the context of the community, and understood by parents.

A number of vocational training programs have attempted to link school and future work more closely. Some succeed; many do not. (World Bank, 1991.) Parents sometimes resist vocational education programs, not wanting their children to be educated for manual labor. Typical was the attempted implementation of a vocational education curriculum in the Sudan. Parents resisted the program and refused to cooperate, fearing that the program would hurt their children's chances on examinations and train their children for a life of manual work. (Ngalamu, 1986.) Again, the mismatch between community needs and school design set the stage for failure.

Successful programs seem to fall into one of two types: They either prepare students for jobs in growth areas of the economy or supplement training with strong placement and guidance. More generalized vocational training programs are generally less successful. (Bellew and King, 1991.) Morocco successfully implemented a technical education program targeting women. (Lycette, 1986; USAID, 1983.) A strong counseling component supplemented by energetic efforts on the part of program staff to place women in apprenticeships enabled many women to get and keep jobs. Given the economic isolation of many peripheral areas, it seems that vocational education programs for peripheral schools need to pay special attention to the needs of local economies.

Use Appropriate Curricula

The benefits of education are obviously heightened by the use of appropriate curricula. However, adapting the content and structure of curriculum to meet the demand in peripheral communities requires creative design (refer to Table 3.6). First, the needs of children in the periphery may differ from those of children in the center. Communities with little experience with education may have a special need to see the utility of what students learn. (Lovell and Fatema, 1989; Republic of Colombia, 1990; UNESCO, 1984a.) There is little sense in providing students unlikely to pursue further education with a curriculum that primarily aims to prepare students for more schooling. At the same time a totally separate curriculum is likely to reinforce the isolation of peripheral children. Certainly the provision of instructional materials in the children's language (and teachers who speak this language) is a key factor in the utility and demand for education, but if the country's dominant language is a different one, students may need instruction in both languages. (See chapter 4.)

Peripheral schools may need curricula that are more flexible than the standard curriculum, adaptable to multigrade classrooms (see chapter 7), self- and peer-instruction, teachers with varying capacities, and children's individual time schedules and learning speeds. Because of their likely isolation from the cultural resources of

Table 3.6. Developing Curriculum to Meet Peripheral Needs

REASONS FOR LOW PARTICIPATION/ INTEREST	MEASURES TO ADDRESS THE PROBLEMS
Curriculum is of little apparent use in children's present and projected future lives.	Include material that is visibly useful in village life.
Specially adapted curricula may not permit children to continue on to higher levels of education.	Include sufficient material from the regular curriculum so that children can continue their education if they so desire.
Instruction is provided in a language the children do not know.	Provide at least initial instruction in the child's home language.
Instruction is not provided in a country's dominant language.	Provide instruction at higher levels also in the dominant language.
The curriculum is structured so that only teachers can use it. Thus, learning depends on the presence and capacity of teacher.	Develop self-instructional materials that can be used by students with minimum professional supervision.
The curriculum is lock-step and geared towards mass instruction; children must keep up with the pace of the class or fail.	Develop modular systems of instruction which students can use at their own pace.

the center, peripheral children need a more self-contained curriculum than do children in the center. As discussed earlier, one of the problems with Nigeria's IEL project and the IMPACT project in Bangladesh was that the materials required more time and supervision than children had access to. *Escuela Nueva*'s curriculum has met these multiple demands remarkably well, by carefully adapting the timing and content of the instructional program to fit the constraints of Colombia's rural schools (refer to Box 3.2).

Even when a curriculum is specially designed for particular needs, it may fail in the classroom if not accompanied by changes in teaching practices. An ethnographic study of a "practical curriculum" implemented in Botswana found very few differences from standard teaching practices. (Prophet, 1990.)

Teachers' efforts to relate national curricula to local needs are supported by certain teacher-training efforts and by measures fostering collaboration among teachers, such as school clusters and instruction-oriented supervision, as opposed to administrative supervision by principals and district officials. (Cummings, Gunawardena, and Williams, 1992.) School personnel may need to be taught the skills required for working well with communities, and assisted in developing positive attitudes toward them, as was done in Sri Lanka and the Philippines (Carino and Valisno, 1992; Ekanayake, 1980.)

Box 3.2. Curriculum in Colombia's *Escuela Nueva*

Recognizing the impracticality of providing each primary school with a multigrade teaching staff, Colombia's *Escuela Nueva* program designed its curriculum for multigrade teaching. Because of children's varying time demands, instructional materials are designed to be studied alone, in groups, or with the teacher. With flexible promotion, children proceed at their own pace; no one must repeat a year. The curriculum emphasizes general principles but places them in the context of daily life. Students are encouraged to find local examples, and teachers are encouraged to elaborate on the material provided. The content of the curriculum permits students to join conventional schools at any time. Each school is equipped with a library consisting of one hundred books, thus ensuring that all children will have access to a number of reference materials.

Evaluation of the program shows very positive results. Children enrolled in *Escuela Nueva* schools scored higher on tests of self-esteem and equally well on tests of creativity as compared with students in conventional rural schools. Interestingly, girls scored as well as boys on tests of self-esteem. In terms of achievement, *Escuela Nueva* students outperformed students in conventional schools on tests of Spanish, mathematics, and socio-civic behavior. Eighty-nine percent of teachers surveyed believed that *Escuela Nueva* schools were better than conventional rural schools, which, it must be remembered, employed a teacher for each grade. (Republic of Colombia, 1990.)

Program developers realized that the training teachers are given in applying the curriculum is as important as the curriculum itself. Thus, teacher training is an essential component of *Escuela Nueva*. New teachers participate in a series of week- long workshops, each focusing on a particular aspect of the program and supplemented by regular visits from supervisors who focus on ways to improve instruction. The emphasis is on practical rather than theoretical training; teachers learn to implement the program. Teachers also learn of the leadership role they are expected to play in the community and ways of fostering school-community collaboration. The program shows that teacher training need not be long term or expensive to be effective. Assuming an average class of 40 students, annual teacher-training costs are estimated at $2.05 per student. *Escuela Nueva*'s curriculum, while difficult to design, is easy to teach. By way of contrast, standard national curricula, teacher training, and supervision are easy to administer—using the same materials and methods everywhere—but difficult for the teacher to adapt to the particular circumstances of the periphery.

Source: Lovell and Fatema, 1989; Republic of Colombia, 1990.

Strengthen Cultural Identity

A final way to stimulate local demand is to use the school to strengthen local culture. When a creative teacher, school, or community organization is able to link education with a devalued or threatened local culture, community interest in education is solidified (refer to Table 3.7). A dedicated teacher can do a great deal to arouse community interest, for example, by creatively drawing on the community as a source of knowledge. A teacher in a rural high school in southern Appalachia (USA) was able to engage his students' interest in learning about their cultural heritage. Initially skeptical, students soon began researching and documenting local handicrafts, customs, and legends; interviewing community members; and eventually publishing a series of books. (Wiggington, 1991.) Community pride and interest in the school blossomed.

Table 3.7. Education to Reinforce Local Cultures

REASON FOR LOW PARTICIPATION	MEASURES TO ADDRESS PROBLEM
Schooling ignores or devalues local culture	Permit/encourage development of curriculum to increase awareness, pride in local culture
Schooling implicitly forces a choice between local and mainstream cultures, economies	Permit/encourage teaching of value of both cultures, skills for bi-cultural survival

In a very different context, the aboriginal Shuar people of Ecuador were able to revive much of their culture through a collaboration between school and community organizations (refer to Box 3.3).

Box 3.3. Shuar Radio Education Project

Like many aboriginal peoples, the Shuar Indians of Ecuador faced a cultural and economic crisis. Purchases of traditional Shuar land by low-land colonists had eroded much of the tribe's sense of community. However, with the assistance of Salesian missionaries, Shuar leaders were able to secure group title to their land. Based on this success, community leaders established a bilingual Spanish-Shuar radio program that enabled children to live with their families and study. Previously, children wanting an education had to leave home for boarding schools, where schooling was carried out in Spanish and children were culturally isolated. Faced with these alternatives, most children stayed out of school. With the new radio program, however, educational participation grew dramatically. Most children stayed in their villages after growing up, and a new pride in local culture emerged. The tribe has since developed several businesses, which will enable the community to survive in the country's larger cash economy.

Source: Merino, 1984.

While the governments played no direct role in either of these cases, they did *permit* the development of special curricula. In some contexts, governments might encourage such work.

Review of these cases suggests that most people believe in education and will enroll their children in school if school is truly accessible. In many cases where children are not in school, there are powerful constraints preventing them from being there. Educational programs able to identify and adapt their delivery around these constraints have gotten enthusiastic responses from children and parents. Children from the periphery are as capable as mainstream children if education is adapted to their needs. The standard model of education, however, does not work well for many peripheral communities: many children remain out of school, are forced to repeat or drop out. In many cases the school's delivery problems are unrelated to the content or goals of education. In such cases consideration of the needs, values, and constraints facing the community may be the only way to reach peripheral children.

USEFUL WAYS TO INVOLVE THE COMMUNITY

In contrast to the contexts discussed earlier, where communities for one reason or another lacked interest in education, there is in many places a great demand for education. Being peripheral has often meant getting less of what others have and of what such communities want. In such contexts, community support can make a great difference in the psychic and material resources schools have to work with. There is little that governments have to do to stimulate such support but channel it in useful ways. For purposes of the discussion, we have grouped community support for schools into three general areas: support for the instructional program, supplements to school resources, and help in managing schools (refer to Tables 3.8 and 3.9).

Table 3.8. How Involvement of the Community Can Improve Education

PROVIDE SUPPORT FOR INSTRUCTIONAL PROGRAM
- Cultivate an environment supportive of school program
- Improve enrollment, retention, attendance
- Monitor study at home
- Ensure all students have adequate study space
- Identify and help students with problems
- Help students with family emergencies
- Boost morale of school staff
- Provide assistant or regular teachers
- Provide instruction in specific areas (where teachers lack expertise)
- Pass on community knowledge
- Provide apprenticeships/work opportunities

SUPPLEMENT SCHOOL RESOURCES
- Donate land for school
- Donate labor/materials to build/help build school building
- Repair/maintain facilities
- Donate equipment, learning aids (eg, books, teaching materials)
- Raise money for school

Supporting the Instructional Program

One of the most important and least discussed contributions of the community is the most nebulous— support of the school's instructional program. Community support is difficult to talk about but easy to recognize. Where there is support, children attend school regularly and are interested in their studies. Where parents support education, schools are able to achieve a great deal, even under very difficult circumstances.

Vietnam's Parents' Associations (PA's) illustrate the positive potential for community involvement in schools, in a context of popular support for education but very little money (refer to Box 3.4). Recognizing the government's financial constraints, yet poor themselves, PA's have contributed time and energy to supporting the school's instructional programs in a variety of ways. As a result, teacher morale and student performance have improved.

Communities can also play more direct roles in support of the school's instructional program by providing instruction in specific skills that teachers cannot teach, by providing connections to the world of work, by giving teachers constructive feedback to help improve pedagogical skills, and, directly, by providing teaching staff. Thus, in addition to the activities described above, Vietnam's PA members teach students their trades, advise students on career options, and provide on-the-job training. In some locations, Vietnam's PA members attend classes, help teachers prepare teaching aids, and offer suggestions on how to improve their teaching.

Box 3.4. Parents' Associations in Vietnam

Vietnam's Parents' Associations were formally authorized by legislation in connection with a series of system-wide reforms begun in 1981. The PA's operate at the school level to improve relations between schools and parents and to help schools improve the quality of education. PA's do a number of things to achieve these objectives. They play an important role in reducing dropout rates, for example, by providing children from poor families or families in crisis with clothes and school equipment. PA's work to improve pupils' studies by ensuring that every house has a quiet "study corner," with table, chair, bookshelf, and light reserved for children to study. Many schools run double shifts; children when not attending school are assigned independent study. PA's monitor and assist students in completing their assignments, offer extra classes to help slower students, and consult teachers and parents when problems are identified. PA's arrange special classes and contests to encourage gifted pupils. PA's organize activities such as school excursions, sports competitions, and arts festivals.

PA's also play an important role in keeping up teacher morale to compensate for low salaries. PA members visit teachers on Vietnam's Teachers' Day with gifts of appreciation. PA's organize teachers' housing, sometimes constructing residences, or arranging land or discounted building materials. PA's organize extra classes for teachers to supplement their incomes, provide special holidays for outstanding teachers and arrange reduced rates at resorts.

Source: Thinh, 1991.

The Philippines' PLSS (Parent-Learning Support System) goes a step further, explicitly drawing parents into the formal classroom to improve the quality of primary education in disadvantaged areas. (Carino and Valisno, 1991.) PLSS is based on three beliefs: 1) the education of children is a joint responsibility of schools and parents; 2) poor children are as capable of learning as wealthier children; 3) with guidance, parents can and should play a significant role in planning, managing, and assessing their children's education. PLSS includes a variety of school-based strategies designed to improve the learning of poor children. Parents are involved in identifying problems and in planning and implementing solutions. Begun in a disadvantaged squatter settlement in Manila and a poor rural area of Leyte, student achievement in PLSS project areas has increased and dropout rates have been reduced.

Some programs have involved parents and other community members directly in teaching, either as teaching aides or as teachers. Pakistan recruited and trained local community residents who had little formal education to serve as assistant teachers. (Verspoor and Leno, 1986.) Nonformal educational programs in India and Bangladesh have recruited and trained community members to staff their programs, paying them a small sum. (UNESCO, 1984a; UNESCO, 1984b.) A typical example is the Maharashtra program discussed earlier, where teachers with some secondary education are recruited from villages and provided with one week of practical training in development and use of locally relevant teaching materials and classroom management techniques. Bangladesh recruits and pays local residents with some education (usually women) to teach in its nonformal programs.

Supplementing School Resources

Pressures to improve the quality of schools and increase enrollment, coupled with stable or decreasing government budgets, have led governments to look to communities to supplement resources available to schools.[1] Communities have supplemented school resources in a variety of ways, many involving donations of labor or in-kind contributions. Governments have asked communities to donate the land and labor to construct school buildings and to maintain school facilities in a number of countries, including Angola, Guyana, Nepal, Malawi, Nigeria, Pakistan, Sri Lanka, Swaziland, Vietnam, and Yemen. Bray and Lillis describe a number of problems related to design, quality control, and costs that governments must resolve in working with communities to build schools. Nonetheless, the larger point remains that communities in many different contexts have been willing to provide considerable assistance in building schools.

Communities can play a considerable role in this. Over half of the school buildings in current use in Vietnam, for example, were built through the Parents Associations. (Thinh, 1991.) In Eastern Nigeria, community cooperation in donating land and labor for school construction enabled the government to build 287 new secondary and technical schools at a minimum cost to the government. As a result, enrollment increased 165 percent between 1975 and 1982. Girls seem particularly to have benefitted from this program; female secondary enrollment in the project state of Anambra was the highest in Nigeria. (Okoye, 1986.)

In the Philippines, communities opened 2000 *barrio* high schools, 1000 preschool classes, 75 community colleges, and a number of multigrade schools in poor and remote areas, at no cost to the government. (Orata, 1977.) In many cases students paid for operational expenses as well by making and selling products for market. The limited evidence available indicates that graduates performed as well as graduates of conventional high schools on national examinations.

In some cases, such as in Bhutan, governments have linked provision of government resources, in this case teachers, to community provision of school facilities. (Bellew and King, 1991; World Bank, 1988.)

Despite a greater influx of resources from the community, however, over-reliance on community resources can result in serious problems with equity or quality. Reliance on community resources tends to exacerbate inequalities across schools and regions. A negative outcome of the Nigerian project was increased regional inequalities in favor of areas with greater willingness and resources. Lillis and Ayot detail the multiple effects of *harambee* schools in Kenya. (Lillis and Ayot, 1988.) While the establishment of *harambee* schools has permitted large numbers of children, especially girls, to attend primary and secondary school, *harambee* schools often suffer from very low quality. Community provision of *harambee* schools has reduced pressure on the government to improve opportunities and quality for all potential students, and has increased rather than decreased regional inequality in education. Similarly, richer communities in Sri Lanka have captured the greater benefit from the loosening of government restrictions on private contributions to schools. (Cummings, Gunawardena, and Williams, 1992.)

At the same time, however, the Sri Lankan study found that most communities, especially those in poor, isolated areas, were eager to help their local schools. Communities provided monetary or in-kind support, averaging 6 percent of the value of school budgets. The poorest communities, however, provided the greatest amounts of money, equivalent to 8 percent of annual school budgets. The form of community support varied according to the resources of particular communities. Wealthier communities tended to contribute money or expensive equipment, while poorer communities donated labor (see Box 3.5).

Community support of schools in Sri Lanka was found to depend on five factors. The first requirement was the existence of a clearly defined community to which the school could relate. Community contributions were highest to two types of schools: elite urban schools with well-organized alumni organizations and schools in poor, isolated villages. Schools that drew students from less clearly defined geographic and social areas showed much lower levels of community support. Community ownership of the school was an important factor in determining community support.

Strong leadership on the part of the principal, along with community respect for the principal, was a second important predictor of community support, particularly in peripheral communities. The more educated and the higher the career status a principal had, the greater the levels of community support. In poor communities, the principal's level of education and career status were even more highly correlated with community support than community socioeconomic status.

Principals' administrative practices also affected community support. In peripheral areas, schools whose principals included community members, public officials and teachers in decision making and who helped students and their families (e.g., by contacting parents if students failed to attend school) received the highest levels of community support.

Box 3.5. School-Community Relations in Sri Lanka

As part of a series of reforms beginning in the late 1970s, the Sri Lankan government set out to improve school-community relations. Legislation authorizing the establishment of local School Development Societies (SDS) was enacted to provide a formal structure for community input and resources into the schools. While previously only parents' and teachers' opinions were solicited, now the entire community was asked to assist in helping develop local schools. At the same time the legislation encouraged schools to play a strong community role.

A survey of schools carried out several years after implementation of the reform found that 69 percent of all communities provided schools with some form of support and that 58 percent of the schools provided support to their communities. Schools helped build roads (29 percent) and places of worship (29 percent); assisted with religious, cultural and recreational events (23 precent); and provided personnel and facilities to teach school dropouts (10 percent). Communities helped organize school functions (56 percent), provided monetary support (56 percent), and helped build and maintain school facilities (42 percent). As one community member stated:

"Here the people are poor, and the funds are poor too. But people show their goodwill in other ways, by labor, by their high respect for the principal and teachers and their feeling of intimacy towards the school."

Source: Cummings, Gunawardena, and Williams, 1992: 30.

A fourth factor was the extent to which the government was making visible efforts to improve the school. School clustering, provision of greater administrative support at the subregional level and greater implementation of improvement projects at the school level were associated with high levels of community support. Again, the effects of government action were clearest in peripheral communities.

The final factor was the degree of support the school gave the community. This support varied in form: In some communities, schools helped build roads or religious buildings. In others, schools helped organize community cultural or recreational events. Some schools provided dropouts with opportunities for further education. It is interesting that peripheral communities, while the poorest in terms of financial resources, provided the greatest percentage and absolute levels of support to their communities. Most schools received greater value than they gave by an average factor of 1.8.[2]

The two most important predictors of community support for schools in peripheral areas were the characteristics and leadership of principals and perceived government interest in local schools. Equally significant is the finding that these two factors played *a much more important role in peripheral areas* than in mainstream communities.

The case of Sri Lanka illustrates that *many of the determinants of community support of schools are under the control of the government.* Also, while it may be argued that Sri Lanka is atypical in both its demand for education and its traditions of community support, it must be recognized that Sri Lanka is one of the poorest countries in the world. For Sri Lanka's poorest communities to provide such high levels of support indicates the potential of school-community collaboration in the periphery.

Help in Managing Schools
Many governments face management as well as financial crises, especially in relation to the periphery. As educational participation has risen and the number of schools increased, most systems have been unable to provide all schools with adequate administrative support. The periphery has typically suffered the most. Thus, a third general area in which communities can help schools is that of management. Raised in professionalized and bureaucratic models of school provision, government officials in the past have often overlooked the management support that schools can draw from communities. With the movement toward decentralization, however, governments have looked for ways to include people at the local level in running schools.

There are several reasons for involving the community in running school. Perhaps the most important reason is that involving parents and community members in the school's efforts is likely to improve the chances of school success. Whether the project involves getting students to do their homework or repairing a school building, community involvement is likely to foster community ownership and cooperation and forestall resistance. Fostering community participation in managing schools emphasizes the joint responsibility of parents and school for children's learning. One ingredient of BRAC's success, for example, is that each community decides when school is to be held.

There are other reasons as well. The extent of material support a community provides a school is likely to depend in large part on whether the community feels it has a stake in the ownership of the school. Formally involving community members in running the school is one way to foster such ownership. Schools, particularly in the periphery, are likely to be understaffed. Community members can take over some of the work of teachers and principals. Finally, community members may have expertise that school personnel lack.

There are a range of options for involving the community in managing schools (summarized in Table 3.9). Most systems have some version of parent-teacher associations. While many systems are unwilling to allow parents to be directly involved in teaching, projects in several countries have encouraged direct community involvement in instruction.

The most common model of community involvement in school management is that of the standard PTA, in which parents and the community play an important supportive role vis-à-vis fund-raising and moral support, but a peripheral role in terms of decision making and instruction. Malaysia provides a typical example: "The role of the PTAs is understood to be one primarily of material support. . . . They are not, in principle, entitled to interfere in matters relating to pedagogical methods or program content." (Dato' Asiah Abu Samah, 1991: 52.)

Table 3.9. Ways the Community Can Help Manage Schools

- Ensure greater likelihood for successful implementation of school plans
- Foster responsibility among parents for children's learning
- Provide greater material support
- Provide manpower to reduce burden on school staff
- Supply expertise
- Assist in fund-raising, provide moral support, general advice
- Provide new ideas, serve trouble-shooting functions
- Serve on advisory/management committees
- Assume joint responsibility (with school) for planning, managing, evaluating local school programs
- Come to assume, over time, major responsibility for local education, formal and informal, with government support and technical assistance
- Take over most of the management functions of the school, with minimal government assistance

It is possible to broaden the role of parent-teacher associations as illustrated earlier by the case of Vietnam. Thus, in addition to providing material support, parent-teacher associations can serve as a formal way of soliciting parents' input on the school's operation. PTA's can serve as a forum where problems can be discussed and solutions sought before problems become serious. PTA's can also be sources of innovation and new ideas. In terms of policy decisions and instruction, however, this version of the PTA remains limited. Indonesia's BP3 parent-teacher associations appear to operate on this model. The BP3's are expected to arrange support for schools, improve relations between school and parents, select local curricula content, offer general advice, and "ensure the school's success by not interfering with technical teaching matters." (Moegiadi, Jiyono, Mudjiman, and Soemardi, 1991: 39.)

A more inclusive model establishes organizations in which community leaders serve an advisory or consultative capacity, as in Sri Lanka's Student Development Societies or the advisory boards of private schools throughout the world. The authority of such bodies can vary but their role is one of arbitration and broad policy making, not involvement in the day-to-day operations of the school. Such advisory groups typically draw their membership from high-status community members. In this model the school and its staff bear the primary responsibility for providing education, based on the advice or policies of the advisory board. A still more inclusive model involves ordinary parents in the school's operation in terms of both school policy and day-to-day operations. This model emphasizes the partnership between school and parents and entrusts the planning and delivery of local education to both groups. The Philippines' PLSS program discussed in the previous section operates on these assumptions: "The entry of parents into formal teaching-learning situations greatly enhances the emerging belief that . . . parents—as partners of teachers and school administrators—are also responsible for the provision of education." (Carino and Valisno, 1991: 34.) Indonesia has also begun to develop a model of education along these lines in its COPLANNER program. Though not yet operational, the project seeks to establish Community Forums for Educational Development (CFED) in each community (Simanungkalit, Moyle, and Bernard, 1991). CFED's will become part of the formal educational bureaucracy and will bring together village leaders, principals, teachers, supervisors, parents, and other community members to plan and meet the educational needs of the area, both formal and nonformal.

A further model views the school as a community-managed enterprise, but one that requires inputs and technical support from the government. India has developed such a program in its PROPEL project. (Naik, 1991.) The project includes a variety of local interventions designed to stimulate local communities to take charge of their own educational destinies. Each village has a Village Education Committee, which plans and oversees local projects and loosely coordinates its efforts with the project as a whole.

A final model turns over the burden of responsibility for the operation of schools to local communities with virtually no support from the government, as in Peru's radical experiments in decentralization. (Malpica, 1980; Ruiz-Duran, 1980; Salazar, 1972.) This model is less useful for two reasons: First, most governments are unwilling to let go of their authority and responsibility for education, particularly at the primary level. Second, the evidence suggests that many communities are unable to provide or manage schooling unaided.

What is most effective is devising ways of cultivating a cooperative relationship between government, school, and community, so that each group can contribute what it does best.

Cultivating Community Support for Schools

It is interesting that the literature has focused most of its attention on material support from communities. While the financial angle is of obvious appeal to governments, greater attention to drawing instruction and management support from communities can help schools become more effective. Thus, we have attempted to highlight the diversity of support communities can offer.

Community support for schools cannot be mandated. However, given an interest in education and the right conditions, many communities are eager to help. Community support is likely to make an important, maybe critical, difference in the quality of peripheral schools. Communities are already involved in the school's work whether or not their involvement is explicit, and anything that encourages parental support is likely to improve the school's instructional program. Governments would do well to encourage positive involvement. Despite the diversity of communities covered by the projects reviewed, several common conditions of community support are clear. Schools with the following characteristics typically received generous support from their communities:

- Openness on the part of the school: "Readiness of the school to welcome changes and to receive and utilize inputs from its local community." (Carino and Valisno, 1991: 36.)
- Personal commitment of school staff, especially the principal: The commitment and leadership of the principal is a crucial factor in determining the degree of community support.

- Regular, structured communication among local actors in the educational process: For long-term improvement of the school, community members, parents, principals and teachers need a regular forum to promote discussion and follow-through on school improvement plans.
- Visible government efforts to improve schools: Communities are more likely to support schools when they see the government taking an interest in the school and when they see the school getting better.
- School involvement in the community: School action on behalf of the community demonstrates the commitment of the school.

WAYS THE SCHOOL CAN HELP THE COMMUNITY

Evidence suggests that both local demand for education and community support of schools are increased when the school helps the community, when there is an exchange, even if it is largely symbolic. Through government provision, schools have sometimes put an unnecessary distance between themselves and the community. While some distance may be essential in avoiding the politics and rivalries of community life, our review suggests that schools do better when they assume leadership roles in their communities. This section focuses on what the local school can do for the local community (refer to Table 3.10). Again, we suspect that the effects of school action are more pronounced in the periphery, given the greater visibility of the school and the relative lack of other government services.

Table 3.10. What Schools Can Do for Communities

COMMUNITY PROBLEM	WHAT SCHOOL CAN DO
Many school dropouts, illiterates	• Offer instruction; • Provide alternative ways for dropouts to obtain educational certificates; • Provide dropouts with ways back into the formal school system
Few learning resources	Share educational resources
Community problem addressable with information	Provide access to information
Low level of community development	Provide ideas, information, leadership, and labor to address specific community problems

There are a number of roles the school can play in the community. At the most basic level, school staff can participate in community activities and projects. In Sri Lanka, for example, school children helped build roads, organize community religious festivals, cultural activities, and educational programs. (Cummings, Gunawardena, and Williams, 1992.) At a slightly greater level of involvement, schools can share resources with the community—school buildings, books, tables and chairs.

Perhaps most importantly, schools can offer instruction—adult literacy classes, classes to prepare children for examinations, classes for school dropouts, and the like. While teachers may be less than willing to devote a lot of time to such activities, even one afternoon a week could have an important impact. Schools have access to information the community may lack. Special community workshops on child care, health, nutrition, and agriculture are relatively easy to arrange, and again can have an important impact. Schools can teach the community about its cultural heritage or document facts of local life. *Escuela Nueva* teachers, for example, are asked to carry out basic community surveys for other government agencies. In other areas as well, schools can help community members in their interactions with the government.

More involved still, schools can initiate community projects, repair of local buildings, development of appropriate technology, and such. At its most involved, the school can serve as the center for community development efforts such as in the *Bunumbu* and PROPEL projects discussed below.

The important point is that schools rarely move beyond the most basic levels of participation in community life, and a little school support for the community can go a long way toward building good ties. There are many things the school can do if it makes the effort.

Two projects in particular provide good illustrations of what the school can offer the community. The *Bunumbu* project in Sierra Leone sought to combine the training of primary-school teachers with community development. The project was coordinated by the *Bunumbu* Teachers' Training College, and twenty villages were selected as pilot-school villages. Community members built schools, and teacher trainees organized a variety of community-development projects while teaching at the village schools. Teacher trainees worked with villagers through all phases of the projects. In addition to educating children, teacher trainees worked with communities to establish village cooperatives, youth clubs, and handicraft shops. The project served as a catalyst for a number of other local development projects. Villages were able to develop the internal leadership necessary to design and implement future self-improvement projects. (Lebby and Lutz, 1982.)

India's PROPEL project's current objective is the universalization of primary education. Ultimately, it hopes to turn the management of education over to local communities. In order to achieve its current objective, PROPEL has undertaken a variety of projects on behalf of the community, including preschools, women's support groups, training of teachers to help children manage the transition to primary school, adult literacy classes and the establishment of People's Education Houses to serve as libraries and local cultural centers. In carrying out these projects, PROPEL has generated local demand for education and an increased capacity on the part of poor villagers to plan and manage their own affairs. (Naik, 1982.) (Refer to Box 3.6.)

> **Box 3. 6. India's Project PROPEL**
>
> High levels of participation in Project PROPEL dispelled the general assumption held by educators and government officials in India that rural communities saw little value in primary education, especially for girls. Girls are reported as having "flocked to the centers." Parents were happy that their daughters were learning to read and write, that schools were free, and that classes were held after the working day. When instructors were unable to attend class, students sometimes took over instruction. PROPEL schools invited community participation and scrutiny and were able to mobilize considerably more community resources than local formal schools. Some students from the formal schools have demanded that they be permitted to attend PROPEL classes in addition to their regular classes. A new sense of collaboration has been fostered among local government officials and the community.
>
> *Source*: Shaeffer, 1992: 156.

Because most discussions of school-community relations concentrate solely on what communities can do for schools, there is little information available on school involvement in communities. However, the relationships are synergistic. What schools give, they get back in kind. Specific projects will depend on school capacities and community needs. This kind of relationship is described in the following quotation about "high-achieving schools" in Thailand:

> The third major dynamic . . . was the strong relationship higher achieving schools had created with their surrounding communities, including the temple. Parents were more involved in school decisions, the curriculum of the school and, probably as a result of such involvement, contributed more to the school, both financially and in in-kind services. School was a part of the community, not a separate government institution. . . . Parents felt comfortable visiting the school whenever they wished. They came to expect the school to educate their children and were willing to support the school in this endeavor. . . . The temple would contribute financially to the school. Finally, both the principal and the teaching staff participated in local community activities, including religious ceremonies. (Shaeffer, 1992: 61.)

POLICY IMPLICATIONS: FERTILE CONDITIONS AND NECESSARY LINKAGES

We set out to identify options for improving education in the periphery through changes in the relationship between school and community. According to the current mode of educational organization, the government bears virtually complete responsibility for the provision of education while the community has been relegated a minor role. This model has not worked well for the periphery. Governments have lacked the resources to provide peripheral populations with adequate educational programs. Even with sufficient resources, however, educational models for the center have not always worked in peripheral areas. The education and development literature has suggested that such populations are **not** disinterested in education. Our review has convinced us that when the delivery and content of education are matched to the values, needs, and constraints of peripheral populations, children and their parents do get involved in formal schooling.

The community has always played an important, though often hidden, role in education. This may be especially true in peripheral areas, where, given the general lack of government infrastructure and services, the school is particularly visible. When the community supports the school, the school does well. When the community opposes or is indifferent to education, the school's task is more difficult. When community resistance or apathy is coupled with relatively poor school resources, as it is in many peripheral areas, the school is unlikely to make much progress. However, when community and school values converge, peripheral communities can offer rich sources of moral, instructional, and material support. According to this view, the task facing government educators is to foster a positive role for the community in the provision of education.

We have suggested a collaborative model of educational provision in which: 1) government considers the constraints, needs, and values of the community and adapts the delivery of education accordingly, 2) the community is actively involved in supporting the school, and 3) the school plays an active leadership and instructional role in the community. While such an approach may improve education in the center, it may be essential for reaching the periphery. Such collaboration can be promoted in a number of ways. If any overall lesson emerges from this review, however, it is that attention to specific contexts is essential in attempting to reach the periphery. Thus, we have identified broad strategies with specific operational components which policymakers can adapt to their particular circumstances. Improvements in school-community relations offer an under-utilized policy space for improving education. Utilizing this space requires imagination, changes in attitudes, sustained and careful attention to implementation, but relatively little money.

Lessons for Improved School-Community Relations

Promote Innovation
The most creative school-community projects developed first as experiments or as nongovernmental initiatives designed to address needs not being met by the regular operation of the school system. While some projects were later expanded or incorporated into the government system, the impetus typically came from outside. Though government has a poor record of initiating innovation, it has an important role to play in supporting it. There are several ways governments can support innovation. They can: publicize the need for innovation, loosening regulations that prevent new experimentation; provide small grants to support new projects; and facilitate the expansion of small-scale projects. Governments can also stress in their training programs the need for innovation at all levels of the education system and provide financial, career, or status incentives to successful innovators.

Work toward Collaborative rather than Competitive or Coercive Relationships among Educational Actors

Virtually all of the changes suggested in this report require cooperation among parents and community members, school staff, and educational authorities. Such cooperation is hindered by competition for resources or status, or by relationships predicated on enforcement. Collaboration is enhanced by regular, structured communication among actors in the educational process and clear delineation of responsibilities and "turf." Openness of the school to ideas from the outside has been cited as one of the single most important determinants of community participation. Teachers are unlikely to attempt new teaching practices if supervisors chastise them for not "going by the book." Negative teacher attitudes toward rural people are cited as a major reason for lack of participation and high dropout rates. (National Council of Educational Research and Training, 1970.)

Treat the Community as Responsible for Education and as a Capable Partner in Providing It

Implicit in most existing educational arrangements is the notion that education is solely the business of government professionals. Here we have argued that community attitudes toward the school determine much of the effectiveness of schooling, and that community interest in education, properly channeled, can endow schools with support that government professionals cannot. Involvement of the community in planning and delivering education can go a long way toward giving the community ownership of the school and a stake in its success. Projects have demonstrated that even the poorest parents will assume responsibility for educating their children if permitted and guided.

Find Ways to Involve the School in Meeting Community Needs

Schools have the potential to offer communities much more than they typically do now. By expanding educational programs beyond the usual school populations, by sharing resources and by assuming a leadership role in the community, schools can make a real difference in community life, especially in the periphery.

Start Where People Are; Adapt the Delivery of Education in the Periphery to Local Values, Needs, Economic Constraints, and Cultures

Lack of participation in education frequently derives from a pedagogically unnecessary mismatch between the form in which education is delivered and the needs and values of peripheral populations. Where educational programs are carefully designed in consideration of local perspectives, children and their parents become strong school supporters. Such design requires careful attention to the constraints facing children and their families, targeting of special subpopulations, and a willingness on the part of government officials to modify their conceptions of what a school must be like.

Make It Easy for Children to Succeed

Repetition and dropout frequently result from children's encounters with systems that require lock-step participation and make education into a series of hoops through which children must jump. If the objective is universal enrollment and learning, governments need to: emphasize positive early encounters with education, minimize the chances of failure, offer second and third chances to learn, and provide multiple ways into the system.

Develop Appropriate Curricula

The content of standard curricula developed for urban, mainstream, further-education-seeking students is often not appropriate to the needs of rural, peripheral children who may end their education early. Similarly, a curriculum predicated on the assumption that one teacher will be teaching one grade often does not fit the reality of peripheral classrooms, where multigrade teaching is often the rule, and where students may come and go according to household demands. The most successful programs have developed instructional programs that are student-centered, of obvious utility, and require only resources that students have access to. Successful curricula lend themselves to self- or peer-instruction and are flexibly structured so that children can stop studying at any point and resume later without penalty. The best instructional materials are adaptable to the varying capacities of teachers yet permit creative adaptation (as opposed to application) by the teacher to local and classroom contexts. At the same time, alternative curricula need to provide students who wish to continue their schooling with an adequate academic background. That all of these requirements can be met is illustrated by the *Escuela Nueva* program.

Train People for Collaboration

The types of collaboration envisioned here do not come naturally to people working in the current system. Every successful school-community program has included a substantial and ongoing training component. System administrators need training for new roles as collaborators in innovation as opposed to enforcers of regulations. Principals need to know how to reach out to and involve the community in the school. Teachers need training in adapting instruction to particular needs. Communities need to be trained in their responsibilities and capacities as partners in education.

Regularly Supervise and Support Peripheral School Staff

Principals and teachers are particularly isolated in the periphery. Innovation is enhanced, principal and teacher behavior improves, student achievement increases, and repetition decreases when sub-district offices are established near schools and when schools receive regular supervisory visits. Supervision is particularly effective when it helps teachers improve instruction in a collegial fashion. In many contexts, school clusters have been useful in promoting innovation and reducing the isolation of small peripheral schools (refer to Bray, 1987, for a more complete treatment of school clusters).

Promote Personal Contact in the Community

Personal relationships are extremely important in most peripheral communities. All successful school-community innovations had at least one committed person at the local level to make contact with community members and parents, to follow through on various tasks involved in project implementation and to solve problems. A project often succeeds or fails because of the personality of the project broker.

Implement Carefully
While most of the projects described here are relatively inexpensive, they require careful attention to implementation, especially during introduction and expansion. All projects require committed local staff to shepherd the project. Projects being implemented across larger areas need sustained leadership from the top and cooperation from actors at all levels of all government agencies involved. (Cummings, Gunawardena, and Williams, 1992.)[3] Successful projects learn from their mistakes (Republic of Colombia, 1990), make adjustments for unanticipated outcomes in-process, and anticipate resistance from those with stakes in current arrangements.

CONCLUSION
In this review, we have attempted to describe strategies for promoting successful school-community interactions. Projects are successful to the extent that they choose a mix of strategies appropriate to the needs and capabilities of government, school, and community. Both government and community are essential to providing more and better education to the periphery. The art is managing appropriate roles for each.

Endnotes

1. Refer to Bray and Lillis, 1988, for an extensive treatment of the issues highlighted in this section.
2. This figure is based on the value of contributions—monetary, labor, and in-kind—principals estimated that communities made to schools divided by the value of contributions of schools to communities. (Cummings, Gunawardena, and Williams, 1992.)
3. For theory and examples of successful and unsuccessful implementation of projects, see, for example, Korten and Klauss, 1984; Rondinelli, 1990; and Warwick, 1982.

Bibliography

Anderson, Mary B. "Improving Access to Schooling in the Third World: An Overview," *BRIDGES Research Report Series,* No. 1. Cambridge, MA: Harvard Institute for International Development, 1988.

Bellew, Rosemary, and Elizabeth King. "Promoting Girls' and Women's Education: Lessons from the Past," *Policy Research, and External Affairs Working Papers (WPS715).* Washington, DC: World Bank, 1991.

Boothroyd, R.A., and D.W. Chapman. "Gender Differences and Achievement in Liberian Primary School Children," *International Journal of Educational Development* 7 (1987): 99-105.

Bray, Mark. *School Clusters in the Third World: Making Them Work.* Paris: UNESCO-UNICEF Cooperative Programme, 1987.

Bray, Mark, and Kevin Lillis. *Community Financing of Education: Issues and Policy Implications in Less Developed Countries.* Oxford: Pergamon Press, 1988.

Carino, Isidro, and Mona Valisno. "Parent-Learning Support System (PLSS): A School and Home-Community Collaboration for Raising Pupil Achievement," in Sheldon Shaeffer, ed., *School and Community Collaboration for Educational Change: Report of an IIEP Seminar.* Paris: International Institute for Educational Planning, 1991.

Coletta, Nat, and Margaret Sutton. "Achieving and Sustaining Universal Primary Education: International Experience Relevant to India," *WPS 166.* Washington, DC: World Bank, 1989.

Cummings, William. *Low-Cost Primary Education: Implementing an Innovation in Six Nations.* Ottawa: International Development Research Centre, 1986.

Cummings, William, G.B. Gunawardena, and James Williams. "The Implementation of Management Reforms: The Case of Sri Lanka," *BRIDGES Research Report Series,* No.11. Cambridge, MA: Harvard Institute for International Development, 1992.

Dove, Linda. "The Deployment and Training of Teachers for Remote Rural Schools in Less-Developed Countries," *International Review of Education,* v 28 (1982): 1- 27.

———. *Teachers and Teacher Education in Developing Countries.* London: Croom Helm, 1986.

Eisemon, Thomas, and Ali Wasi. "Koranic Schooling and its Transformation in Coastal Kenya," *International Journal of Educational Development* , v 6 (1987): 257-70.

Ekanayake, S.B. "Training Teachers for Changing Roles in Sri Lanka," *Prospects*, v 10 (1980).

Enquist, O. *Education and Training in Sri Lanka: A Sector Analysis*. School of Education, Malmo, Sweden, No. 77, 1982.

Haddad, Wadi. "Educational and Economic Effects of Promotion and Repetition Practices," *World Bank Staff Working Paper*, No. 319. Washington, DC: World Bank, 1979.

Halpern, Robert. "Effects of Early Childhood Intervention on Primary School Progress in Latin America," *Comparative Education Review,* v 30 (1986): 193-215.

Improving the Efficiency of Educational Systems (IEES). "The Feasibility of Integrating Programmed Learning with Conventional Instruction in Liberian Primary Education." Tallahassee, FL: Florida State University , 1986.

Jolly, Richard, and Giovanni A. Cornia. *The Impact of the World Recession on Children*. Oxford: Pergamon Press, 1984.

Kelly, Gail. "Setting State Policy on Women's Education in the Third World: Perspectives from Comparative Research," *Comparative Education Review,* v 23 (1987): 95-102.

Korten, David and Rudi Klauss, *People-Centered Development: Contributions Toward Theory and Planning Frameworks*. West Hartford, CT: Kumarian Press, 1984.

Latif, Abu Hamid. "A Case Study on Bangladesh Rural Advancement Committee's Facilitation Assistance Programme on Education." Mimeo, 1991.

Lebby, Sam, and Jack Lutz "Education and Productive Work: The *Bunumbu* Approach," *Prospects,* v 12 (1982): 485-93.

Lee, Valerie, and Marlaine Lockheed. "The Effects of Single-Sex Schooling on Achievement and Attitudes in Nigeria," *Comparative Education Review,* v 34 (1990): 209-231.

LeVine, Robert, and Merry White. *Human Conditions: The Cultural Basis for Educational Development*. New York: Routledge and Kegan Paul, 1986.

Lillis, Kevin, and Henry Ayot. "Community Financing of Education in Kenya," in Mark Bray, and Kevin Lillis, eds., *Community Financing of Education: Issues and Policy Implications in Less Developed Countries*. Oxford: Pergamon Press, 1988.

Lillis, Kevin and M.E. Sinclair, eds. *School and Community in Less Developed Areas*. London: Croom Helm, 1985.

Lockheed, Marlaine, and Adriaan Verspoor, et al. *Improving Primary Education in Developing Countries*. Washington, DC: World Bank , 1990.

Lovell, Catherine and Kaniz Fatema. *The BRAC: Non-Formal Primary Education Programme in Bangladesh*. New York: UNICEF, 1989.

Lycette, Margaret. "The Industrial and Commercial Job Training for Women Project in Morocco." Washington, DC: United States Agency for International Development, 1986.

Mallon, Nacha. "The Community Classroom," *World Education Reports*, v 28 (1989): 15-18.

Malpica, C. "Education and the Community in the Peruvian Educational Reform," *International Review of Education*, v 26(1980): 357-367.

Merino, Jose. *Mirando al Manan: Una Educacion Shuar*. Sucua, Ecuador: Mundo Shuar, 1984.

Meyer, John, Francisco Ramirez, Richard Rubinson, and John Boli-Bennett. "The World Educational Revolution, 1950-1970." *Sociology of Education*, v 50(1977): 242-58.

Moegiadi, Jiyono, Mudjiman, and Soemardi. "Experiences in School and Community Collaboration," in Sheldon Shaeffer, ed., *School and Community Collaboration for Educational Change: Report of an IIEP Seminar*. Paris: International Institute for Educational Planning, 1991.

Naik, Chitra. "An Action-Research Program on Universal Primary Education—The Plan and the Process," in Gail Kelly and C. Elliot, eds., *Women's Education in the Third World: Comparative Perspectives*. Albany, NY: State University of New York, 1982.

————. "Promoting Primary and Elementary Education (PROPEL)," in Sheldon Shaeffer, ed., *School and Community Collaboration for Educational Change: Report of an IIEP Seminar*. Paris: International Institute for Educational Planning, 1991.

National Council of Educational Research and Training (NCERT) in India. "Attacking Educational Wastage at the Primary Level in India." *Education in Asia: Reviews, Reports, and Notes.* Bangkok: UNESCO Regional Office for Education in Asia, 1970.

National Institute of Education. Case Studies of School-Community Relations. Colombo, Sri Lanka: Ministry of Education. Mimeos, 1986.

Ngalamu, J. "Integrated Rural Education Centers (IRECs) as Basis of Vocationalization at Primary School Level: The Southern Sudanese Experience." London: Institute of Education, London University , 1986.

Nielsen, H. Dean, and William Cummings. "The Impact of 'IMPACT': A Study of the Dissemination of an Innovation in Six Countries." Mimeo. Ottawa: International Development Education Centre, 1985.

Nkinyangi, John. "Access to Primary Education in Kenya: The Contradictions of Public Policy," *Comparative Education Review*, v 26(1982): 199-217.

Okoye, Mary. "Community Secondary Schools: A Case Study of a Nigerian Innovation in Self-Help," *International Journal of Educational Development*, v 6 (1986): 263-74.

Orata, Pedro. "Barrio High Schools and Community Colleges in the Philippines," *Prospects,* v 7(1977): 401-12.

Pollitt, Earnest. *Malnutrition and Infection in the Classroom*. Paris: UNESCO, 1990.

Prophet, Robert. "Curriculum-In-Action: The Practical Dimension in Botswana Classrooms," *International Journal of Educational Development*, v 10 (1990): 17- 26.

Ramirez, Francisco, and John Boli. "The Political Construction of Mass Schooling: European Origins and Worldwide Institutionalization," *Sociology of Education,* v 60 (1987): 2-17.

Ramirez, Francisco, and Richard Rubinson . "Global Patterns of Educational Institutionalization," in Philip Altbach, Robert Arnove, and Gail Kelly, eds., *Comparative Education*. New York: Macmillan , 1982.

Rasmussen, P.E. "The Mass Educational Program of the IRDP/DANIDA Project, Noakhali, Bangladesh: A Success Story So Far," *International Journal of Educational Development*, v 5 (1985): 27-39.

Republic of Colombia. "The New School Programme: More and Better Education for Children in Rural Areas." Bogota: Ministry of Education, 1990.

Robinson, Wade, Nadia Makery, and Andrea Rugh. "Fourth Annual Report of the Study of USAID Contributions to the Egyptian Basic Education Program." Washington, DC: Creative Associates, 1987.

Rondinelli, D.A. *Planning Educational Reforms in Developing Countries: The Contingency Approach.* Durham, NC: Duke University Press, 1990.

Ruiz-Duran, G. "Experience of Educational Microplanning in Peru Through Nuclearisation" in D. Malpica and S. Rassekh, eds., *Educational Administration and Multilevel Plan Implementation: Experiences From Developing Countries.* Paris: UNESCO, IIEP, 1980.

Salazar, A. "On Educational Reform in Peru," *Prospects*, v 2 (1972): 383-391.

Shaeffer, Sheldon, ed. *School and Community Collaboration for Educational Change: Report of an IIEP Seminar.* Paris: International Institute for Educational Planning , 1991.

————. *Collaborating for Educational Change: The Role of Teachers, Parents and the Community in School Improvement.* Paris: International Institute for Educational Planning, 1992.

Simanungkalit, Dr., Colin Moyle, and Doran Bernard. "Community Participation in the Planning and Implementation of Educational Resources (COPLANNER)," in Sheldon Shaeffer, ed., *School and Community Collaboration for Educational Change: Report of an IIEP Seminar.* Paris: International Institute for Educational Planning, 1991.

Singh, R.P. "An Indian Experiment in Earning While Learning," *Prospects,* v 12 (1982): 495-8.

Stromquist, Nelly. "A Review of Educational Innovations to Reduce Costs," in Sivasailam Thiagarajan, and Aida Pasigna, eds., *Financing Educational Development.* Ottawa: International Development Research Center, 1981.

Thiagarajan, Sivasailam, and Aida Pasigna. "Literature Review on the Soft Technologies of Learning," *BRIDGES Research Report Series,* No. 2. Cambridge, MA: Harvard Institute for International Development, 1988.

Thinh, Bui Gia. "Qualitative Improvement in Basic Education through the Collaboration and Co-operation of Parents' Associations," in Sheldon Shaeffer, ed., *School and Community Collaboration for Educational Change: Report of an IIEP Seminar*. Paris: International Institute for Educational Planning, 1991.

Thobani, Mateen. *Charging User Fees for Social Services: The Case of Education in Malawi*. Washington, DC: World Bank, 1983.

Tilak, Jandhyala. "Female Schooling in East Asia: A Review of Growth, Problems and Possible Determinants," *PHREE Background Paper Series, No. PHREE/89/13*. Washington, DC: World Bank, 1989.

UNDP. "Nepal: Teacher Training (Equal Access of Women to Education)." Project Findings and Recommendations. New York: UNDP, 1982.

UNESCO, Asian Programme of Educational Innovation for Development. "Towards Universalization of Primary Education in Asia and the Pacific, India Country Study." Bangkok: UNESCO Regional Office, 1984a.

————. "Towards Universalization of Primary Education in Asia and the Pacific, Bangladesh Country Study." Bangkok: UNESCO Regional Office, 1984b.

————. "The Dropout Problem in Primary Education: Towards Universalization of Primary Education in Asia and the Pacific—Some Case Studies: China, India, Peninsula Malaysia, Socialist Republic of Vietnam, Sri Lanka and Thailand." Bangkok: UNESCO Regional Office, 1984c.

USAID. "Industrial and Commercial Job Training for Women in Morocco, Final Report." Washington, DC: U.S. Agency for International Development, 1983.

Verspoor, Adriaan, and Janet Leno. "Improving Teaching: A Key to Successful Educational Change, Lessons from World Bank Experience." Washington, DC: World Bank, 1986.

Wan, U Thien. "A Study of Educational Wastage in Burma." *Education in Asia: Reviews, Reports, and Notes*, No. 7. Bangkok: UNESCO Regional Office, 1975.

Warwick, Donald. *Bitter Pills: Population Policies and Their Implementation in Eight Developing Countries*. Cambridge: Cambridge University Press, 1982.

Warwick, Donald, Fernando Reimers, and Noel McGinn. "The Implementation of Reforms in the Primary Schools of Pakistan." Cambridge, MA: Harvard Institute for International Development, 1989.

Weick, Karl. "Administering Education in Loosely-Coupled Systems," *Phi Delta Kappan*, v 63 (1982): 673-676.

Weiner, Myron. *The Child and the State in India*. Princeton: Princeton University Press, 1991.

Wiggington, Eliot. *Foxfire: 25 Years*. New York: Anchor Books, 1991.

Windham, D.M. "Cost Analysis of the Improved Efficiency of Learning Project." Monrovia, Liberia: Ministry of Education , 1983.

World Bank. "Colombia Staff Appraisal Report. Subsector Project for Rural Basic Education." Washington, DC, 1982.

————. "Staff Appraisal Report Bangladesh Secondary Primary Education Project." Washington, DC, 1985.

————. "Project Completion Report, Fourth Education Project (Credit 892-Pak)." Washington, DC, 1987a.

————. "Staff Appraisal Report: Islamic Republic of Pakistan Third Primary Education Project." Washington, DC, 1987b; also cited in Bellew and King, 1991.

————. "Staff Appraisal Report, Bhutan Primary Education Project." Washington, DC, 1988.

————. "Staff Appraisal Report, The Gambia Education Sector Project." Washington, DC, 1990a.

————. "Staff Appraisal Report, The Sind Primary Education Project." Washington, DC, 1990b.

————. *Vocational and Technical Education and Training*. Washington, DC: World Bank, 1991.

CHAPTER 4

School-Language Policy Decisions for Nondominant Language Groups

Zeynep F. Beykont

INTRODUCTION

This paper is a survey of issues involved in the choice of school- language policies for nondominant language groups. The term "nondominant language group" refers to groups whose native languages are *different from* a country's:

- official language(s);
- prestige language(s);
- language(s) of wider communication;
- language(s) of upward mobility; and/or
- standard dialect.

The widely used term "language minority" is inaccurate because it implies that a language group does not enjoy linguistic and educational rights due to their small number in a society. In many countries, such as Cameroon, Indonesia, Luxembourg, and Mali, nondominant language groups constitute the numerical majority. In more extreme cases, such as in Senegal, Liberia, Sierra Leone, and South Africa, more than 80 percent of the population are native speakers of languages or dialects *other than* the respective official languages or standard dialects. The terminology used here broadens the definition of "minority groups" to include all language groups that have *unequal access to educational opportunities* because they speak a native language or dialect different from the official language or the standard dialect.

The main goal of this review is to synthesize different lines of research to inform school-language policy decisions for nondominant language groups. The discussion focuses on nondominant language groups only; readers are referred to Genesee (1991) for an extensive review of research on school-language policies and programs for dominant language groups. Throughout the text, nondominant/first/native language refers to a language or a dialect that nondominant language groups speak and learn at home. Dominant/second/official language refers to the "prestige" and "power" language in a society that nondominant language groups learn at school.

In many educational contexts, children from nondominant language groups exhibit disproportionate school failure and dropout and repetition rates, compared with dominant language groups. (Cummins, 1986; Gibson, 1991; Hakuta, 1986; Ogbu, 1987.) This pattern was observed in high-income countries such as Canada (Swain, 1984), Holland (Appel, 1983), England (Tosi, 1988), and the United States (Hakuta and Gould, 1987), as well as in lower-income countries such as Burundi (Eisemon, Prouty, and Schwille, 1989), Namibia (Haasbroek and Botha, 1989), Paraguay (Corvalán, 1988), and Jamaica (Craig, 1985). In some other contexts, nondominant language groups, such as Chinese in Malaysia, Koreans in the United States, and Vietnamese in Australia, perform as well as or better than dominant language groups. (Barrington, 1991; Gibson, 1991; Lee, 1991; Ogbu, 1991; Shimahara, 1991.)

The disproportionate school failure of nondominant language groups has been attributed to various factors, including the children's inadequate linguistic and intellectual abilities; their families' low socioeconomic backgrounds and unstimulating home environments; and their parents' lack of formal education. (See J. Gonzalez, 1975, and Padilla, 1982, for reviews.) These children were claimed to be "semilinguals," with no proficiency in either native language or official language, due to continual code-switching behavior in their communities and use of nonstandard languages at home. (See Cummins, 1983, for a review.) Bilingualism was argued to cause confusion in language use and cognitive functioning, and therefore to inhibit their academic progress. (See Kessler and Quinn, 1982, and Hakuta, 1986, for a review.) Home-school discontinuity in terms of language and culture was assumed to create school adjustment problems for children, with a consequent achievement gap. (Tharp, 1989; Wong-Fillmore and Valadez, 1986.) Another conjecture was that children from certain racial and ethnic groups were genetically inferior and that their lower intelligence caused lower school performance. (See Padilla, 1982, for a review.) Families' lack of formal education in the official language and their low income levels were other explanations for the disproportionate school failure of some nondominant groups. (Bernstein, 1970; Laosa, 1984.) Finally, persistent school problems were attributed to the unfavorable power relations between nondominant and dominant language groups. (Macedo, 1994.)

In the following pages, I give an overview of the rationales for widely used school-language policies and the characteristics of language programs. I then survey psycholinguistic, sociopolitical, and sociohistorical perspectives on school-language policies for nondominant language groups. I examine psycholinguistic research in order to highlight pedagogical considerations involved in choosing and implementing a sound educational language policy and program. The discussion on sociopolitical issues focuses on the varied governmental orientations toward linguistic diversity, with implications for their choice of language of instruction, amount of intergroup contact in schools, community involvement, and educational objectives. The review of sociohistorical factors highlights the varied educational expectations, motivations, and goals of nondominant communities in relation to their support for a school-language policy. The chapter ends with a summary of findings from three decades of research on school-language policies. Case studies and boxes exemplify different facets of the education of nondominant language groups in diverse policy contexts.

SCHOOL-LANGUAGE POLICIES FOR NONDOMINANT LANGUAGE GROUPS

Broadly speaking, two different educational language policies have been adopted in the education of nondominant language groups. The first policy is the use of an official language, a standard dialect, or a metropolitan language such as English, French or Spanish, as the medium of instruction. The main argument for this policy is that nondominant language groups need to acquire literacy skills in a language of upward mobility or of worldwide communication so that they have competitive advantages in the economic world. (Spencer, 1985.) Accordingly, the sooner children are exposed to the dominant language as the medium of instruction, the more rapidly they acquire it and can participate in the mainstream. (Glazer and Moynihan, 1970; Porter, 1990.)

Some of the advantages of adopting a metropolitan or an official language as the medium of instruction are the following. In countries like Nigeria or Sri Lanka, where there is more than one influential ethnic group and more than one local language widely spoken, use of a metropolitan, "politically neutral" language as the language of instruction may prevent ethnic cleavage that could arise from favoring one regional language or ethnic group over another. (Dada, 1985.) Furthermore, this policy may promote linguistic unity because it makes nationwide communication possible in linguistically heterogeneous countries, such as South Africa, that would otherwise lack a common language (see Box 4.1). This policy also promises financial advantages because it allows standardization in planning, preparing or importing textbooks, other teaching materials, and teacher education programs. (Spencer, 1985.)

One disadvantage of using a metropolitan or official language as the medium of instruction is the resultant lack of parental help and community involvement in children's education. (Cummins, 1986.) Furthermore, children are overburdened, in trying to gain literacy and academic skills through a language that they are not fluent in, and therefore are more likely to be tracked out of the academic path, to repeat a grade, and to drop out of school. (Hakuta, 1986.) From a developmental perspective, this school-language policy is disadvantageous because it does not build on children's existing native language skills. (J. Gonzalez, 1975.) Finally, from an ecological and moral perspective, this language policy is catastrophic because it results in steadily decreasing numbers of languages and cultures across the world and a consequent loss of major human potential and rich cultural knowledge. (Crawford, 1991.)

The second-language policy is the use of children's native languages as a medium of instruction. The main argument for this policy is that acquisition of basic literacy skills and comprehension of academic content is easier if instruction is in the native language. (Cummins, 1981; Mikes, 1986; Skutnabb-Kangas, 1984.) Accordingly, the argument goes, insofar as elementary education is a basic human right, every child has the right to be taught in their native language or local dialect— at least until they learn the official language. (UNESCO, 1953.)

Proponents of this policy emphasize pedagogical, cognitive, motivational, and economic benefits of native-language instruction. They argue that early conceptual and perceptual development can be built upon by instruction in children's native language. (Haasbroek and Botha, 1989; Pattanayak, 1986.) Another important

Box 4.1. Metropolitan Language Policy in South Africa: An Interview [1]

Depending on the region, we speak a different mother tongue. So, for example, in the Cape, the Western Cape, the mother tongue is Xhosa. Up in the East Coast region, people speak Zulu as the mother tongue. In the north, the Johannesburg area, they speak Sutu. . . .

The official languages of South Africa are English and Africaans. There's a lot, I think, of reflection about whether one shouldn't add an African language as the official language. . . . Here [in the U.S.], Spanish would be a minority language. In our country, African languages are the majority language because there are forty million people, that's the population. Of that forty million, say five to six million are whites and Indians, five million are colored, and the rest are black. But, again, apartheid has so destroyed intergroup communication. There isn't one language that everybody throughout the whole country speaks besides the official languages, and that is [only] because they've been forced to learn it in school. So even though there are similarities in the languages, the people in the north, for example, don't speak Xhosa. The people in the south don't speak Zulu. And if they choose one of those as an official language, it is going to alienate the other groups. . . .

In the black community, parents actually are in favor of English rather than Africaans as the medium of instruction because of all the economic and practical reasons. It's seen as the language of social mobility, educational mobility. You know, it is the language that you would use to get ahead. You can't go to another country and speak Africaan because they won't understand you. You can't import textbooks in Africaan, you can't export students to go abroad and come back and introduce new ideas. The universities don't know students' home languages, the qualified teachers don't know their languages. I think that maybe that will change with time, but for the next decade, I would say that probably people are looking to English until that time.

argument for using the native language is that parents can be involved in children's education, can help with and monitor homework, and can communicate with teachers about their children's academic progress. (Moll, 1992.) Furthermore, instruction in the native language legitimizes nondominant groups' home culture and language, and therefore has motivational effects on children's school attendance and performance. (McGroarty, 1992.) Finally, this policy has long-term economic benefits because children who are instructed in their native language generally do not repeat grades or drop out of school. (Hornberger, 1987; Pattanayak, 1986.)

Nevertheless, there are certain practical problems associated with using native language as the language of instruction in the education of nondominant groups. For instance, some languages (such as the hundreds of languages spoken in Papua New Guinea), although widely spoken, do not have a written script or an established written literacy tradition. The development of alphabets, standardization of languages, and expansion of vocabulary for use in academic matters require a long-term financial investment and time commitment from governments. (Haasbroek and Botha, 1989; Mackey, 1984.) Furthermore, native-language instruction can pose logistical problems, especially in countries with a high linguistic heterogeneity, such as India or Nigeria, where hundreds of languages are spoken. Implementing teacher education programs and preparing instructional materials in so many languages may be impractical. (J. Edwards, 1984.) Finally, in many countries, where the language of higher education and upward mobility is a metropolitan or an official language, it may seem more efficient to teach children in that language from early on (e.g., Eisemon et al., 1989). (See Box 4.2 on next page.)

LANGUAGE PROGRAMS FOR NONDOMINANT LANGUAGE GROUPS

The positive effects of prolonged bilingual instruction are cumulative, showing themselves most distinctly and robustly after five to seven years of instruction. (Dolson and Mayer, 1991: 124)

School-language policies discussed above are implemented through a choice of five commonly used language programs in the education of nondominant language groups: submersion programs, immersion programs, transitional bilingual programs, maintenance language programs, and home-language programs. In the following, these programs are discussed with regard to their instructional features and objectives, community involvement, and intergroup contact.

Submersion Programs

In a submersion program, nondominant language groups are instructed in mainstream classrooms through the official language, a nonnative language to them. The official language is the exclusive language of instruction and children's native languages are not used for instructional purposes. Teachers are monolingual speakers of the official language, which prevents children from asking questions for clarification and comprehension. Furthermore, the program is *not* designed for nondominant language

Box 4.2. Native Language Policy in Papua New Guinea

Native-language literacy programs in Papua New Guinea illustrate what is possible if governments are willing to respond to the educational needs of nondominant language groups and to utilize community resources in this effort. Papua New Guinea is a linguistically heterogenous country with eight hundred language groups of different sizes, which have no written literacy tradition. More than 90 percent of the country speaks a native language different from the official language.

A large-scale, community-based literacy program was launched in 1989 to introduce native language instruction to more than eight hundred language groups in Papua New Guinea. S.E. Malone described the importance of community involvement as follows:

> Community people are involved in each phase of planning, implementing, expanding, and maintaining their programme. They decide who the learners will be. They select and support their own teachers. They are involved in the production of their own reading materials and in building and maintaining classrooms. Because community people plan and implement their own programmes, the programmes are developed to meet the specific interests, needs and goals of the learners. (Malone, 1992: 2)

Use of previously unwritten languages as a medium of instruction involves developing new alphabets, curriculum, textbooks, teaching materials, and teacher-education programs. However, what once seemed impractical, inefficient, formidable, and expensive is now possible with new translation capabilities and innovative use of technologies and materials.

> There is little to read besides basic primers and a few story books on the elementary level, with very little for the intermediate reader. . . . As a partial solution to producing a greater variety of reading material, the concept of "shell books" was introduced. A shell is a book framework which contains illustrations and the mechanical details of a book layout but lacks the text which can be supplied in the specific language. It promises to be an inexpensive approach, easy to produce, and easily adopted across the 800 languages of Papua New Guinea. . . .
>
> Although the idea started as a computer-related phenomenon, it has moved beyond that and now utilizes whatever technology is appropriate and available in the local community setting—typewriters, silkscreening, handwriting, etc. Shell technology has been tested among 25 different language groups. . . .
>
> Since the introduction of the concept of shell books, the National Department of Education has come to view the production of vernacular books as a foreseeable possibility in many languages for the nation's 2600 community schools. Their goal is to build a library of 200 well-tested, well-used titles which can then be translated into many other languages. (Summer Institute of Linguistics, Annual Report 1990: 18.)

The task is seemingly expensive. Long-term consequences "of malnourished children, of unproductive labor, of noncompetitive businesses, of high attrition rates in existing schools of a discouraged and lethargic populace," however, can be more costly. (Summer Institute of Linguistics, 1989: 20.) An earlier evaluation study conducted in Tokples schools in Papua New Guinea, for example, demonstrated the motivational effects of native-language instruction on children's school retention. (Davis, 1986.) In this study, children instructed in their native language were much less likely to drop out of school, compared with children instructed in the official language.

groups. Regular curriculum, textbooks, and teaching materials are used to teach the subject matter. Generally, there is no teaching of the official language as a second language. In other words, with no support, nondominant language groups in submersion programs learn basic literacy skills as well as content areas in a language that they do not speak fluently. Because of the lack of accommodation to children's linguistic and academic needs, submersion programs are known as the "sink or swim" approach to the education of nondominant language groups. (Hakuta, 1986; Skutnabb-Kangas, 1983.)

A variant of submersion programs may entail some second-language support. For example in Sweden, immigrant children are offered an intensive second-language program *prior to* their placement in all-Swedish mainstream classrooms. (Skutnabb-Kangas, 1983.) In some other contexts, like the United States or Canada, children are pulled from mainstream classes and given instruction in English as a second language for part of the day. (J. Gonzalez, 1975.)

Submersion programs are used worldwide. For example, they are used in Morocco with the Berber-speaking group; in Paraguay with Guarani speakers; in Guam with Chamarro speakers; in Britain with West Indians; in Hungary with the Roms; and in Denmark, Norway, France, Holland, Germany, Sweden, and the United States with various immigrant groups.

Immersion Programs

Immersion programs were originally developed in Canada to foster balanced bilingualism in English-speaking children (dominant language group) by instructing them first exclusively through French (nondominant language) and then bilingually through French and English. *All* children in immersion classes are second-language learners. Academic instruction is integrated with teaching of French. The teacher is typically a native speaker of French. Native language instruction is introduced three to four years into the program; English literacy development is gradually emphasized, and an increasing number of content areas are taught in English. By the sixth grade, half of the instruction is in English and half in French and the program goal is bilingualism.

The original immersion program model was adopted to teach nondominant language groups in various parts of the world. In some contexts, such as Cameroon, Mali, Zambia, Senegal, Sierra Leone, and Liberia, a former colonial language is used as the sole language of instruction, even though the majority of children and teachers speak a different language at home. The program resembles the original immersion program in that all students in the class are second-language learners of the language of instruction. Consequently, teachers can accommodate their instructional language to children's linguistic ability and level of understanding. In contrast to the original model, children have little exposure to native speakers of the colonial language and no access to bilingual materials. Textbooks and teaching materials are usually published in the former colonizing country, and therefore are not culturally relevant. Unlike the original immersion model that aims to foster bilingualism, the goal of the immersion program in postcolonial states is monolingualism in the former colonial language. Children's native language is not introduced as an additional instructional medium.

Another form of immersion program, called the *structured immersion* program, is used in the United States in the education of nondominant language groups. The language of instruction in these programs is English throughout children's schooling. In structured immersion programs, teaching of English and other subjects are integrated and presented at a linguistic level that is comprehensible to nondominant language groups. For the first few years, nondominant language groups are instructed separately from native-English-speakers. Children are mainstreamed once they are judged to be fluent in English. Teachers in structured immersion programs are usually bilingual; consequently, children can ask and answer questions in their native language, if necessary. Typically, teachers use English exclusively, and pace their lessons according to children's linguistic needs and levels. Structured immersion programs have been used for Mexican, Puerto Rican, Mexican American, Cuban, and Chicano students in different parts of the United States.

Immersion programs are also used for language *revival purposes*, i.e., to revive languages that are in danger of extinction. Communities usually initiate language-revival programs to (a) alter the negative effects of mainstream education on children's knowledge and appreciation of their native language; (b) ground children in their cultural traditions; and (c) develop heritage languages. Language-revival programs are sometimes taught by older members of the community, and have been used with preschool-age children, such as those established in New Zealand to revive the Maori language. (See Box 4.3; also Benton, 1986, and Cazden, Snow, and Heise-Baigorria, 1990, for a review.) After-school language revival programs have been used to develop native-language literacy skills in addition to the literacy skills in the official language, such as all-Hawaiian and all-Japanese after-school programs in Hawaii. (Huebner, 1985.)

Transitional Bilingual Programs

In transitional bilingual programs, nondominant language groups are taught basic literacy and academic skills, including reading, writing, and math, in their native language while learning the official language as a second language. As soon as children are somewhat fluent in the official language, they are placed in mainstream classrooms. Native-language instruction is discontinued.

The main pedagogical assumption of the program is that the more quickly children are placed in mainstream classrooms, the more they are exposed to the official language and to native speakers of it, and the faster they learn it. (See Wong-Fillmore and Valadez, 1986, for a review.) The decision about the appropriate time to mainstream children is often based on teachers' evaluation of children's fluency in the official language. Generally, children are mainstreamed within two to four years, and teaching of the official language as a second language is discontinued. Once mainstreamed, children may be allowed to ask questions and speak with friends or teachers in their native language. Teachers may be fluent in both languages, or may rely on bilingual teaching assistants.

UNESCO (1953) advocated and advised the use of transitional bilingual programs in linguistically diverse countries. Many countries that followed UNESCO

Box 4.3. Language Revival Programs in New Zealand

The indigenous Maori population in New Zealand has been educated in all-English programs since the Native School Act was introduced in 1867. (Barrington, 1991.) For about a century, Maori children continued to be instructed in English only because the European settlers (Pakeha) perceived the use of Maori for instructional purposes as a hindrance to Maori children's academic and economic advancement. Maori children were forbidden to use their native language at school, even among friends.

In 1969, Maori and Pakeha schools were desegregated in the hopes that race relations would improve and that academic disparities between the dominant and nondominant language groups would decline. (Barrington, 1991.) The instructional medium continued to be English, with no extra second-language support for Maori children. Desegregation efforts did not bring about the hoped-for changes in Maori children's academic performance; school achievement disparities between Pakeha and Maori children remained the same.

The government attributed Maori children's underperformance to the discontinuity between the culture and language of the community and the culture and language of the school. In the 1970s, steps were taken to incorporate Maori language and culture into the curriculum and to train teachers and administrators about Maori traditions. Small adjustments were made in the teaching of Maori children to compensate for their cultural and linguistic "deficiencies."

The Maori community was convinced that public schools were not providing children with proper knowledge of their history, language, and the cultural practices of the community. In addition, the Maori community had concerns about the survival of their language and culture. In the 1980s, parents and community members decided to take charge of their children's education and started establishing their own preschools and primary schools, called "Kura Kaupapa Maori" (total immersion in Maori language and culture). (Smith, 1992: 89.) Children in these community-based educational programs are immersed in Maori language and culture. Since the pressure outside of the school is to learn the Pakeha culture (i.e., the dominant culture) and use English (the official language), all-Maori immersion programs result in bilingualism.

The outcome of the total immersion experience for pupils is bilingualism and biculturalism and includes Maori parents assuming power to choose those aspects of Pakeha culture which are to be incorporated in the curriculum. (Smith, 1992: 97.)

guidelines adopted these programs, including Burundi for Kirundi speakers; Nigeria for Yoruba, Hausa, and Igbo speakers; Malaysia for Chinese speakers; Ecuador for Quichua speakers. Transitional bilingual programs were also adopted by Britain for Asian groups and the United States for Puerto Ricans, Asian Americans, and Mexican Americans.

Maintenance Bilingual Programs

In maintenance bilingual programs, children are instructed in their native language while the official language is gradually incorporated as an additional instructional medium. The basic academic skills of reading, writing, and numeracy are taught first in the native language and later bilingually. One important difference between maintenance bilingual programs and transitional bilingual programs is that in maintenance bilingual programs, the emphasis on native-language literacy development is continued throughout schooling.

In maintenance bilingual programs, teachers are often bilingual and children are allowed to use native language in class with friends and teachers. Even after children are fluent in the official language, they are not mainstreamed. Bilingual instruction continues throughout schooling: part of the time, nondominant groups are instructed separately in the native language, and part of the time, in the official language in mainstream classrooms.

Compared to other language programs, maintenance bilingual programs are used less frequently. The French in Quebec; Swedes in Finland; Germans and French in Italy; and Cubans, Mexican Americans, and Puerto Ricans in some parts of the United States are instructed in these programs.

Another form of maintenance bilingual programs, called two-way bilingual programs, is being used in the United States primarily with Spanish-speaking children. The two-way bilingual model differs from the maintenance bilingual model in that native Spanish-speaking children in these programs (nondominant language group) are instructed together with native English-speaking children (dominant language group) and are not segregated from the rest of the school. Half of the instruction in two-way bilingual programs is in English and half of the instruction is in Spanish. All students in the program acquire literacy skills and academic knowledge bilingually.

Home-Language Programs[2]

Home-language programs are specifically designed for nondominant language groups. All instruction in home-language programs is through children's respective native languages. The official language may be taught as a second language for a few hours a week. Only native-language literacy development is emphasized.

The curriculum in these programs is usually different from that in mainstream classrooms. Home-language programs serving children of "guest workers" in some parts of Europe, for example, use curriculum and instructional materials imported from the immigrants' country of origin. (McLaughlin and Graf, 1985: 245.) Teachers are sent by embassies. They are trained to teach in their home countries and often are not fluent in the language of the host country. Home-language programs in other contexts, such as for blacks in South Africa, use a curriculum that is supposedly designed to enable the child to serve his/her community upon graduation. Whether in Europe or South Africa, however, children in home-language programs are instructed through their native language in segregated schools and taught by teachers from the same linguistic and cultural background as their own. The use of the official language for entrance examinations effectively bars children instructed in home-language programs from continuing their education.

Home-language programs have been used to educate many nondominant language groups, including Indians in Peru; Creoles in Haiti; blacks in South Africa and Namibia; Burakamins and Koreans in Japan; and Turkish people in some parts of Germany.

Table 4.1 below summarizes the discussion above by comparing programs in terms of the medium of instruction, the teaching of the official language as a second language, and children's use of their native languages in each language program.

Table 4.1. Characteristics of Widely Used Language Programs for Nondominant Language Groups

Language Program	Medium of Instruction	L2* as a Subject	Children's Use of L1
Submersion	L2	No	No
Immersion:			
Post-Colonial	L2	Rarely	Yes
Structured	L2	No	Yes→No
Revival	L1	No	Yes
Transitional Bilingual	L1→L2	Yes→No	Yes→No
Maintenance Bilingual	L1→L1&L2	Yes	Yes
Two-Way Bilingual	L1 & L2	Yes	Yes
Home Language	L1	Yes	Yes

*L2 corresponds to official/dominant/second language in a country
*L1 corresponds to native/nondominant/first language
*→ transition from one characteristic to another, e.g. L1→L2 corresponds to transition from instruction

Variations Across Programs

Submersion and structured immersion programs may seem similar. In both of these programs, children have maximum exposure to the official language, because it is the language of instruction from the beginning. It is important to note that submersion programs are *not* designed for nonnative speakers of the official language. Nondominant language groups in these programs are at a considerable disadvantage. With no extra support in mainstream classrooms, children are doubly burdened to learn academic content and the language through which it is taught at the same time. Furthermore, native and nonnative speakers of the official language are instructed together in mainstream classrooms. Typically, teachers in submersion programs do not alter their instructional language to accommodate the proficiency level of a few second-language learners in their classrooms.

Structured immersion programs, on the other hand, are specifically designed for nondominant language groups. Children are placed in classrooms in which all students are second-language speakers of the official language. Teachers can pace their instruction and accommodate students' linguistic needs. In other words, even though children's native language is not used for instructional purposes, there is some accommodation to their linguistic needs.

In both of the bilingual programs, transitional and maintenance, children are instructed in their native language for the first few years. The linguistic goals of the programs are different. Maintenance bilingual programs aim at promoting balanced bilingualism defined as "the alternate use of two languages, either vernacular or standard varieties, manifested in complete and meaningful utterances in each of the languages." (Kessler and Quinn, 1982: 54.) Transitional bilingual programs aim at promoting monolingualism in the official language. One of the leading researchers, Skutnabb-Kangas, maintains that

> .... we cannot examine and compare outcomes of programmes unless we first analyze and compare the goals, both explicit and implicit. Outcomes of using the same methods (e.g. the same language of instruction) can be different if the goals are different. (Skutnabb-Kangas, 1984: 18.)

Skutnabb-Kangas suggests that, for comparative purposes, a sole focus on language of instruction is deceptive. To illustrate this notion, Table 4.2 below summarizes different programs in terms of the medium of instruction, contact between native and nonnative speakers of the official language, and program objectives. Notice that the linguistic objectives of language programs include monolingualism in the official language, monolingualism in the native language, and bilingualism in the official and native languages. The reader should also note that there is variation across language programs regarding the extent of contact between native and nonnative speakers of the official language.

Table 4.2 illustrates that native language can be used as a medium of instruction to realize different linguistic objectives, ranging from bilingualism (as in the case of a maintenance bilingual program) to monolingualism in the official language (as in the case of a transitional bilingual program) or monolingualism in children's native language (as in the case of a home language program). The table also illustrates that structured immersion, submersion, and transitional bilingual programs have similar linguistic goals. Despite the variation in the medium of instruction and level of integration of nondominant groups, all of these programs aim at promoting literacy skills in the official language.

Table 4.2. Language Programs for Nondominant Language Groups and Their Linguistic Objectives

Language Program	Medium of Instruction	L2* as a Subject	Children's Use of L1
Submersion	L2	Yes	Mono in L2
Transitional Bilingual	L1 →L2	No →Yes	Mono in L2
Immersion			
Post-colonial	L2	No	Mono in L2
Structured	L2	No →Yes	Mono in L2
Revival	L1	No	Bilingualism
Maintenance Bilingual	L1 →L1&L2	Gradual	Bilingualism
Two-Way Bilingual	L1 & L2	Yes	Bilingualism
Home Language	L1	No	Mono in L1

Adopted from Fishman and Lovas (1970) and Skutnabb-Kangas (1983, 1984)

*L2 corresponds to official/dominant/second language in a country
*L1 corresponds to native/nondominant/first language
*L1→L2 corresponds to transition from instruction in native language to instruction in second language
*L1→L1 & L2 corresponds to transition from instruction in native language to bilingual instruction

Variation Within Programs
The program descriptions above are "ideal types" that show the range of commonly used programs. The comparisons drawn are based on these prototypical descriptions of programs. In practice, programs may differ from these prototypes and incorporate characteristics from other programs. For example, in practice, transitional bilingual programs vary in the extent of second-language use, the length of native- language instruction, and the proportion of hours spent in mainstream classrooms versus native-language classes. All transitional bilingual programs, however, share an intensive second-language teaching component, a shift in the medium of instruction from native language to second language, and a time limit in the use of native language for instructional purposes.

A recent national evaluation project portrayed the great variation in the extent of first- and second-language use in bilingual classrooms in the United States.

(Ramirez, Ramey, Yuen, and Pasta, 1991.) Classroom observations indicated that some transitional bilingual programs operated more like submersion programs in that the instruction in these programs was almost exclusively in English. Similarly, some maintenance bilingual programs operated more like transitional bilingual programs in terms of the length and extent of teachers' second-language use. Systematic classroom observations can help to "gauge . . . the fidelity of treatment" and "conclusiveness of the results" of program comparisons. (Ramirez, et al., 1991: 23.) In other words, it is crucial that the program implementation be closely observed before any conclusions are drawn about the effectiveness of a program in the education of nondominant language groups.

The next section examines psycholinguistic issues in decisions on school-language policies. This line of research highlights pedagogical considerations involved in choosing and implementing a sound educational language policy and program for nondominant language groups.

A PSYCHOLINGUISTIC PERSPECTIVE ON SCHOOL-LANGUAGE POLICIES FOR NONDOMINANT LANGUAGE GROUPS

> *Sensitivity to meaning that comes with bilingualism deepens one's understanding of concepts. . . . Bilinguals are better able to think beyond the bounds of linguistic systems and to play and create with words and concepts. It is as though bilingualism provides persons with a mental stereoscope, enabling them to see concepts in perspective.* (Lambert, 1981: 3.)

There has been much research on cognitive and academic development of bilingual children. This line of research has important implications for the choice of school-language policies and programs in the education of nondominant language groups. (Cummins, 1981.) Balanced bilingual children—i.e., children who are fully proficient in two languages—demonstrate a wide range of cognitive and analytical skills and academic abilities that monolingual children seem to lack. (See Hakuta, 1986; Kessler and Quinn, 1982, for comprehensive reviews.) These abilities include an analytic orientation (Ben-Zeev, 1977), cognitive flexibility (McLaughlin, 1984), awareness of linguistic operations (Vygotsky, 1962), concept formation (Kessler and Quinn, 1982), and divergent thinking[3] (Kessler and Quinn, 1982.) Pedagogical and programmatic factors that promote or inhibit development of balanced bilingualism in school contexts are reviewed below.

The optimal time to introduce a second language as an instructional medium is one important factor in promoting or inhibiting development of balanced bilingualism. (Lenneberg, 1967; Cummins, 1981.) Early studies supported the folk wisdom that children should be exposed to a second language as early as possible because the younger the child, the easier it is for him/her to achieve a proficiency in two languages. (See McLaughlin, 1984, for an extensive review.) It has been argued that after a "critical period," specified as two to ten years of age, a child's brain rapidly loses its plasticity with regards to second-language development. The policy implication of this belief has been to instruct nondominant language groups in mainstream classrooms and provide maximum exposure to the official language and the native speakers of it as early as possible. (See Hakuta, 1986, for a review.)

The critical-biological-period theory has been discredited, based on more current studies in Israel, Holland, Canada, and the United States that did not indicate a "sudden decline" in second-language development at around ten years of age. (See Hakuta, 1986, for a review.) With the exception of pronunciation skills, older children and adults were found to be equally fast, if not faster, learners of a second language. (Snow and Hoefnagel-Hohle, 1978.) Studies also indicated that children who have well-developed literacy skills in their native language gain literacy skills in a second language quickly. (See Cummins, 1986, for a review.) The policy implication of these findings is that the optimal time to introduce the official language as an instructional medium is after children have developed native-language literacy skills.

There appears to be a close relationship between first- and second-language literacy skills. (Cummins, 1981; Snow, 1981.) Numerous studies have shown that immigrant children who had had several years of schooling in their home country performed well at school in the host country. (Cummins, 1981; Skutnabb-Kangas, 1984; Medina and Escamilla, 1984.) For example, studies of Finnish immigrant children in Sweden have indicated that their level of Finnish reading skills upon arrival is the most stable predictor of a child's Swedish reading development. Finnish children with high Finnish academic language skills, e.g., Finnish reading skills, upon entering school showed rapid progress in acquiring Swedish academic language skills, e.g., Swedish reading skills. (Cummins, 1986; Skutnabb-Kangas and Toukomaa, 1976; Troike, 1978.) Native-language literacy skills supported development of second-language literacy skills. (Cummins, 1981; Snow, 1981.)

These findings were explained by the famous linguistic-interdependence hypothesis and common-underlying-proficiency notion. (Cummins, 1981, 1983, 1986, 1989.) Accordingly, provided children have enough exposure and motivation to learn a second language, most academic language skills acquired in the native language form part of a common underlying proficiency that supports the progress of second-language academic language skills. (Cummins, 1981.) Similarly, academic language skills in the second language support the progress in the native language. (Cummins, 1981.) In terms of school performance of nondominant language groups, then, the crucial determinant is academic language skills in the native language, because skills gained in the native language transfer to the second language.

The linguistic-interdependence hypothesis and common-underlying-proficiency notion were supported by evaluation studies of bilingual programs conducted in many countries with various nondominant language groups, including Finnish immigrants in Sweden (Skutnabb-Kangas and Toukomaa, 1976); Ukrainian children in Canada (Cummins, 1986); Navajo children (Holm and Holm, 1990), Puerto Rican students (Beykont, 1994; Velasco, 1989), and other Hispanic groups (Egan and Goldsmith, 1981; Evaluation Associates, 1978) in the United States. Researchers examined the relationship between the reading comprehension skills in the native language and the official language in the respective countries, and found that children who had well-developed native-language reading skills rapidly developed second-language reading skills. Research is inconclusive about the effects of second-language literacy skills on the subsequent progress of first-language literacy skills. (Cummins, 1981.) Inconclusive results were attributed to "the greater exposure to literacy in the majority language outside of school and the strong pressure to learn the second language." (Cummins, 1989: 44.)

Other studies suggest that native-language literacy skills do not always transfer quickly to the second language and that there may be a delay in the transfer of literacy skills from children's native language to the second language. Research on Tagalog speakers in the Philippines (A. Gonzalez, 1989), Shona speakers in Zimbabwe (Roller, 1988), and Guarani speakers in Paraguay (Valadez, 1984) suggests that transfer effects may not be seen until after five to seven years of bilingual instruction. In other words, children need to be instructed in their native language *and* the second language for *five to seven years* before the beneficial effects of first-language literacy skills on second-language literacy skills is observed.

Relevant here is a distinction made by Cummins (1981) and Snow (1981) between the language used in everyday conversations—i.e., contextualized language skills—and the language that is demanded in formal academic settings—i.e., context-reduced language skills. Performance on contextualized language tasks is supported by many contextual cues such as gestures, intonation, and shared information, whereas decontextualized academic language tasks rely on linguistic cues almost exclusively. When children have exposure to native speakers of the second language, they can practice their contextualized language skills and develop a good command of everyday usage in two to three years. (See Hakuta, 1986, for a review.) Developing context-reduced academic-language skills in the second language, on the other hand, may take five to seven years. (Cummins, 1983.)

In many contexts, decisions to mainstream children are based on their contextualized, everyday oral language skills rather than on their academic/decontextualized language skills in the official language. (Cummins, 1983.)

> The common sense of urgency about . . . mainstreaming [linguistic minority children] as early as possible, has no basis in linguistic fact. . . . Prematurely mainstreamed students run the risk of being diagnosed as slow, disabled, or even retarded because of their language handicap. (Hakuta and Gould, 1987: 41-42.)

When placed in mainstream classrooms before they have developed the requisite academic language skills in the official language, children fall behind both in literacy development and content-area learning.

More recent work delineates specific conditions under which literacy skills in native language transfer to second-language literacy skills and vice versa. (Galema and Hacquebord, 1985; A. Gonzalez, 1989; Moll, Diaz, Estrada, and Lopez, 1992; Roller, 1988; Valadez, 1984.) The prerequisites for transfer of literacy skills from the native language to a second language are identified as participation in a bilingual program, like the maintenance bilingual program, which provides (a) enough time to develop solid literacy skills in the native language before introducing a second language as an instructional medium (Cummins, 1981, 1983; Skutnabb-Kangas, 1983, 1984); (b) continual instruction in both languages (Cummins, 1981); (c) a continual instructional context that elicits literacy skills in both languages for at least five to seven years (Hakuta and Gould, 1987); (d) conditions of acquisition for second-language literacy skills that mimic conditions of acquisition of native-language literacy skills (Moll, et al., 1992; Snow, 1990); and (e) an active instructional context in which children can apply their newly developing academic language skills in both native and second language to discussions of content. (See Beykont, 1990, and Garcia, 1993, for reviews.)

The review above highlights consistent empirical evidence that suggests cognitive and developmental benefits of balanced bilingualism over monolingualism. There is now substantial counter-evidence to two commonly held beliefs that have guided policy decisions in many countries: the younger the child, the more rapid the second-language acquisition; the more exposure to the second language, the faster children will learn it. Instead, a growing body of literature suggests that well-developed native-language literacy skills support development of second-language literacy skills and the optimal time to introduce the official language as an instructional medium is after children have acquired native-language literacy skills.

These findings have important implications for the design and implementation of bilingual programs for nondominant language groups. In terms of second-language literacy development, the crucial determinant seems to be literacy skills in the native language. Native-language literacy skills act as an important support for development of second-language literacy skills and therefore need to be emphasized and built upon throughout the elementary-school years. Children can be expected to develop biliteracy skills in five to seven years if the transition from native- to second-language academic skills is facilitated through similar conditions of acquisition in first- and second-language literacy skills and continual bilingual instruction. Transfer effects from one language to the other are likely to be observed in later grades, after the child has developed native-language literacy skills.

From a purely pedagogical and linguistic perspective, then, maintenance bilingual programs and community-based immersion (language-revival) programs that aim to develop a strong foundation in native language *in addition to* the official language can be expected to boost nondominant language groups' academic performance. Unfortunately, the importance of pedagogical and linguistic considerations is often overlooked in choosing one language policy or program over another. Social and political agendas and practical and economic considerations have driven the educational goals and choices of many parents and governments. In the next section, I examine the prominent characteristics of sociopolitical contexts in which school-language policies are implemented. The discussion focuses on the features of a political context, such as the predominant attitude toward ethnic and linguistic diversity in a country, in their implications for governmental choices of school-language policies in the education of nondominant language groups.

A SOCIOPOLITICAL PERSPECTIVE ON SCHOOL-LANGUAGE POLICIES FOR NONDOMINANT LANGUAGE GROUPS

Language decisions are made during the history of a nation: decisions are primarily made on political and economic grounds and reflect the values of those in political power. Linguistic issues per se are of minor concern. (Paulston, 1983: 55.)

Governmental responses to the education of nondominant language groups have been varied. Governments may choose to ignore the linguistic needs of nondominant language groups and instruct them in mainstream classrooms or accommodate them temporarily or for a long period of time by providing special programs. Sociological analyses suggest that a government's response to the education of nondominant language groups reflects its orientations to ethnic and linguistic diversity. Berry (1983, 1984), J. Gonzalez (1975), and Ruiz (1984) developed useful frameworks that typify governmental orientations to diversity. These frameworks are synthesized in their implications for the choice of language of instruction, extent of intergroup contact in schools, community involvement, and educational goals in the education of nondominant language groups.

The discussion below is grounded in Ruiz's (1984) notion of orientations. Ruiz's original discussion of "orientations toward languages" in a society can be extended to include orientations toward ethnic and linguistic diversity. Accordingly,

Orientation . . . refers to a complex of dispositions . . . toward languages and their role in society. . . . they constitute the framework in which attitudes are formed: they help to delimit the range of acceptable attitudes toward languages and to make certain attitudes legitimate. (Ruiz, 1984: 16).

Table 4. 3 below summarizes different governmental orientations toward ethnic diversity, linguistic goals, perception of languages, and the choice of language programs. Reading the first row from left to right, notice that governments with explicit assimilation orientations toward ethnic diversity perceive "languages as a problem." (Ruiz, 1984: 18.) They aim for linguistic unity and adopt submersion programs in which all children are instructed through the official language only. Reading down the table, the reader will notice that governments with varied orientations toward ethnic diversity employ different language programs.

Throughout the world, the most common governmental orientation toward linguistic and ethnic diversity has been assimilationist. According to this orientation, national unity has to be ensured by "the absorption of a non-dominant group into an established mainstream" with no tolerance for their unique cultural identity, values, customs, and languages. (Berry, 1983: 68.) Diversity and heterogeneity in values, beliefs, traditions, and languages are perceived as threats to national unity. (Berry, 1983; Crawford, 1991; J. Gonzalez, 1975.)

Table 4.3. Orientations to Diversity and the Choice of Language Programs

Orientation to Ethnic Diversity	Linguistic Goals	Perception of Languages	Language Program
Assimilation (explicit)*	Linguistic Unity	Problem	Submersion
Assimilation (implicit)*	Linguistic Unity	Remedy	Transitional Bilingual; Immersion
Multiculturalism	Multilingualism	Resource	Maintenance/ Two-Way Bilingual
Segregation	Linguistic Partitioning	Partition	Home Language

Synthesized from Berry (1983, 1984), Ruiz (1984), and J. Gonzalez (1975).
*Anderson's terminology (1990)

A government with an assimilation orientation to diversity does *not* tolerate linguistic diversity. (J. Gonzalez, 1975.) Linguistic diversity is perceived as an obstacle to intergroup communication and to national unity:

> From a central government's standpoint, a common language forges a similarity of attitude and values which can have important unifying aspects, while different languages tend to divide and make direction from the center more difficult. (Leibowitz, 1971: 1, quoted in J. Gonzalez, 1975: 6.)

Education is perceived as an important channel through which linguistic unification in a country can be sought by teaching all children through the official language. One language, the official language, is imposed in schools as part of a larger nation-building agenda. (Crawford, 1991; J. Gonzalez, 1975.)

Assimilation orientations range from "explicit assimilation" to "implicit assimilation." (Anderson, 1990: 128.) An explicit assimilation orientation entails no accommodation to the linguistic and educational needs of nondominant language groups. The existence of many languages is perceived as a "problem" to be dealt with as quickly as possible. (Ruiz, 1984: 18.) Language programs that prohibit the use of all other languages for educational purposes, i.e., submersion programs, are chosen to instruct nondominant language groups. The common rationale for adopting submersion programs is that these programs provide maximum exposure to the official language and speakers of it in mainstream classrooms. "Equal treatment" of dominant and nondominant groups (by exposing children to the same facilities, textbooks, and curriculum in integrated mainstream classrooms) is assumed to ensure equal opportunity for all children in the educational system and later in the economic system. (Paulston, 1978; Navarro, 1985.) Since every child is "equally" treated, school failure of nondominant language groups in submersion programs is attributed to (a) their language problems and intellectual abilities (see Hakuta, 1986, for a review); (b) their resistance to assimilation (see J. Gonzalez, 1975, and Padilla, 1982, for reviews); (c) their bilingualism that results in mental confusion and inhibits cognitive and academic development. (See, e.g., Kessler and Quinn, 1982, for a review.) An explicit assimilation school-language policy has been employed, for example, in the education of Roms in Hungary, Maoris in New Zealand, West Indians in England, and various immigrant groups in parts of Germany and Belgium.

Implicit assimilation entails some accommodation to the needs of nondominant language groups for a limited amount of time. Within the framework of an implicit assimilation orientation, the role of nondominant languages in public services, including schools, is perceived as a "remedy" for children's lack of proficiency in the official language. (Ruiz, 1984: 22.) Language programs that allow use of nondominant languages temporarily until children are ready to be instructed in mainstream classrooms, i.e., transitional bilingual programs, are therefore employed.

The common rationale for adopting transitional bilingual programs is that it "helps equalize ... shortcomings of opportunity" and provides a remedy for students' lack of proficiency in the official language. (Paulston, 1978.) In a transitional bilingual model, (a) children are taught basic literacy skills through native language until they learn the official language; (b) content areas are taught in children's native language until third to fourth grade, because presumably, instruction in their native language prevents them from falling behind in content matter; (c) second-language support is provided through classes that teach the official language as a second language, thereby preparing children for instruction exclusively in the official language; and (d) a temporary recognition of different cultures, history, arts, and literature of nondominant groups in schools facilitates a smoother transition from home to school.

Governments with an implicit assimilation orientation to diversity can also adopt another language program model, i.e., structured immersion programs. In these programs, children are instructed using the official language in classes in which all students are second-language learners, until they are ready to be mainstreamed. (See Swain and Lapkin, 1982, for a review.) Teachers can pace their instruction and teach the content matter through the official language at a linguistic level that is comprehensible to all children. (Lambert and Tucker, 1972.)

Within the implicit assimilation orientation, then, there is a recognition that equal treatment of different language groups cannot be realized "merely by providing students with the same facilities, textbooks, teachers and curriculum," and that the educational system needs to accommodate the linguistic needs of nondominant-language groups. (Navarro, 1985: 293.) It is assumed that, in order to reverse the pattern of school failure of nondominant-language groups, schools need to compensate for "deficiencies" in their language and culture, and a lack of intellectual stimulation in their "deprived" home environments. (See Lubeck, 1985, for a review.) Children are argued to be "semilinguals," with no proficiency in either native language or the official language, due to continual code-switching behavior and use of nonstandard varieties in their communities. (See Cummins, 1983, for a review.) An implicit assimilation policy has been utilized, for example, in the education of Yoruba, Hausa, and Igbo speakers in Nigeria; Chinese speakers in

Malaysia; Asian groups in England; Mexican and Asian groups in some parts of the United States; and Kirundi speakers in Burundi.

Another governmental response toward linguistic and ethnic diversity has been a multicultural orientation "in which own-group and other-group cultures are valued and in which major common social and political institutions are developed to tie them all together." (Berry, 1984: 105.) Within this orientation, varied values, customs, and languages in a country do not threaten national unity. Loyalties to home cultures and languages do not constitute serious obstacles to language groups' adoption of mainstream values. (Crawford, 1991; J. Gonzalez, 1975.)

A multicultural orientation to ethnic diversity implies a positive attitude toward multilingualism. Nondominant groups maintain and develop their respective native languages in addition to the official language. The preservation of nondominant languages is seen as a "resource" or an "asset" for the whole society and nondominant language groups are viewed as a repository of this valuable resource. (Ruiz, 1984: 25.) The challenge is to find a balance between accepting and valuing the cultural distinctiveness of different groups while also seeking some shared values. (Berry, 1983,1984.)

Language programs that employ the dominant and nondominant languages as instructional media throughout the school years, i.e., maintenance bilingual programs, are chosen to educate nondominant language groups. The rationale for adopting maintenance bilingual programs is to recognize and reinforce equally both dominant and nondominant cultures and languages. Unlike transitional bilingual programs, the use of nondominant languages for instructional purposes is not perceived as an "unfortunate necessity," but rather as "an opportunity for enrichment." (J. Gonzalez, 1975: 11.)

Within the multicultural framework, school failure of nondominant language groups is attributed to historically unfavorable relationships between dominant and nondominant groups, teachers and students, and schools and nondominant language communities. (Cummins, 1981, 1986; Gibson, 1991; Ogbu, 1978, 1991.) This framework suggests that education *can* alter school failure of nondominant groups by using culturally responsive pedagogy, i.e., by reinforcing children's cultural identity and values, recognizing and responding to the varied educational needs and goals of different nondominant language groups, seeking parental support and involvement in children's education, and using culturally appropriate instructional approaches and materials. (Cummins, 1989; Diaz, Moll, and Mehan, 1986; Erickson, 1987.) A multicultural orientation is exemplified in Canada toward the French, in Finland toward the Swedish, and in Italy toward the German and French.

Another governmental response to diversity has been a segregation orientation, which embodies an attitude of rejection toward nondominant groups and aims "to keep people in 'their place' (as in slavery or 'apartheid' situations)." (Berry, 1983: 69.) A segregation orientation reflects disturbed intergroup relations between dominant and nondominant groups. Intergroup contact is not desirable: nondominant language groups are segregated from the mainstream both in terms of the areas that they live in and in their educational institutions. They maintain their group identity and customs separately from the rest of society. (Berry, 1983, 1984; Skutnabb-Kangas, 1983, 1984.)

Box 4.4. Segregation of African Language Groups in South Africa[4]

African language groups in South Africa have been instructed in home-language programs through their native language and a curriculum different from other groups. Access to educational and economic opportunities are severely inhibited because the official languages, Africaan and English, are used for entrance exams and subsequent classroom instruction in secondary schooling. An informant described home- language programs under the apartheid system as follows:

> In South Africa, in the black schools, all classes are taught in the mother tongue until grade five. Thereafter, they've got to switch to English as the medium of instruction. For colored students, white students, and Indian students, it's not so much of a problem because either English or Africaan is likely to be their mother tongue, and the language of instruction is English or Africaan all throughout schooling; so, it doesn't cause a problem. But the black students ... have to switch from indigenous languages to English. Also, black students have really limited access to either English or Africaan because they live in segregated communities. So that is why there is a real problem for black students ... especially in high school, when all the textbooks are in English and students are expected to write all their examinations in English.
>
> Everybody is in segregated classes. The whites are in their own school, the coloreds are in their own school, the Indians are in their own schools, and the blacks are in their own schools. Because of the severe segregation, people interact only with people in their own communities who only speak the mother tongue, so that gets reinforced. . . .
>
> I'm classified colored, which means that I'm in the mixed-race group and I speak one of the two official languages, which are English and Africaan. Because of the way I'm classified, I can only teach to students who are also classified colored, a sort of mixed race, and they speak either English or Africaan.
>
> When the Dutch came, the colored people were slaves of the Dutch and they spoke Africaan. So now they speak Africaan or English, depending on where they live. My family is in the south where the English or British came, and so my home language is English. . . .
>
> The hierarchy goes like this: whites, Indians, colored, and blacks. Each group has a different department of education, with different administrations and different curriculums. For example, in the black elementary schools, the kids actually don't have any study cards. They do gardening, they do agricultural studies even though they live in cities. They do things like that. These policies, I think, came in the early twentieth century. Blacks had to be given an education that would only prepare them for working on their own and for the whites. So, they had to be equipped with skills that would allow them to work on farms, for example, or allow them to work as gardeners for the whites or allow them to do tasks which basically the country needed at a cheap labor rate. Not enough skills to make you educated enough to demand more, but also educated enough to be able to do things. So that was really part of the new policies.
>
> In high school, black students have to buy their own textbooks, which white students don't have to do. For black students, the government provided about a quarter of the funds that they would provide for white students. So let's say, $1000 per white child, you would have only $250 per black child. So the community has to pay for the rest, basically, for the books. And it's the most deprived community in terms of economics. The government and the rulers are actually depriving the people their rights and opportunities in every way.

A segregation orientation to ethnic diversity typically incorporates language-partitioning goals. The use and maintenance of local languages in schools works as a "partition" to keep nondominant groups away from each other. (See Beykont, 1992a, for a review.) Language programs that teach literacy skills in children's native language only, i.e., home-language programs, are chosen to instruct nondominant groups. In these programs, nondominant groups maintain their cultural values and traditions. The rationale for adopting home-language programs is that "education must train and teach people in accordance with their opportunities in life." (Horrell, 1978: 297, cited in LaBelle and White, 1985: 55.) For example, in the case of the education of guest workers in Europe, the rationale for employing home-language programs is to prepare children for the educational system in their home country. (Skutnabb-Kangas, 1984: 307.) Home-language programs serving indigenous groups, e.g., black groups in South Africa, use a curriculum that is supposedly designed to enable the child to serve his/her community. Community involvement in education is sometimes encouraged.

Within the segregation orientation, children's disproportionate school failure is attributed to their genetic inferiority. It is assumed that education cannot alter children's life opportunities and provide equal chances in society. Therefore, children from different language groups are educated in segregated schools separately from each other, in home-language programs using only their native language. They are denied the opportunity to learn the official language or to join the inner circles of the larger society. The usage of the official language(s) for entrance exams and subsequent classroom instruction effectively bars nondominant language groups from upward mobility and further education. The dominant groups' orientations toward Indians in Peru, Creoles in Haiti, Burakamins in Japan, and Turkish people in some parts of Germany, for example, are segregational.

Table 4.4 below compares orientations to diversity and language programs in their implications for intergroup contact in schools, native-language development, and community involvement in children's education. Reading the first row from left to right, governments with an explicit assimilation orientation to ethnic diversity typically adopt the submersion program model that is characterized by continual intergroup contact between native and nonnative speakers of the official language. In these programs, native-language development is not emphasized and the program is not conducive for community involvement in children's education. Reading down the table, the reader will notice that the relative emphasis placed on intergroup contact, native-language development, and community involvement varies across different language programs.

As can be seen in Table 4.4, programs that serve assimilation and multicultural orientations are designed to instruct children from different linguistic backgrounds in mixed classrooms. At least for part of the day or in upper grades, there is intergroup contact with the assumption that continuous intergroup contact reinforces positive relations between groups, which in turn results in a common set of beliefs and values. Positive relations between groups and a common set of values are desirable from a nation-building perspective. In segregational home-language programs, there is no intergroup contact.

Table 4.4. Dominant Groups' Orientations to Diversity and Educational Processes and Goals

Orientation to Diversity	Language Program Development	Intergroup Contact	Native Language	Community Involvement
Assimilation (explicit)*	Submersion	Yes	No	No
Assimilation (implicit)*	Transitional Bilingual; Structured Immersion	No→Yes	No	No
Multiculturalism	Maintenance/ Two-Way Bilingual	Gradual	Yes	Yes
Segregation	Home Language	No	Yes	Sometimes

Synthesized from Berry (1983, 1984), J. Gonzalez (1975), and Moll (1992).
*Anderson's terminology (1990)

Programs also vary regarding the relative value placed on the maintenance and development of native languages and community involvement in children's education. In programs that serve an assimilation orientation, i.e., submersion, structured immersion, and transitional bilingual programs,

> . . . . few efforts are made to involve parents in a meaningful partnership with the schools. Home language, culture and child rearing practices are often perceived as detrimental to a child's performance in school. (J. Gonzalez, 1975: 14.)

Community involvement in children's education is not encouraged, and development of native languages is not considered the school's responsibility. Advocates of these language programs assume that due to continuous contact between different language groups and lack of parental involvement, home culture and language will have less influence on children. Over time, children will learn the official language and assimilate into the dominant culture. Lambert (1981) referred to this second-language learning situation as "subtractive bilingualism." Subtractive bilingualism is observed when the relative cultural and economic value of a native language is much lower than that of the official language, and maintenance of the native language is not valued in the larger society. In these contexts, native language competence is gradually lost and replaced by the official language in a society. Children often develop an ambivalent attitude toward their native language and home culture. (Cummins, 1986.)

In programs that serve a multicultural orientation, however, namely maintenance bilingual programs, prolonged use of the native language as an instructional medium facilitates parental involvement, and community members are actively sought as partners in their children's education. As says, "Parental involvement is recognized as a potential asset. Attention is given to community resources as sources for curricular content and programmatic direction." (J. Gonzalez, 1975: 14.)

In contrast to subtractive bilingualism, maintenance of the native language is valued by the larger society while a second language is learned. (Lambert, 1981.) This learning situation, called "additive bilingualism" (Lambert, 1981), results in a high degree of proficiency in both languages. Over time, children learn literacy and academic skills in the official language in addition to their respective native languages.

As discussed above, orientations to diversity influence governments' decisions on educational and linguistic goals, language programs, degree of intergroup contact in schools, and degree of community involvement in children's education. In the next section, I examine sociohistorical factors in school-language policy decisions. In particular, the factors that influence nondominant groups' educational goals, their attitudes toward the language(s) of instruction, and their support of their children's education in a particular language program are discussed. I also explore different sociohistorical conditions under which dominant and nondominant groups' orientations and goals are in congruence or in conflict with each other in their implications for children's school performance.

A SOCIOHISTORICAL PERSPECTIVE ON SCHOOL-LANGUAGE POLICIES FOR NONDOMINANT LANGUAGE GROUPS

Minorities differ in the type of cultural model that guides them, that is, in the type of understanding they have of the workings of the larger society and of their place as minorities in that working order. . . . because of differences in their histories. (Ogbu, 1991: 8.)

Sociological and anthropological literature suggests that there is great variation in nondominant groups' educational expectations and goals for their children. (Baratz-Snowden, Rock, Pollack, and Wilder, 1988; Ogbu, 1978, 1991.) Depending on the particular set of expectations and goals, nondominant groups support different kinds of language policies and programs. (Taylor, 1991; Ogbu, 1978.) Furthermore, it appears that community support for or resistance to educational policies has a direct impact on the success of the language policy, as well as on children's academic performance. (Gibson and Ogbu, 1991; Laosa, 1984; Ogbu, 1981b, 1985, 1991.) In the following, I discuss these conjectures as they relate to decisions on school-language policies for nondominant groups.

In recent years, research has revealed the heterogeneity in the educational goals, attitudes, and expectations across nondominant language groups. (See Baratz-Snowden, et al., 1988; Gibson, 1991; Lambert and Taylor, 1986; Ogbu, 1987, for reviews.) Language groups differ in their expectations regarding exactly what the school is responsible for teaching children. For example, parents have varied views on whether or to what extent the school is responsible for teaching home culture, developing native-language literacy skills, providing bilingual teachers, allowing children to use their native language in school, and so on. (Baratz-Snowden, et al., 1988; Lambert and Taylor, 1988; Ramirez, et al., 1991.)

A nationwide study of language groups in the United States illustrates the point. (See Baratz-Snowden, et al., 1988.) Nondominant language communities expressed varying expectations regarding the school's responsibility in teaching children from non-English-speaking homes. (Baratz-Snowden, et al., 1988.) In a survey of Asian, Puerto Rican, Mexican American, and Cuban groups, parents overwhelmingly agreed that the schools should be responsible for developing children's English literacy skills. (Baratz-Snowden, et al., 1988.) With respect to parental attitudes toward the use of native language as an instructional medium and the development of native-language literacy skills as an educational goal, there was great variation across groups. Controlling for educational background, family income, patterns of language use at home, and children's school achievement, Puerto Rican and Mexican American parents differed from other groups: they expected that schools also develop native-language literacy skills and teach children about their cultural heritages, history, and traditions. (Baratz-Snowden, et al., 1988: iii-iv.)

In another large U.S. study, Polish Americans, Arab Americans, Albanian Americans, Puerto Ricans, Mexican Americans, Anglo Americans, and African Americans were asked about their attitudes toward multiculturalism, bilingualism, and assimilationist policies. (Lambert and Taylor, 1988.) Groups varied greatly in terms of their responses. Along with Arab Americans, the Puerto Rican group ranked one of the highest in their support for multiculturalism and bilingualism. (Lambert and Taylor, 1988, 1990; Taylor, 1991.)

Many factors influence parental goals and expectations. Discerning the reasons for this variation, as well as the impact of such differences on children's academic performance, is important. (Gibson, 1991; Ogbu 1981a, 1981b; 1983.) Certain sociohistorical and sociopolitical factors appear to influence language groups' attitudes and responses toward the school-language policies and programs, including language groups' economic motivations, political goals, literacy traditions, historical relations with the dominant group, degree of mobility, length of establishment in the dominant culture, intention to stay in the country, demographic characteristics of the country, and so on. (Baratz-Snowden, et al., 1988; Berry, 1983, 1984; Gibson, 1991; Ogbu, 1978, 1981a, 1991.) For example, a group with a long-established written literacy tradition might have a different set of expectations compared to a group with no written literacy tradition. These factors, in turn, appear to have an impact on a nondominant language group's (a) willingness to maintain positive relations with other groups (Berry, 1984: 12); (b) preservation of their languages, cultural identities, and traditions (Berry, 1984: 12; Ogbu, 1978, 1991; Taylor, 1991); (c) views of the role of school in teaching native languages and traditions (Baratz-Snowden, et al., 1988; Lambert and Taylor, 1988, 1990; Taylor, 1991); (d) definition of differences in languages, cultural identities, and traditions (Gibson, 1991; Ogbu, 1981b); (e) views of success (Ogbu, 1978, 1991); and (f) views of the role of schooling in realizing success (Ogbu, 1978, 1991).

Anthropological studies link success of a school-language policy with community response, expectations, and attitudes toward education. The main premise of this line of work is that community support for a particular program or policy is a crucial determinant of policy success or failure. (Ogbu, 1978, 1981b, 1985, 1991; see Gibson, 1991, for a review.) In particular, studies of bilingual school-language policies have shown that the success or failure of a bilingual policy is a function of parental support and parental involvement. (See Beykont, 1992a, for a review of case studies.) Case studies of Quechua speakers in Peru and Navajo speakers in the United States illustrate these points.

Box 4.5. Community Resistance to School-language Policy in Peru

An ethnographic study of Quechua speakers in Peru illustrates the importance of community support in the success or failure of educational language policies. (Hornberger, 1987.) The Peruvian government's efforts to initiate native-language instruction, standardize the Quechua language, develop first- through fourth-grade textbooks, and provide inservice training for elementary school teachers were fruitless. There was little community support or input in the planning of this new school-language policy. The community resisted the use of Quechua for schooling purposes, even though there were positive changes in children's school performance and motivation to attend classes

In her ethnographic study, Hornberger uncovered that communities wanted to preserve the "school/community distinction" by keeping the languages separate. She maintained that:

Communities that had survived through centuries of exploitation and dominance by developing strategies of internal cohesion and exclusion of the larger society were not inclined to easily permit within their midst an institution representing the larger society. It was only when the communities perceived that Spanish literacy might be to their [economic] advantage. . . . that they began to seek to have schools. . . . but the school was not to be part of the community. (Hornberger, 1987: 219.)

It appears that, historically, the route of upward mobility for Indian-language speakers in Peru was to learn Spanish, move to big cities and immerse themselves in the Spanish-speaking culture. Everybody in the community aspires to bilingualism in the Quechua-speaking areas due, in part, to immigration patterns, e.g., the need for at least one family member to work in the city and earn money. The community interpreted the government's efforts to initiate native-language instruction as yet another way of denying access to the "power" language, upward mobility, and employment possibilities. Even though children exhibited rapid academic progress when taught through their native language, the community resisted Quechua-language instruction and demanded Spanish-language instruction.

Box 4.6. Community Support for Bilingual Language Policy: Navajo Children in Maintenance Bilingual Programs

A longitudinal study by Holm and Holm (1990) demonstrates the importance of community support and involvement in the success of a bilingual school-language policy. The researchers studied Navajo children in Rockport, Arizona, who were enrolled in an experimental maintenance bilingual program from first through sixth grade. Navajo students in all-English programs had generally performed two years behind their grade levels in English reading comprehension skills and underperformed in content areas. Their dropout rates had been extremely high (80-85 percent).

The maintenance bilingual program aimed to provide quality education in both languages and develop literacy skills in both Navajo and English, with a strong emphasis on the relevance of the content to the children's lives. Community and parental involvement were thought to be crucial in developing culturally relevant curriculum, and were encouraged and sought for. At every stage of program development, community members played a central role as a resource in decisions on content and curriculum.

The use of Navajo for instructional purposes continued throughout the program, with a gradually increasing use of English. Children first gained literacy skills in Navajo. English reading classes were delayed until reading skills were developed in Navajo (fourth semester). Thereafter, reading, writing, and math were taught in both Navajo and in English. The study indicated that students graduating from the maintenance bilingual program performed above the grade norms in English reading-comprehension skills. The authors attributed this overwhelming improvement in Navajo children's school performance to an educational program:

that went back to parental involvement and community control, that went back to the native language and to the community and Reservation as a source of content and curriculum, and that went forward to a more appropriate, more effective education for their children. (Holm and Holm, 1990: 170.)

Another important finding in anthropological literature is that community response to a school-language policy is a crucial determinant in children's academic performance. (Gibson and Ogbu, 1991; Ogbu, 1978, 1979, 1981a, 1991.) When a community supports a particular school-language policy, children tend to do well in school and, conversely, when the community does not support a particular school-language policy, children underperform in school. (Lee, 1991; Ogbu, 1991; Shimahara, 1991.) Specifically, when parents have favorable attitudes toward native-language development and consider it the school's responsibility to promote academic and literacy skills in native language, children tend to do well in bilingual programs. (See Beykont, 1992b, for a review.) When parents support instruction through the official language only, children tend to do well in monolingual programs. (Beykont, 1992b.) Case studies of Berber children in Morocco, and Puerto Rican children in the United States illustrate the point.

Box 4.7. Congruent Goals: Monolingual School-language Policy in Morocco

A longitudinal study conducted by Wagner, Spratt, and Ezzaki (1989) illustrates a situation where there is fundamental agreement between the dominant and nondominant groups' goals. Both groups favor linguistic assimilation, and children perform well in submersion programs that have generally resulted in catastrophic failure.

Berber- and Arabic-speaking groups were followed from first through fifth grade in an all-Arabic submersion program in a rural area of Morocco. This study indicated that any academic differences between native and nonnative speakers of Arabic "disappeared" by fifth grade (p. 31). Fifth-grade Berber-speaking students achieved just as well as Arabic-speaking students in all Arabic classes. The authors explained this finding by referring to the social and historical relations between the two groups and their congruent orientations toward the official language.

A close look at the sociohistorical conditions indicates that "Arabic is the language of Islam" and "a symbol of unity in Arabic-speaking countries," consequently, "standard Arabic enjoys great acceptance and respect among Berber speakers." (Wagner, et al., 1989: 44-45.). Furthermore, after a long competition with French for schooling purposes, Arabic has been the language of instruction since 1983, which symbolizes a victory over European colonizers (p. 45). Finally, there is no preceding literacy tradition in Berber. For these reasons, parents support their children's schooling in Arabic, and children's motivation for learning in Arabic is generally high. Children's relatively good school performance in a submersion program can be attributed to the congruent goals of linguistic assimilation of the government and the Berber community.

Box 4.8. Congruent Goals: Puerto Rican Children in Bilingual Programs in the United States

Persistent school failure of Puerto Ricans in the United States has long been a concern. Provisions that have been made since the civil-rights movement have failed to alter the patterns of school failure of these children. Puerto Ricans achieve at the lowest levels when compared with other minority groups and mainstream children. (Gibson, 1991.) School persistence rates of Puerto Ricans are among the lowest, while repetition rates are the highest of all minority groups. One of the most pervasive consequences of schools' inability to meet their educational needs is the high incidence of Puerto Ricans in special-education classes.

A recent nationwide evaluation study, conducted by Ramirez and his associates (1991), documented the effectiveness of varied bilingual programs in promoting school performance of Hispanic children in the United States. A secondary analysis of this nationwide study focused on Puerto Rican children's academic progress in a bilingual program, with prolonged emphasis on Spanish literacy development. (Beykont, 1994.) The analyses indicated that Puerto Rican children showed rapid academic progress in English and Spanish reading classes from third through sixth grade.

Surveys of parents of participating students suggested Puerto Rican parents' agreement that schools should teach English and Spanish literacy skills, and that their children should be part of both English and Spanish cultures. Puerto Rican parents also emphasized that the school should provide bilingual teachers, allow children to use Spanish in classes, use Spanish in teaching of content matter, and teach about home culture. Children's progress in both English and Spanish reading from third through sixth grade was positively associated with favorable parental attitudes toward bilingual education. (Beykont, 1994.) Academic growth in English-and Spanish- reading classes was faster for children whose parents expressed favorable attitudes toward bilingual education and slower for children whose parents expressed unfavorable attitudes toward bilingual education. (Beykont, 1994.)

This line of research indicates that nondominant language groups have varied educational expectations and goals. Nondominant language groups may or may not consider it the school's responsibility to teach their children native-language literacy and academic skills in addition to the official language academic skills. In other words, it is possible for dominant and nondominant language groups to have congruent or incongruent educational goals and expectations. Case studies indicate that school-language policy reforms that do not address the educational goals and expectations of parents tend to fail. Furthermore, it appears that when there is incongruence between the goals of dominant and nondominant language groups, children underperform.

CONCLUSIONS

This paper has presented a survey of research of the school-language policies for nondominant language groups. Psycholinguistic, sociopolitical, and sociohistorical perspectives were examined in decisions on school-language policies and programs. The most widely used programs—submersion, structured immersion, transitional bilingual, maintenance bilingual, language revival, and home-language programs— were described and compared in terms of their instructional features and program objectives. Pedagogical considerations involved in the choice and implementation of sound school-language policies were discussed. Sociological and anthropological frameworks were then explored to identify the prominent characteristics of sociopolitical and sociohistorical contexts that shape educational goals of dominant and nondominant groups. Conclusions and research implications are summarized below:

1) *Balanced bilinguals compared with monolinguals are superior in many verbal and analytical skills, such as concept formation, cognitive flexibility, and divergent thinking, which are closely associated with academic and intellectual skills.* From a developmental and linguistic perspective, educational programs that aim to develop children's first- and second-language literacy skills promote greater intellectual and academic progress.

2) *Political and economic motivations seem to override pedagogical and linguistic considerations in the choice of school-language policies for nondominant language groups.* Social and political agendas and short-term economic considerations continue to drive the educational decisions of many parents and governments and lead them to choose programs that aim for monolingualism in the official language.

3) There is *great variation in governmental response to education of nondominant language groups.* The dominant group's orientation to diversity in a particular political context has an impact on educational and linguistic goals; on the choice of language program; on the choice of language of instruction; on the degree of integration of nondominant groups in schools; and on the degree of community involvement in the education of children.

4) There is *great variation in nondominant groups' educational orientations, expectations, and goals.* Numerous factors influence the educational goals and motivations of nondominant communities. These factors include a written literacy tradition, historical relations with the dominant group, socioeconomic status, geographic mobility, degree of establishment, etc. Based on their orientations, expectations, and goals, communities may or may not support a particular school-language policy or program.

5) *Community support of or resistance to a language policy has an impact on the success of school-language policy as well as children's school performance:*

- When nondominant groups support a particular school-language policy children tend to perform well in school.
- When nondominant groups do not support a school-language policy, children are less likely to perform well in school.

6) *Dominant and nondominant groups may have congruent or incongruent goals and agendas*:

- When there is congruence in the goals and orientations of dominant and nondominant language groups, nondominant groups support their children's education in a particular language program, and children are likely to perform well in school.
- When there is incongruence in the goals and orientations of dominant and nondominant language groups, parents may resist their children's education in a particular program, and children are less likely to perform well in school.

This review supports the argument that there is no one school-language policy that can be recommended as the best choice across different contexts. (Paulston, 1978; Skutnabb-Kangas, 1984.) Three decades of research indicate that the effectiveness of school-language policies or programs has to be assessed within their unique sociopolitical and sociohistorical contexts. One school-language policy can not respond to the great variety of goals and agendas of nondominant and dominant language groups across the world. Decisions on a school-language policy for a particular nondominant language group need to be based on an examination of (a) the educational goals of dominant and nondominant groups, and (b) the social, economic, political, and historical reasons for congruence or incongruence of these goals. Furthermore, the choice of a good school-language policy for a particular nondominant language group needs to be guided by pedagogical considerations, and the linguistic research in its support for bilingualism and biliteracy development.

Endnotes

1. The informant, Denise Zinn, is a doctoral candidate at Harvard University. She taught English as a Second Language in South Africa, where she was born and raised. This interview was conducted in March 1992.

2. Home language programs should not be confused with home schooling in which children are taught by parents.

3. Divergent thinking is "a special type of cognitive flexibility reflecting a fertile imagination and ability to generate rapidly a wide range of possible solutions to a problem." (Guilford, 1956, cited in Kessler and Quinn, 1982: 56.)

4. Based on the interview with Denise Zinn mentioned in note 1 above.

Bibliography

Anderson, A. "Comparative Analysis of Language Minorities: A Sociopolitical Framework." *Journal of Multilingual and Multicultural Development,* v. 11, n. 1-2 (1990): 119-136.

Appel, R. "Minority Languages in the Netherlands: Relations between Sociopolitical Conflicts and Bilingual Education," in B. Bain, ed., *The Sociogenesis of Language and Human Conduct.* New York: Plenum, 1983.

Bain, B. "The Illusion of Choice in Ethnic Bilingual Education." *Integrated Education,* v. 20, n. 1-2 (1982): 64-69.

Baratz-Snowden, J., D. A. Rock, J. Pollack, and G. Z. Wilder. Parent Preference Study. Final Report. ERIC Clearinghouse. ED320444, 1988.

Barrington, J. M. "The New Zealand Experience: Maoris," in M. A. Gibson and J. U. Ogbu, eds., *Minority Status and Schooling: A Comparative Study of Immigrant and Involuntary Minorities.* New York: Garland, 1991.

Benton, R. A. "Schools as Agents for Language Revival in Ireland and New Zealand," in B. Spolsky, ed., *Language and Education in Multilingual Societies.* Clevedon, England: Multilingual Matters Ltd., 1986.

Ben-Zeev, S. "The Influence of Bilingualism on Cognitive Strategy and Cognitive Development." *Child Development,* v. 48, n. 3 (1977): 1009-1018.

Bernstein, B. "A Sociolinguistic Approach to Socialization: With Some Reference to Educability," in F. Williams, ed., *Language and Poverty: Perspectives on a Theme.* Chicago: Markham, 1970.

Berry, J. W. "Acculturation: A Comparative Analysis of Alternative Forms," in R. J. Samuda and S. L. Woods, eds., *Perspectives in Immigrant and Minority Education.* Lanham, MD: University Press of America, 1983.

―――. "Multicultural Attitudes and Education," in R. J. Samuda, ed., *Multiculturalism in Canada: Social and Educational Perspectives.* Toronto: Allyn & Bacon, 1984.

Berry, J. W., R. Kalin, and D. Taylor. *Multiculturalism and Ethnic Attitudes in Canada.* Ottawa: Minister of State for Multiculturalism, 1977.

Beykont, Z. F. *Cognitive and Behavioral Processes in Cross-Group Cooperative Learning.* Unpublished Qualifying Paper. Cambridge: Harvard University, 1990.

―――. *The Politics of Linguistic Diversity in Education.* Paper presented at the SIDEC, San Francisco, CA, November 1992(a).

————. *Sociopolitical and Sociohistorical Contexts of School Language Policies.* Paper presented at the World Congress of Comparative Education, Prague, Czechoslovakia, July 1992(b).

————. "The Choice of Language Policies and Programs: A Comparative View," in P. Altbach, ed., *Special Studies in Comparative Education,* 31. Buffalo, NY: State University of New York, 1994.

————. *Academic Progress of a Nondominant Group: Education of Puerto Rican Children in New York City's Late-Exit Bilingual Programs.* Doctoral dissertation, Harvard Univeristy, Cambridge, MA, 1995.

Cazden, B. C. *Classroom Discourse: The Language of Teaching and Learning.* Portsmouth, NH: Heinemann Press, 1988.

Cazden, B. C., C. E. Snow, and C. Heise-Baigorria. *Language Planning in Preschool Education with Annotated Bibliography.* Report prepared at request of Consultative Group on Early Childhood Care and Development, UNICEF, 1990.

Corvalán, G. "Bilingualism in Paraguay." In C. B. Paulston (Ed.), *International Handbook of Bilingualism and Bilingual Education.* New York: Greenwood Press, 1988.

Craig, D. R. "The Sociology of Language Learning and Teaching in a Creole Situation," in N. Wolfson and J. Manes, eds., *Language of Inequality.* Berlin: Mouton, 1985.

Crawford, J. *Bilingual Education: History, Politics, Theory and Practice.* Los Angeles: Bilingual Education Services, Inc., 1991.

Cummins, J. "The Role of Primary Language Development in Promoting Educational Success for Language Minority Students," in California State Department of Education, ed., *Schooling and Language Minority Students: A Theoretical Framework.* Sacramento: California State Department of Education, Office of Bilingual Bicultural Education, 1981.

————. *Heritage Language Education: A Literature Review.* Toronto: Ontario Ministry of Education, 1983.

————. "Empowering Minority Students: A Framework for Intervention." *Harvard Educational Review,* v. 56 (1986): 18-36.

————. *Empowering Minority Students.* Sacramento, CA: California Association of Bilingual Education, 1989.

Dada, A. "The New Language Policy in Nigeria: Its Problems and Its Chances of Success," in N. Wolfson and J. Manes, eds., *Language of Inequality*. Berlin: Mouton, 1985.

Davis, P.M. *Vernacular literacy and pre-school training. Final Evaluation Report.* Ukarumpa, Papua New Guinea: Summer Institute of Linguistics, 1986.

Diaz, R. M. "Thought and Two Languages: The Impact of Bilingualism on Cognitive Development," in E. W. Gordon, ed., *Review of Research in Education: Vol. 10*, (1983): 23-45. Washington, DC: American Education Research Association, 1983.

Diaz, S., L. C. Moll, and H. Mehan. "Sociocultural Resources in Instruction: A Context-Specific Approach," in *Beyond Language: Social and Cultural Factors in Schooling Language Minority Students*. Los Angeles: Evaluation, Dissemination and Assessment Center, California State University, 1986.

Dolson, P. D., and J. Mayer. "Longitudinal Study of Three Program Models for Language Minority Students: A Critical Examination of Reported Findings." *Bilingual Research Quarterly,* v. 16, n. 1, (1991): 105-156.

Dua, H.R. "Sociolinguistic Inequality and Language Problems of Linguistic Minorities in India," in N. Wolfson and J. Manes, eds., *Language of Inequality*. Berlin: Mouton, 1985.

Edwards, J. "Language, diversity and identity," in J. Edwards, ed., *Linguistic Minorities, Policies and Pluralism*. London: Academic Press, 1984.

———. "Notes for a Minority Language Typology: Procedures and Justification." *Journal of Multilingual and Multicultural Development,* v. 11, n. 1-2 (1990): 137-151.

Edwards, V. "Language Policy in Multicultural Britain," in J. Edwards, ed., *Linguistic Minorities, Policies and Pluralism*. London: Academic Press, 1984.

———. "Expressing Alienation: Creole in the Classroom," in N. Wolfson and J. Manes, eds., *Language of Inequality*. Berlin: Mouton, 1985.

Egan, L. A. "Bilingual Education: A Challenge for the Future," *NABE News,* March, 1981.

Egan, L. A., and R. Goldsmith. "Bilingual Bicultural Education: The Colorado Success Story." *NABE News,* v. 4, n. 3 (1981): 1, 4, 12-14.

Eisemon, T., R. Prouty, and J. Schwille. "What Language Should be Used for Teaching?: Language Policy and School Reform in Burundi." *Journal of Multilingual and Multicultural Development,* v. 10, n. 6 (1989): 473-497.

Erickson, F. "Transformation and school success: The policies and culture of educational achievement." *Anthropology and Education Quarterly,* v. 18 (1987): 335-6.

Evaluation Associates. *Nestor School Bilingual Education Program Evaluation.* Unpublished research report, San Diego, CA, 1978.

Fishman, J. A. and J. Lovas. "Bilingual Education in a Sociolinguistic Perspective." *TESOL Quarterly,* v. 4, n. 3 (1970): 215-222.

Galema, C., and H. Hacquebord. "Text Comprehension of Bilingual Turkish Children in Dutch Primary and Secondary Schools," in G. Extra and T. Vallen, eds., *Ethnic minorities and Dutch as a second language.* Dordrecht: Foris Publications, 1985.

Garcia, E. E. "Instructional Discourse in 'Effective' Hispanic Classrooms," in R. Jacobson and C. Faltis, eds., *Language Distribution Issues in Bilingual Schooling.* Clevedon, England: Multilingual Matters Ltd., 1989.

———. *Education of Linguistically and Culturally Diverse Students: Effective Instructional Practices* (Educational Practice Report No. 1). Santa Cruz, CA: National Center for Research on Cultural Diversity and Second Language Learning, 1991.

———. "Language, Culture, and Education," in L. Darling-Hammond, ed., *Review of Research in Education, vol. 19.* Washington, DC: American Educational Research Association, (1993): 51-98.

Garcia, E. E., and R. V. Padilla, eds. *Advances in bilingual education research.* Tucson, AZ: University of Arizona Press, 1985.

Genesee, F. "Second Language Learning in School Settings: Lessons from Immersion," in A. G. Reynolds, ed., *Bilingualism, Multiculturalism, and Second Language Learning.* Hillsdale, NJ: Lawrence Erlbaum, 1991.

Gibson, M. A. "Minorities and Schooling: Some Implications," in M. A. Gibson and J. Ogbu, eds., *Minority Status and Schooling: A Comparative Study of Immigrant and Involuntary Minorities.* New York: Garland, 1991.

Gibson, M. A., and J. Ogbu, eds. *Minority Status and Schooling: A Comparative Study of Immigrant and Involuntary Minorities.* New York: Garland, 1991.

Glazer, N., and D.P. Moynihan. *Beyond the Melting Pot.* Cambridge, MA: MIT Press, 1970.

Gonzalez, A. "Evaluating Bilingual Education in the Philippines: Towards a Multidimensional Model of Evaluation in Language Planning," in M. Halliday, ed., *Learning, Keeping, and Using Language: Selected Papers from the 8th World Congress of Applied Linguistics*. Amsterdam: Benjamins, 1989.

Gonzalez, J. "Coming of Age in Bilingual/Bicultural Education: A Historical Perspective." *Inequality in Education*, v. 19 (1975): 5-17.

Haasbroek, J. B., and P. Botha. *The Medium of Instruction in Developing Countries* (Report No. 0-317). Pretoria, South Africa: Human Sciences Research Council. ERIC Document Reproduction Service No. ED 311 740, 1989.

Hakuta, K. *Mirror of Language: The Debate on Bilingualism*. New York: Basic Books, 1986.

Hakuta, K., and L. J. Gould. "Synthesis of Research on Bilingual Education." *Educational Leadership*, v. 45 (1987): 38-45.

Holm, A., and W. Holm. "Rock Point, A Navajo Way to Go to School: A Valediction." *Annals of the Academy of Political and Social Science*, v. 508, (1990): 170-184.

Hornberger, N. "Bilingual Education Success, but Policy Failure." *Language in Society*, v. 16, n. 2 (1987): 205-226.

Huebner, T. "Language Education Policy in Hawaii: Two Cases and Some Current Issues." *International Journal of the Sociology of Language*, v. 56 (1985): 29-49.

Keller, G. D., and K. S. Van Hooft. "A Chronology of Bilingualism and Bilingual Education," in J. A. Fishman and G. D. Keller, eds., *Bilingual Education for Hispanic Students in the United States*. New York: Teachers College Press, 1982.

Kessler, C., and M. E. Quinn. "Cognitive Development in Bilingual Environments," in B. Hartford and A. Valdman, eds., *Issues in International Bilingual Education*. New York: Plenum Press, 1982.

La Belle, T. J., and P. S. White. "Educational Policy Analysis and Intergroup Relations: International and Comparative Analysis," in J. N. Hawkins and T. J. La Belle, eds., *Education and Intergroup Relations*. New York: Praeger, 1985.

Lambert, W. E. "Bilingualism: Its Nature and Significance." *Bilingual Education Series*, 10. Washington, DC: The Center for Applied Linguistics, 1981.

Lambert, W. E., and D. M. Taylor. "Greek Canadians' Attitudes towards Own Group and Other Canadian Ethnic Groups: A Test of the Multiculturalism Hypothesis." *Canadian Journal of Behavioral Science*, v. 18, n. 1 (1986): 35-51.

————. "Assimilation Versus Multiculturalism: The Views of Urban Americans." *Sociological Forum,* v. 3, (1988): 72-88.

————. *Coping with Cultural and Racial Diversity in Urban America*. New York: Praeger, 1990.

Lambert, W. E., and G. R. Tucker. *Bilingual Education of Children: The St. Lambert Experience*. Rowley, MA: Newbury House, 1972.

Laosa, L. M. "Social Policies Toward Children of Diverse Ethnic, Racial, and Language Groups in the United States," in H. W. Stevenson and A. E. Siegel, eds., *Child Development Research and Social Policy*. Chicago: University of Chicago Press, 1984.

Lee, Y. "Koreans in Japan and the United States," in M. A. Gibson and J. Ogbu, eds., *Minority Status and Schooling: A Comparative Study of Immigrant and Involuntary Minorities*. New York: Garland, 1991.

Leibowitz, A. H. "Educational Policy and Political Acceptance: The Imposition of English as the Language of Instruction in American Schools." ERIC Clearinghouse for Linguistics: ED047321, 1971.

Lenneberg, E. H. *The Biological Foundations of Language*. New York: Wiley, 1967.

Leyba, C. F. *Longitudinal Study, Title VII Bilingual Program, Santa Fe Public Schools, Santa Fe, New Mexico*. Los Angeles: National Dissemination and Assessment Center, California State University, 1978.

Lubeck, S. *Sandbox Society: Early Education in Black and White America*. London: Falmer Press, 1985.

Lyons, J. J. "The Past and Future Directions of Federal Bilingual Education Policy," in C. B. Cazden and C. E. Snow, eds., *English Plus: Issues in Bilingual Education. The Annals of the American Academy of Political and Social Science*: v. 508, Newbury Park, CA: Sage, 1990; 66-81.

Macedo, D. *Literacies of Power: What Americans Are not Allowed to Know*. Boulder, CO: Westview Press, 1994.

Mackey, W. F. "Bilingual Education and Its Social Implications," in J. Edwards, ed., *Linguistic Minorities, Policies and Pluralism*. London: Academic Press, 1984.

Malone, S. E. *Vernacular Literacy in Multi-Language Societies*. Paper presented at the Eighth World Congress on Comparative Education, Prague, Czechoslovakia, July 1992.

McGroarty, M. "The Benefits of Cooperative Learning Arrangements in Second Language Instruction." *NABE Journal,* v. 13, n. 2 (1989): 127-143.

————. "The Societal Context of Bilingual Education." *Educational Researcher,* v. 21, n. 2 (1992): 7-9.

McLaughlin, B. *Second Language Acquisition in Childhood: Vol. 2. School-Age Children,* 2nd ed. Hillsdale, NJ: Lawrence Erlbaum, 1984.

McLaughlin, B., and P. Graf. "Bilingual Education in West Germany: Recent Developments." *Comparative Education,* v. 21, n. 3 (1985): 241-255.

Medina, M., and K. Escamilla. "Language Acquisition and Gender for Limited-Language-Proficient Mexican-Americans in a Maintenance Bilingual Program." *Hispanic Journal of Behavioral Sciences,* v. 16., n. 4 (1984): 422-437.

Mehan, H. *Learning Lessons.* Cambridge, MA: Harvard University Press, 1979.

Mikes, M. "Towards a Typology of Languages of Instruction in Multilingual Societies," in B. Spolsky, ed., *Language and Education in Multilingual Societies.* Clevedon, England: Multilingual Matters Ltd., 1986.

Moll, L. C. "Educating Latino Students." *Language Arts,* v. 64 (1988): 315-324.

————. "Funds of Knowledge for Change: Developing Mediating Connections between Homes and Classrooms." Paper presented at the conference on "Literacy, Identity and Mind," University of Michigan, Ann Arbor, 1991.

————. "Bilingual Classroom Studies and Community Analysis: Some Recent Trends." *Educational Researcher,* v. 21, n. 2 (1992): 20-24.

Moll, L. C., and S. Diaz. "Ethnographic Pedagogy: Promoting Effective Bilingual Instruction," in E.E. Garcia and R.V. Padilla, eds., *Advances in Bilingual Education Research.* Tucson, AZ: University of Arizona Press, 1985.

Moll, L., S. Diaz, E. Estrada, and L. Lopez. "The Organization of Bilingual Lessons: Implications for Schooling." *Laboratory of Comparative Human Cognition Newsletter,* La Jolla, CA, 1980.

————. "Making Contexts: The Social Construction of Lessons in Two Languages," in Saravia-Shore and S. F. Arvizu, eds., *Cross-Cultural Literacy: Ethnographies of Communication in Multiethnic Classrooms.* New York: Garland, 1992.

Navarro, R. A. "The Problems of Language, Education and Society: Who Decides," in E. E. Garcia and R. V. Padilla, eds., *Advances in Bilingual Education Research.* Tucson, AZ: University of Arizona Press, 1985.

Ogbu, J. *Minority Education and Caste: The American System in Cross-Cultural Perspective*. New York: Academic Press, 1978.

―――. "Minority Education and Caste: The American System in Cross-Cultural Perspective." *Crisis*, v 86, n 1 (1979): 17-21.

―――. "Origins of Human Competence: A Cultural-Ecological Perspective. *Child Development*, v. 52 (1981a): 413-429.

―――. "Schooling in the Ghetto: An Ecological Perspective on Community and Home Influences." Paper presented at the National Institute of Education Follow Through Planning Conference. Philadelphia, PA, February 10-11, 1981b.

―――. "Minority Status and Schooling in Plural Societies." *Comparative Education Review*, v. 27 (1983): 168-190.

―――. "Research Currents: Cultural-Ecological Influences on Minority School Learning." *Language Arts*, v. 62 (1985): 860-869.

―――. "Variability in Minority School Performance: A Problem in Search of an Explanation." *Anthropology and Education Quarterly*, v. 18, n. 4 (1987): 312-334.

―――. "Immigrant and Involuntary Minorities in Comparative Perspective," in M. A. Gibson and J. Ogbu, eds., *Minority Status and Schooling: A Comparative Study of Immigrant and Involuntary Minorities*. New York: Garland, 1991.

Padilla, A. M. "Bilingual Education: Gateways to Integration or Roads to Separation," in G. D. Keller and K. S. Van Hooft, eds., *Bilingual Education for Hispanic Students*. New York: Teachers College Press, 1982.

Pattanayak, D. P. "Diversity in Communication and Languages Predicament of a Multilingual State: India. A Case Study: The Unequal Equation," in N. Wolfson and J. Manes, eds., *Language of Inequality*. Berlin: Mouton, 1985.

―――. "Educational Use of the Mother Tongue," in B. Spolsky, ed., *Language and Education in Multilingual Societies*. Clevedon, England: Multilingual Matters Ltd, 1986.

Paulston, C. B. *Implications of Language Learning Theory for Language Planning: Concerns in Bilingual Education*. Arlington, VA: Center for Applied Linguistics, 1974.

―――. "Rationales for Bilingual Education Reforms: A Comparative Assessment. *Comparative Education Review*, v 22, n 3 (1978): 402-419.

————. *Swedish Research and Debate about Bilingualism: A Critical Review of the Swedish Research and Debate about Bilingualism and Bilingual Education in Sweden from an International Perspective: A Report to the National Swedish Board of Education*. Stockholm: National Board of Education, 1983.

Porter, R. P. *Forked Tongue: The Politics of Bilingual Education*. New York: Basic Books, 1990.

Ramirez, J. D., S. D. Yuen, D. R. Ramey, and D. Pasta. *Longitudinal Study of Structured English Immersion Strategy, Early-Exit and Late-Exit Transitional Bilingual Education Programs for Language-Minority Children. Final Report to the U.S. Department of Education, Vol. I and Vol. II*. San Mateo, CA: Aguirre International, 1991.

Ray, D. *Education and Cultural Difference: New Perspectives*. New York: Garland, 1992.

Roller, C. "Transfer of Cognitive Academic Competence and L2 Reading in a Rural Zimbabwean Primary School." *TESOL Quarterly,* v. 22, n. 2 (1988): 303-318.

Ruiz, R. "Orientations in Language Planning." *NABE Journal,* v. 8, n. 2 (1984): 15-34.

Shimahara, N. "Social Mobility and Education: Burakumin in Japan," in M. Gibson and J. Ogbu, eds., *Minority Status and Schooling: A Comparative Study of Immigrant and Involuntary Minorities*. New York: Garland, 1991.

Skutnabb-Kangas, T. "Why Aren't All Children in the Nordic Countries Bilingual?" *Journal of Multilingual and Multicultural Development,* v. 2, n. 3-4 (1983): 301-315.

————. "Children of Guest Workers and Immigrants: Linguistic and Educational Issues," in J. Edwards, ed., *Linguistic minorities, policies and pluralism*. London: Academic Press, 1984.

Skutnabb-Kangas, T., and P. Toukomaa. *Teaching Migrant Children's Mother Tongue and Learning the Language of the Host Country in the Context of the Socio-Cultural Situation of the Migrant Family*. Helsinki: Finnish National Commission for UNESCO, 1976.

Smith, G. H. "Kura Kaupapa Maori: Contesting and Reclaiming Education in Aotearoa," in D. H. Poonwassie and Douglas Ray, eds., *Education and Cultural Differences: New Perspectives*. New York: Garland, 1992.

Snow, C. E. "English Speakers' Acquisition of Dutch Syntax," in H. Winitz, ed., *Native Language and Foreign Language Acquisition,* v 379. New York: Annals of New York Academy of Sciences, 1981.

————. "Rationales for Native Language Instruction: Evidence from Research," in A. M. Padilla, H. H. Fairchild, and C. M. Valadez, eds., *Bilingual education: Issues and strategies*. Newbury Park, CA: Sage, 1990.

Snow, C. E., and M. Hoefnagel-Hohle. "Age Differences in Second Language Acquisition," in E. Hatch, ed., *Second Language Acquisition*. Rowley, MA: Newbury House, 1978.

Spencer, J. "Language and Development in Africa: The Unequal Equation," in N. Wolfson and J. Manes, eds., *Language of Inequality*. Berlin: Mouton, 1985.

Spolsky, B. "Overcoming Language Barriers to Education in a Multilingual World," in B. Spolsky, ed., *Language and Education in Multilingual Settings*. Clevedon, England: Multilingual Matters Ltd, 1986.

Summer Institute of Linguistics. *Literacy in the 90's*. Dallas, Texas, 1989.

————. *Annual Report for 1990*. Dallas, Texas, 1990.

Swain, M. "A Review of Immersion Education in Canada: Research and Evaluation Studies," in California State Department of Education, ed., *Studies on Immersion Education: A Collection for United States Educators*. Sacramento: California State Department of Education, Office of Bilingual Bicultural Education, 1984.

Swain, M., and S. Lapkin. *Evaluating Bilingual Education: A Canadian Case Study*. Clevedon, England: Multilingual Matters Ltd, 1982.

Taylor, D. M. "Social Psychological Barriers to Effective Childhood Bilingualism," in P. Homel, M. Palij, and D. Aaronson, eds., *Childhood Bilingualism: Aspects of Linguistic, Cognitive, and Social Development*. Hillsdale, NJ: Lawrence Erlbaum Associates, 1987.

————. "The Social Psychology of Racial and Cultural Diversity: Issues of Assimilation and Multiculturalism," in A. G. Reynolds, ed., *Bilingualism, Multiculturalism, and Second Language Learning*. Hillsdale, NJ: Lawrence Erlbaum Associates, 1991.

Tharp, R. G. "Psychocultural Variables and K Constants: Effects on Teaching and Learning in Schools." *American Psychologist*, v. 44 (1989): 349-359.

Tosi, A. "The jewel in the crown of the Modern Prince: The new approach to bilingualism in multicultural education in England." In T. Skutnabb-Kangas and J. Cummins (Eds.), *Minority Education: From Shame to Struggle*. Clevedon, England: Multilingual Matters Ltd, 1988.

Toukomaa, P., and T. Skuttnab-Kangas. *The intensive teaching of the mother tongue in migrant children of pre-school age and children in the lower level of comprehensive school.* Helsinki: Finnish National Commission for UNESCO, 1977.

Troike, R. C. "Research Evidence for the Effectiveness of Bilingual Education." *Bilingual Education Paper Series,* v. 2, n. 5. Los Angeles: National Dissemination and Assessment Center, California State University, 1978.

UNESCO. *The Use of Vernacular Languages in Education.* Paris: UNESCO, 1953.

————. *Workshop on Problems Relating to the Language of Instruction in Multilingual Countries in Asia and the Pacific.* Paris: UNESCO, 1981.

Valadez, C. M. *Informe final evaluación formativa y sumativa: Proyecto educacion bilingüe, Paraguay.* Asunción: Ministry of Education and Culture, 1984.

Velasco, P. *Cross-Language Relationships in Oral Language Skills of Bilingual Children.* Unpublished dissertation thesis submitted to Harvard Graduate School of Education, 1989.

Vygotsky, L. S. *Thought and Language.* (E. Hanfmann and G. Vakar, eds. and trans.). Cambridge, MA: MIT Press, 1962. (Original work published 1934.)

Wagner, D.A., J.E. Spratt, and A. Ezzaki. "Does Learning to Read in a Second Language Always Put the Child at a Disadvantage? Some Counterevidence from Morocco." *Applied Linguistics,* v. 10 (1989): 31-48.

Willig, A. "A Meta-Analysis of Selected Studies on the Effectiveness of Bilingual Education." *Review of Educational Research,* v. 55, n. 3 (1985): 269-317.

————. "Examining Bilingual Education Research Through Meta-Analysis and Narrative Review: A Response to Baker." *Review of Educational Research,* v. 57 (1987): 363-376.

Wong-Fillmore, L. "Language Minority Students and School Participation: What Kind of English is Needed?" Journal of Education, v. 164(1982): 143-156.

————. "When Learning a Second Language Means Losing the First." *Early Childhood Research Quarterly,* v. 6 (1991): 323-346.

Wong-Fillmore, L. and C. Valadez. "Teaching bilingual learners," in M. C. Wittock, ed., *Handbook of research on teaching* (3rd ed.). New York: Macmillan, 1986.

CHAPTER 5

School Curriculum in the Periphery
The Case of South India

Prema Clarke

This presentation portrays the dysfunctionality of Indian formal education for the major portion of its population living in the "periphery." In agreement with educators, who attest to the importance of contextual embeddedness for effective education, it argues that one of the principal causes of this dysfunctionality is the irrelevance of the curriculum to the world of the children living in peripheral areas and communities. Through an examination of the curricular messages in primary-school social-studies textbooks in Tamil Nadu, South India, this study will demonstrate the predominance of the center's physical and sociocultural ideas and images and a concomitant scarcity of the elements related to the physical and sociocultural world of the periphery. Such biases in the curriculum serve to restricts the appropriateness and usefulness of the education that children in the periphery receive at school.

The chapter contains three sections. After a few brief introductory comments on the Indian educational sector, the first section portrays the differences between the center and periphery in contemporary India and sociohistorical factors which shaped them. A second section juxtaposes the environment and lifestyle of a child from the periphery with the images of reality that are portrayed in school textbooks. In the final section, proposals are made concerning ways of better representing cultural realities of the periphery in the school curriculum.

EDUCATION IN THE CENTER AND PERIPHERY IN CONTEMPORARY INDIA

The Indian educational system is the second largest in the world. Schooling consists of eight years of elementary education and four years of secondary education. Elementary education includes lower primary school (grades one through five) and upper primary school (grades six through eight). In 1991, according to government statistics, there were about 132.4 million children enrolled in primary school. Though a variety of problems characterize primary education in India, this chapter attempts to address the problem of inefficiency as shown by indicators such as levels of enrollment, dropout, and cohort survival rates.

Low enrollment rates and the failure to complete even the lower primary cycle are endemic to the Indian rural situation. Myron Weiner has pointed to the level of elementary school participation in the Indian educational system as documented and published by the census bureau: "Only 52.2 million of India's 123.7 million rural children ages six to fourteen were in school." (Weiner, 1991: 8.) About 35 percent male and about 54 percent female of the rural elementary school age cohort have never been enrolled in school. In addition to the low enrollment rates, low retention and high dropout rates are also characteristic of India's rural population. John Desrochers refers to the marginal decrease of the dropout rate since the 1950s. In fact, in 1983 the rate of dropouts and stagnation was as high as 63 percent in classes one through five. (Desrochers, 1987: 76-80.)

There are various explanations that highlight the economic, social, and cultural factors distinct to the Indian situation, which contribute to the problems just discussed. P. L. Malhotra, a leading educator in India, identifies a compelling reason for the problems of nonenrollment and dropout at an elementary level. He says, "Apart from socio-economic factors which prevent children from enrolling in schools or result in their premature withdrawal, education unrelated to specific needs of specific communities and segments of population is seen to be a major hindering factor in reaching the goal of universal elementary education." (Malhotra, 1983: 53.) Malhotra's analysis is highly relevant to this discussion of education in the periphery. Furthermore, it should be noted that education which takes into consideration "specific needs of specific communities" in the Indian context must expand itself to include the physical and sociocultural world of those in the periphery. By creating a new curriculum which reclaims the world of marginal communities, school managers will be in a better position to convince parents of the value of formal schooling for their children, and the children themselves will become more interested and engaged in their subjects, two developments which could drastically reduce school dropout and repetition.

The relationship of the center and periphery in India has been largely fashioned by two sociohistorical factors: the indigenous structures of social stratification, and the strategies and results of British colonial rule. Indian society has traditionally operated within the framework of a five-tier caste hierarchy. In hierarchical order the castes are as follows: the Brahmin (priests); the Kshatriya (warriors); the Vaisya (traders); the Sudra (laborers); and the Outcaste (the untouchables). The twice-born status of the first three castes gave them ritual privileges that were over the centuries transformed into social, cultural, political, and economic empowerment determining the features of the center. (Dumont, 1979: 66; Smith, 1989: 93.) This left the other castes, not twice-born, the problem of developing for themselves a different realm of social and cultural discourse constituting a distinctive periphery. The upper castes continue to be invested with considerable economic, religious, political, and social power, which supports ongoing efforts to deculturate those in the periphery. It must be kept in mind that in Tamil Nadu, the Kshatriyas and Vaisyas are virtually nonexistent. Therefore, the Brahmins aligned themselves with the upper crust of the Sudras (*sat* Sudras), who were not twice-born but accepted as ritually adequate. This alliance cooperatively carved out the features of the center. The marginated periphery constituted the lower rung of the Sudras (*asat* Sudras) and the Untouchables.

The second factor which influenced center-periphery relationships in India has been the strategies nation-building worked out and sharpened during British colonial rule.[1] In order to establish its political and economic influence in India, the British consciously strengthened and perpetuated precolonial centers of control, which also functioned effectively as instruments of westernization. These centers were further validated as they became hubs of industrialization and modernization. In postindependence India, the nucleus of power continues to reside in such urban centers. Ashish Nandy has analyzed this latter phenomenon, namely, the preeminent evolution of the western nation-state with cores of power concentrated in metropolitan centers and administered by the "high culture." He attributes the formation of these authoritative centers not only to the situation of postindependence leaders inheriting western statecraft, but also to their own fascination with the functioning of a modern nation-state. (Nandy, 1989.) This preoccupation with the centers in India has resulted in a neglect of and disinterest in its extensive rural populations.

Moreover, the absorption with the center and the resulting disregard for the periphery had a particularly pronounced effect on elementary schooling in the periphery during the period of direct colonial rule (1834-1947). During that period, Indian education was dominated by the British, signifying not only a dependence on the British Eurocentric curriculum (see Kaur, 1985), but also a neglect of indigenous systems of education and a refusal to promote free education among the masses.[2]

Mohandas K. Gandhi is well known for his advocation of an alternative to the British model of education called "basic education."[3] With regard to the domain of education, Gandhi was perhaps the most powerful voice for the displaced periphery. In his life and work (which includes his educational efforts) he attempted to bring back India's peripheral population into the center of its emerging national agenda. For Gandhi, "basic education" involved a curriculum grounded in the mastering of a craft with the twin goals of producing a self-sufficient economy and developing the village. Prior to this time, crafts such as pottery and weaving were confined to lower castes; by introducing this form of learning as the primary focus of the curriculum he was encouraging upper castes to become familiar with forms of knowledge among the lower castes: "Thus it sought to alter the symbolic meaning of 'education' and thereby to damage the established structure of opportunities for education." (Kumar, 1991: 171.)

Gandhi is also known for his crusade against untouchability and his support for the intrinsic worth of all persons, which contributed to a redefinition of some of Hinduism's basic categories. However, one can identify two reasons for the limited impact of his policies in the field of India education. First, in spite of the rhetoric of basic education and the campaign against untouchability, Gandhi still believed in a reformed version of the caste system: "He was still in favor of its basic principles of functional differentiation and hereditary occupation, but thought that the social groups involved need not be exclusive and hierarchical." (Parekh, 1989: 227.) Thus, his emphasis was not taken seriously by the lower castes and the people in rural India. Second, he redirected independent India toward unifying, empowering and strengthening its own fragile nation-state, which undercut and depreciated the country's obligations to the majority of its rural and low caste people living in the periphery.

In contemporary, postcolonial India the nation-state exerts considerable influence over important aspects of education, including the curriculum. Thus, although constitutionally education comes under the "Departments" or "Directorates" of Education in the various states, curriculum content—except for the small amount contributed by state elites—largely reflects central or national government stipulations.

National guidelines have been enumerated in a core curriculum contained in the document called "The Curriculum for the Ten Year School—a Framework," which was put out by the National Council for Educational Research and Planning in 1973. (UNESCO, 1984.) National objectives of secularism, unity, and national integration are accorded important places in this curriculum. Secularism has been defined so as to preclude the incorporation of explanatory aspects of culture and religion. Furthermore, the devotion to unity and national integration imposes an artificial homogeneity defined by the higher caste.[4] Aspirations for such homogeneity are evident in textbook content, particularly that which stresses concepts like a common cultural heritage, unity of states through a common government, flag and anthem, and the portrayals of a good citizen as one who is obedient and passive. This assertion of homogeneity ignores the reality of highly diverse cultures and environments in India. Even when the curriculum includes the idea of diversity, it portrays this plurality at state, national, and international levels, effectively bypassing the microlevel where difference are the most concrete and substantial.

Another significant notion of the hegemonic nation-state, which regional centers have adopted and portrayed through textbook content, is the idea of progress being represented by the country's level of industrialization and technological development. This notion is made explicit in the Ministry of Education's goal "[to] prepare the manpower to enable the country to participate vigorously in the technological revolution sweeping the world." Most states have also adopted this link with industrialization and modernization, further legitimizing an urban and high-caste- centered ideology. The detailed treatment of themes in the textbooks, such as transportation, industries, agricultural technologies, and communication, conveys the value of this variety of modernity, and a concomitant disregard for village life.

THE STANDARD SCHOOL TEXTBOOK COMPARED TO EVERYDAY LIFE IN THE PERIPHERY

Thus far most of what has been said has primarily been at an abstract level. In this section, I shall focus specifically on the Indian school curriculum as contained in the "textbook" in order to demonstrate the continued tendency of the school system to validate the world of the urban and high-caste peoples and depreciate peripheral cultures embedded in low-caste villages. The textbook based on the Tamil Nadu primary-school social-studies curriculum will be analyzed and juxtaposed with the lifestyle of a rural low-caste child representing the periphery.

The "Textbook Culture"

A point of clarification about the focus on the textbook is needed at this point. In India official textbook is the primary, indeed often, the sole teaching instrument in the schools. Krishna Kumar has pointed this out by drawing attention to the "textbook culture" which he defines in the following words: "The basic norm of this culture was to treat the prescribed textbook as the de facto curriculum, rather than as an aid. The teacher taught the text by elucidating it, by asking children to copy and memorize it, and finally by drilling them to answer and memorize questions that were based on it." (Kumar, 1991: 64.) Thus textbook is seen to dominate the classroom. Neither the teacher nor the student deems it germane to digress from the prescribed textbook, perhaps, for the following reasons: the unavailability of other material; the traditional Hindu reverence for the written Scriptures; and the celebrated status of examinations, which are a necessary and unavoidable culmination of the school year.

This study is based on the primary-school social-studies curriculum prescribed for educational institutions in Tamil Nadu, South India. Social studies was selected for this study, instead of subjects like math or science, because of its strong concern with human values. The social-studies curriculum houses the world of the people, stimulating them to continuously assess its values and remake its social arrangements, tasks which are interpretation-bound. (Bragaw and Hartoonian, 1988: 10.) Preceding an analysis of the social-studies textbooks, the vicissitudes of a child's life, both in school and at home, based on videotapes and interviews in a village called Vallarpurai in Tamil Nadu will be presented.

Life in a Dalit "Colony"

I shall focus on the daily life of a young girl to whom I give the fictitious name "Sundari." Sundari is a fifth grader who lives in the colony of Vallarpurai, which is about fifty miles (a three-hour bus ride) from the city of Madras in South India. Vallarpurai is situated in an area characterized by a few green rice fields and vast stretches of arid land spotted with thorny bushes. Sundari belongs to an outcast community referred to as Untouchables or the Dalits,[5] which numbers about 200 million in India.[6] The Dalits in Tamil Nadu primarily belong to the subcaste called the "*Praiyans.*" They reside in rural areas called the "*cheri*"or the "colony" situated at some distance from the "*Ur*" or village. While the latter is exclusively inhabited by the high caste, the *cheri* is occupied only by the Dalits. (Moffat, 1979: xxiii, 59-85.) The gulf between the Dalits and the higher-caste people is real and seems almost unbridgeable.

Sundari's parents are both Dalit agricultural laborers employed by "village" caste landlords. Sundari and her family live together in a thatched hut with mud walls. The village does have electricity. Every morning Sundari and her mother have to fetch water from a nearby well. There are 46 families in this colony. Sundari's family owns a cow and a couple of goats.

Sundari's day begins at five in the morning. Her first chore is to smear the cow dung which has been collected the previous day onto the ground just outside the door of her home and on the floor of the hut. Interestingly, cow dung, which is made into a watery paste, is thought of as having qualities that keep the floor hygienic and clean. Her father leaves for work early, around six o'clock.

After smearing the cow dung, Sundari goes on to her next chore, which is collecting dry twigs to cook a meal. She usually enlists the services of her younger sibling for this task, which could take her a small distance from her home. She is expected to bring back these twigs, which would serve as fuel to cook a rice-based meal that will be both breakfast and lunch primarily for the working members of the family since the children are given a hot lunch at school. When the meal is prepared she is asked to take it to her father in the fields. By the time she returns home there is just enough time for a hurried breakfast consisting of rice and some lentils or chilies. Her dash to school fortunately is not too long since her school is in the colony itself.

Her return home from school in the afternoon initiates a very similar routine to the one which took place before school. This time she has to search the village for cow dung. She also has to go and bring home the cow, which has been grazing nearby. Because food has to be bought daily with the wages that are paid at the end of the work day, provisions for the evening meal need to be procured. So inevitably Sundari walks to the village store to buy a few things. The colony itself does not have any shops. Her mother then requests her to assist in the preparation of the evening meal. She goes to bed as soon as the sun sets since there are only a few lights in the whole village. During certain weeks through the rice-growing season, Sundari gets to be a wage earner. Generally children are illegally hired at a lower wage to sow, weed, and harvest. She works from about six in the morning to one in the afternoon. She does not go to school during these weeks.

Entertainment for Sundari usually involves playing with her girlfriends and about once a week, watching parts of a weekly television film that is broadcast on Sunday evenings. To watch this movie without the interruption of her family asking her to do a chore for them is indeed a rare treat. The village religious festival to the goddess *Gangamma* takes place once a year and comprises a two- or three-day celebration. This is always a fun time for Sundari. She gets to see a drama, a film on video, and a two-day-long religious ceremony which includes a lively procession. Mostly this festival time is fun because Sundari gets to see her relatives. They bring good food and she gets to stay up late with them.

Textbook Images

This rather cursory sketch of Sundari's world, taken to represent some aspects of a child's life in the Tamil Nadu periphery, will now be juxtaposed against the content of the grade one to five social-studies textbooks.[7] Each textbook consists of a set of lessons, with every lesson being followed by a list of questions pertaining specifically to the lesson. The lessons themselves are descriptive and the questions require factual answers contained in the lessons. The number of lessons in each textbook ranges from about fifteen to twenty.

The stated objective in the prefaces to the grades one and two textbooks is to "help the child to understand and enjoy his relationship with his environment . . . [through which] the learner is bound to gain self-confidence besides knowledge." While the environment is treated as one cohesive whole in the curriculum in grades one and two, it later branches into two broad areas of study: natural environment and physical/social environment. Thus from grade three onward the natural environment deals with the field of science, and the physical/social environment constitutes the social-studies curriculum.

A primary focus in grades three and four is to introduce the student to the different ways that people live in various parts of the country in order "to appreciate the heritage of our country and to become responsible and good citizens of the future." (Preface, grade three.) In grade five this aim is broadened to include lifestyles in various parts of the world, in addition to inculcating "in the child values relating to [India's] cultural heritage, freedom struggle, democracy, socialism and secularism." (Preface, grade five.) In the rest of this section, the physical and sociocultural world of the child from the periphery will be discussed in relation to the physical and sociocultural world reflected in the textbooks.

Physical World

Most of the physical objects presented in the grade one and two textbooks are either unfamiliar or nonexistent in the environment of a village child. For instance, in the chapters about the home, apart from a reference to village life in a single sentence ("Most people in villages live in thatched mud houses and these houses are called huts"), all the references authenticate the urban situation. These excerpts from a grade one lesson entitled "Our House" serves to illustrate this point: "Houses have floors, roofs, walls, doors and windows. Some houses are big. Others are small. Big houses have many rooms. They have a big hall or living room, a sitting room, a dining room, a kitchen and bedroom. All modern houses have bathrooms and toilets." (Grade one, p.10.) Again, in a chapter on "Things in our House," the textbook states: "We have a lot of things in our house. Each thing has its use. We sit on chairs and sofas. We write on tables. We sleep on beds. We keep our books and other things in cupboards or on shelves. We put our clothes on stands." (Grade one, p.13.)

In addition to the text, most of the illustrations also draw attention to an urban situation, with pictures of large concrete homes with driveways and rooms that contain plush furniture. Information on clothes that are worn and games that are played also contain a similar bias. With reference to clothes, lessons draw attention to neat, clean uniforms worn to school by children; men putting on coats and ties when they go out to work, and woman wearing pants and dresses. In contrast, Sundari and her friends usually possess just two sets of clothes, which are tattered and worn out. Uniforms and western clothes are unreal in such a setting. Apart from a game called "Kabadi," which is played by village children, the games that are mentioned in the textbooks are characteristic of an urban, high-caste culture: football, hockey, cricket, and volleyball (outdoor games) and carom board, Ping Pong, and chess (indoor games). Usually only schools in urban areas possess facilities for playing such games.

The grade three textbook has two sections, which are entitled "our district" and "our state" (Tamil Nadu). The district section has four chapters entirely focusing on the city of Madras, namely its location, physical features, history, climate, natural resources, population, and forms of transportation. The descriptions and illustrations cover the different areas in the city, its hills and rivers. The chapter on natural resources focuses on the city's fisheries and industries, as follows:

People living near the sea have fishing as their chief occupation. Some of them have been using Catamarans. But now-a-days trawlers are being used. There is one aquarium in Madras and a fish farm near Adyar. . . . Madras is an industrially advanced city. Many major industries are located here because of the following reasons. 1. Electricity is easily available for factories. 2. Laborers with experience live here. 3. Madras is a port and hence raw materials can be imported. 4. Export of finished products is also easy because of the port. 5. Madras is well connected with inland towns by road and rails. (Grade three, p.20.)

Further, in a lesson on "History and Places of Importance," detailed descriptions, along with many illustrations, are provided about the many places of interest in the city of Madras such as Fort St. George, Washermanpet, Rajaji Hall, Santhome, Valluvar Kottam, Ripon Buildings, and Chintadripet. A chapter entitled "Transportation" delineates the harbor, railway stations, airport, and the roads in Madras. The section on the state also deals with these same categories, again focusing on other cities and towns in Tamil Nadu . In addition to these chapters on the district and the state, the grade-three textbook also has a few chapters on the whole country.

The textbooks for grades four and five elaborate the same topics presented in the grade-three textbook with reference to the whole country and the world. Grade four explains the physical features, natural resources, transport, life, traditions, culture, and administrative structure of the Indian subcontinent in great detail. The grade-five textbook moves the focus of study onto the world.

Sociocultural World
A significant theme appearing in the grade-one and -two textbooks is the role of parents and families. The father is depicted as the bread-winner and the mother as a housewife, cooking and giving the children "nice things to eat." Parents are also shown helping their children with their homework and as being responsible for buying books, paying the special fees at school, and escorting children to exhibitions, fairs, the zoo, the circus, the cinema, and picnics. This is in juxtaposition to the situation in the periphery, where mothers are not only responsible for providing all the meals, but also are significant earning members of the family. Mothers generally go to the fields particularly when it is time to sow, and work as long or longer than their husbands. Further, parents are usually illiterate or are too busy with daily chores to be of any help with their children's homework. Additionally, it would not be financially possible for them to take their children to exhibitions, fairs, etc. The reference to a family picnic is unreal in the rural areas, keeping in mind the problems of transportation. Therefore, the whole picture that is evolving in the textbook about parents and families is in contrast with the experiences of a peripheral child.

The grade-one and -two textbooks also examine in some detail the occupations of various people in the nation and again, the predominance of those vocations relevant to the center is evident. For instance, the occupations delineated in these textbooks include doctors, engineers, teachers, lawyers, office clerks, typists, and accountants. Historically, the stipulated responsibilities[8] of the Dalit community included "the most despised and defiling jobs of their society, exhausting unskilled physical labor, scavenging, cleaning latrines and carrying off dead animals." (Freeman, 1979: 5) There can be no doubt that this situation has changed among the Dalits in that they no longer are characterized as solely handling such jobs.[9] However, it would be fair to say that most of the Dalits in rural South India fall into the category of agricultural laborers by occupation. It is significant to note how the agricultural occupation is dealt with in the textbooks.

Agriculture, the main occupation of the people, is referred to in connection with the rich soil and natural vegetation of the state. This excerpt from a chapter entitled "Life and Occupation of the People" (grade three) will serve to illustrate this point: "Of the total area of the State, a major portion is under cultivation. About 15 percent of the land is covered with forests. The soil in most regions in the State is fertile. It is well suited for cultivation. More and more lands are brought under cultivation. Hence the main occupation of the people is agriculture. The coastal plains are made up of the rich alluvial soil brought down and deposited by the rivers." (Grade three, p.12.)

Again, in the grade-four textbook, agriculture is mentioned in association with "Soil, the carpet of the Earth." Tamil Nadu and India are referred to as being an agricultural state and country respectively: "70 percent of the people are engaged in agriculture." (Grade four, p. 36.) The discussion emphasizes soil and vegetation (as opposed to farming). The credibility and status of farming as an occupation is not a weighty part of this lesson nor is it dealt with in other parts of the textbooks. Further, in both grades three and four the information on farming focuses on how advances in technology, such as machines, pesticides, and fertilizers have benefitted agricultural production.[10] The role of the landless agricultural laborer working for the farmer who owns the land, or the value of subsistence farming, are ignored. Thus Sundari's world, dominated by wage labor and subsistence agriculture—her only comprehensible milieu—is not recognized at all.

In the grade-three textbook there are three chapters on the state of Tamil Nadu: Tamil Nadu's "Life and Tradition," "History and Culture," and "Places of Importance." These themes are developed further in grade four. In the explication of these themes, the devaluing of peripheral culture is particularly noticeable. In the chapter on "Life and Tradition," the art and architecture of Tamil Nadu is emphasized. To its credit, folk music and dances, in addition to the national music and dance, are mentioned. However, when referring to places of worship and places to visit, only the temple, the mosque, and the church are depicted. Further, in a paragraph on unity, the holy rivers and places of worship are stated as contributing to the unity of the country. For many communities of Dalits, though they are Hindus, the temple is a forbidden locality.[11] They hardly possess temples of their own and their own places of worship are usually positioned under a tree in their own village. The icons of goddesses in these places of worship are small, usually a few feet high, and made out of stone, as opposed to the big and colorful structures within the caste Hindu temples. The unity that is referred to is an enigma for the Dalit community.

From Sundari's viewpoint, it would be pertinent to inquire into whether the important elements of her social world are represented at all in the textbooks. Two dominant components determine Sundari's life: the extended family and the caste system. According to the Indian psychologist Sudhir Kakar, "the psycho-social world encountered by Indian children as they reach the 'age of accountability' is governed by the principle of the inviolable primacy of the family and secondarily jati (or caste) relationships." In his view, "from the beginning, participation and acceptance in this world entail strict observance of a traditionally elaborated hierarchical social order and the subordination of individual preferences and ambitions to the welfare of the extended family and jati communities." (Kakar, 1978: 126.) Though the urban situation today is increasingly characterized by the impersonality and fragmentation of industrialization and modernization, there can be little doubt that Kakar's interpretation is still extremely relevant to rural India.[12] The recent work of Fuller on popular Hinduism attests to the vitality of one of these factors: "Caste is not an abstract, hidden principle of social organization; it is a visible dimension of everyday life in rural India, which is part of everyone's social and personal identity in a very real sense." (Fuller, 1992: 13.)

Both these organizing principles are seemingly nonexistent, or, at least, inadequately dealt with in all of the textbooks. Descriptions of family affiliations and interactions in the textbooks are limited to urban nuclear configurations such as the mother, father, siblings, and grandparents. Moreover, the whole chapter on the "Neighborhood" is incapable of capturing the intimate dynamic that characterizes relationships in village communities. Rather it conveys the ideal of an urban community, characterized by impersonal but friendly relationships. Reference to the caste system occurs in a chapter on social reformers focusing on Gandhi. In the grade-four textbook it records that "all his life Gandhi fought for the removal of many social evils. He worked against untouchability. He did not like the idea of high and low caste. He said 'all are children of God.' He called the depressed class as Harijans which means "Children of God." It is surprising that prior to this rather concise reference to the caste system there is no explanation about the history, rationale, and functioning of the caste system in any of the earlier grades or within the context of this paragraph. In addition to this, the portrayal of these significant words by Gandhi, without any explanatory details, appears to communicate the idea that "untouchability" and caste discrimination is a redundant phenomenon no longer operant in contemporary India. Such a depiction denies the continued reality of caste within the periphery.

The above contrast between the world that Sundari inhabits and the world that is portrayed through the textbooks serves to communicate the extent to which the textbooks impede the active participation of a peripheral child. The distant situation presented to a child in the periphery through the textbook prevents the possibility of achieving its stated objective of facilitating the student to "understand and enjoy [her] relationship with [her] environment." (Grade one, preface.) The section in the grade-three textbook on "our district" might have been a suitable place to introduce Sundari to her own environment. Instead, the grade-three textbook begins a process of gradual alienation by which Sundari is taken further and further away from her felt and perceived reality. Sundari is inundated with information reiterating a world with which she is unfamiliar: starting with the city of Madras it gradually and calculatingly moves her to the state and then to the country, finally culminating in the world. This dissociation of textbook content with the environment of a peripheral child affects the child's incentive to learn and remain in school. In addition, by encountering over and over again images and messages which are alien to their lifestyles and culture, parents of school-age children in the periphery will feel little inclination or motivation to enroll their children in schools.

REPRESENTING REALITIES OF LIFE IN THE PERIPHERY: NEW DIRECTIONS
In the light of the above discussion it would be expedient to enumerate possible directions that curriculum revision could take in order to take into account the world of its periphery. The government's perception of the problem concerning the elementary school curriculum, which is laid out in the 1990 document "Towards an Enlightened and Human Society," is noteworthy. It criticizes Indian education on the following grounds:

a)   For viewing the curriculum mostly in the cognitive domain; there, too, by and large in recalling facts, particularly at the time of examinations;
b)   For being inflexible and unresponsive to the local needs and environment;
c)   For being devoid of the component of skill formation;
d)   For lacking in social and cultural inputs from the community;
e)   For being unrelated to the world of work which exercises a strong pull on the life of a large number of children after the age of 10 years;
f)   For the mode of transaction being mostly through lectures in a non-participative mode;
g)   For the near-absence of activity-based learning; and
h)   For discouraging exploration, inquiry, creativity and initiative on the   part of the student.

It is apparent that the Indian government has identified pertinent and critical problems concerning the curriculum. However, in order for the above problems to be adequately addressed with reference to its periphery, two avenues need to be further explored.

First, a decentralized process of curricular content formation needs to be cultivated. Though India's educational system could be defined as a decentralized system with individual states being responsible for their own curriculum, this model of decentralization needs to go further, specifically by the formation of curricular content at district levels in collaboration with their microcommunities. A practical way by which this could be implemented is to set up institutions at district levels which would bring together select groups of teachers who are involved in educating peripheral communities in order to explore curriculum resources that would be representative of their communities as a whole. Having said this, one has to acknowledge the importance of a national and state core curriculum within the social studies area. Perhaps, both these areas (the national and state components in the curriculum) could occupy around one-half of the textbook. Therefore, while around one-half of the curriculum contains input by microcommunities, providing opportunities for the active appropriation of the local environments of the periphery, the other is worked upon by the national and state departments. The latter would facilitate the awareness of issues at a larger level by the inclusion of national and state agendas.

Secondly, and relatedly, there needs to be systematic effort put into identifying and delineating the emotional and cultural factors affecting peripheral lifestyles. With regard to this point it would be useful to discuss the role of culture in curricular formation, contained in the later part of the same above document. Its recommendations relevant to this discussion include the following two statements:

> (i) The cultural content of education should include not merely the common cultural heritage of India as a whole but also diversities of cultural traditions of all parts of India, particularly those symbolized by the oral and folk traditions. (ii) In conveying to the student community, through the content of education, the cultural traditions of the country the needs for acceptance/rejection for the same based on critical analysis should also be inculcated.

In my view, these statements indicate that educational theorists in India are moving in an appropriate direction. However, two issues need to be further clarified. On the one hand, research methods by which these cultural traditions can be identified need to be re-examined. The National Council for Educational Research and Training has initiated research in this direction. These programs mainly encourage faculties of teacher-training institutions and teachers of primary schools to undertake community surveys. (Malhotra, 1983: 53.) Utilizing this occasion for encounter between the policy implementers of curriculum and peripheral communities, perhaps, efforts could be directed toward including more qualitative studies which would allow for the environment, experiences, and narratives of the periphery to emerge. On the other hand, the notion of "cultural traditions as symbolized by oral and folk traditions" needs to be further clarified. Many potentially fruitful questions need to be pondered: Does "traditions" refer only to the customs and rituals of peripheral communities or does it includes the religious and philosophical underpinnings of the same? Can the essence of the diverse cultural traditions be communicated without valuation and promotion of any one particular tradition?

This chapter has been an attempt to demonstrate, through the analysis of curricular content as contained in the social-studies textbooks in Tamil Nadu, the dynamic of the center-periphery relationship within the Indian situation. It unveils the significant presence of the "high culture" of the center and a concomitant absence of the physical and sociocultural world of the periphery within the textbooks. Such a situation restricts the sustained interest of the peripheral child and affects parental motivation to enroll their children in school. The chapter concludes by suggesting alternative methods of reclaiming the peripheral way of living, thinking, and understanding, thereby allowing for the active involvement of the peripheral child within the education scenario.

Endnotes

1. Here I am influenced by the seminal work of Burton Stein, *Peasant State and Society in Medieval South India*, New Delhi: Oxford University Press, 1980. In contrast to prevailing notions of an authoritative and centralized South Indian state, which was ruled by powerful kings from C.E. 800-1300, Stein argues for the existence of a kind of "segmentary model" in order to explicate political, social, and economic life during the medieval era. In such a segmentary state, power was held by chiefs or leaders at the micro levels with the king and his central authority functioning merely ritually. He further proposes that through these centuries, cities were unimportant with most people living a peasantry lifestyle; thus, political and economic power were primarily local and rural-based. In appropriating Stein's interpretation, this chapter presupposes that the period of British colonization was responsible for the development and rationalization of central bureaucracies.

2. See Desrochers, 1987: 29. It is interesting to note a point that this author makes: Kerala, the only state to have achieved 100 percent literacy in India, still maintained the predominance of vernacular schools during the colonial period.

3. See Krishna Kumar, *Political Agenda of Education*, New Delhi: Sage, 1991, Ch. 5. Also, Rogoff's discussion of the social and cultural underpinnings affecting both learner and instructor when learning a particular skill could be an interesting parallel to Ghandi's ideas on basic education. See Barbara Rogoff, *Apprenticeship in Thinking*, New York: Oxford University Press, 1990.

4. This idea of homogeneity is similar to the notion of "cultural hegemony" expressed by Michael Apple, *Idealogy and Curriculum*, New York: Routledge, 1990, Ch.5.

5. See Parekh, p. 234. Mahatma Gandhi coined the term "Harijan" or "Children of God" to refer to the Untouchable castes of India. This was intended to give them respectability, which they were denied for centuries. However, because this was taken to be a patronizing term given by persons from the high-caste communities, the Untouchable rejected this appellation. They have claimed the term "Dalit." The sanskrit word *Dal,* from which the word "Dalit" comes, bears connotations such as broken, rend asunder, oppressed.

6. In spite of official prohibition against "untouchability" and Government attempts at economic upliftment, this community still remain in a desperate situation in India. "Most of them despite legislation, the expenditure of millions of rupees, and two and a half decades of federal and state efforts to improve their economic and social position, remain desperately poor, semiliterate or illiterate, and subject to brutal discrimination and economic exploitation, with no realistic prospects for economic or social gain." (Freeman, 1979: 5.)

7. I shall be using the English version of textbooks in this discussion. The textbooks that are used by state and municipal schools both in cities and in the villages are translations of the English version into the vernacular language.

8. Each caste is assigned its specific duties or "Dharma." See the chapter "Dharma in the Self-Understanding of Traditional Hinduism" by Wilhelm Halbfass in *India and Europe*, New York: SUNY Press, 1988.

9. See Kumar, 1991: 107. Kumar uses two criteria, representation in the job market and retention rates in school, for judging the efficacy of government policies of positive discrimination or "reservation" stipulated for the periphery. With regard to employment in urban areas, he states that there is a "solid representation" in the lower ranks but few in the middle and higher ranks.

10. It is possible that these references are made in connection with the "Green Revolution" in the sixties. However, many believe that there are already signs of the revolution's decline, as evidenced by a decrease in production of many commodities and an increase in rural unemployment.

11. To be sure, this is not legal. According to the Indian constitution, all public places are open to all people in India. However, at local levels through the force of social pressure, Dalits are kept away from Hindu temples. See Moffat, 1979: 219f.

12. Alan Roland in his psychoanalytic book , *In Search of Self in India and Japan* (Princeton: Princeton University Press, 1988), has described the conflict within urban upper-class Indians between traditional and western values.

Bibliography

Apple, Michael. *Ideology and Curriculum.* New York: Routledge, 1990.

Bragaw, Donald H., and H. Michael Hartoonian. "Social Studies: The Study of People in Society." *Content of the Curriculum*, ASCD Yearbook, 1988.

Desrochers, John. *Education for Social Change.* Bangalore, India: Center for Social Action, 1987.

Dumont, Louis. *Homo Hierarchicus.* New Delhi: Chicago University Press, 1979.

Freeman, James M. *Untouchable: An Indian Life History.* Stanford, CA: Stanford University Press, 1979.

Fuller, C.J. *The Camphor Flame: Popular Hinduism and Society in India.* New Delhi: Penguin, 1992.

Halbfass, Wilhelm. "Dharma in the Self-Understanding of Traditional Hinduism," in *India and Europe.* New York: SUNY, 1988.

Kakar, Sudhir. *The Inner World: A Psychoanalytic Study of Childhood and Society in India.* New Delhi: Oxford University Press, 1978.

Kaur, Kuldip. *Education in India (1781-1985).* New Delhi: CRRD, 1985.

Kumar, Krishna. *Political Agenda of Education.* New Delhi: Sage, 1991.

Malhotra, P.L., *Textbooks and Reading Materials,* v. 3. UNESCO, 1983.

Moffat, Michael. *An Untouchable Community in South India.* Princeton: Princeton University Press, 1979.

Nandy, Ashish. "The Political Culture of the Indian State." *Daedalus*, v. 118, n. 4 (Fall 1989).

Parekh, Bhikku. *Colonialism, Tradition and Reform: An Analysis of Ghandi's Political Discourse.* New Delhi: Sage, 1989.

Rogoff, Barbara. *Apprenticeship in Thinking.* New York: Oxford University Press, 1990.

Roland, Alan. *In Search of Self in India and Japan.* Princeton: Princeton University Press, 1988.

Smith, Brian K. *Reflections on Resemblance, Ritual, and Religion.* New York: Oxford University Press, 1989.

Stein, Burton. *Peasant State and Society in Medieval South India.* New Delhi: Oxford University Press, 1980.

UNESCO. *Towards Universalization of Primary Education in Asia and the Pacific: Country Studies, India.* Bangkok: UNESCO Regional Office, 1984.

Weiner, Myron. *The Child and the State in India.* Princeton: Princeton University Press, 1991.

CHAPTER 6

Teachers Working in the Periphery
Addressing Persistent Policy Issues

Maria Teresa Tatto

INTRODUCTION

Recently the focus of educational policy has shifted from providing educational access to improving educational quality. This shift is reflected in policy changes directed at teachers. Increasingly researchers, educators, and policymakers point to the teacher as a, if not *the*, key actor in the successful implementation of quality-improvement policies, in both developed and developing countries. (Beeby, 1966; Cohen, 1988; Cohen and Spillane, 1992; Fuller and Snyder, 1991; International Development Research Centre, 1981; Lockheed and Verspoor, 1991; Rust and Dalin, 1990; USAID, 1990; Verspoor and Leno, 1986.) Recently, international agencies, such as the World Bank and the United States Agency for International Development (USAID), have highlighted the importance of teacher preparation in improving the quality of education. This emphasis is evident both in these institutions' research agendas and in the initiatives they support in a number of countries. (Avalos and Haddad, 1981; Fuller, 1986; Lockheed and Verspoor, 1991; Nielsen and Chan, 1990; USAID, 1990; Williams, 1979.) The importance given to the teacher in improving the quality of education is also evident in a recent informal review of World Bank's 93 basic education projects over the last ten years. (World Bank, 1992.) Although this emphasis on teachers represents a remarkable departure in educational policy and budget-allocation priorities in the countries included in this review, it should be noted that only six out of the 93 projects reviewed include provisions to address teachers' recurrent concerns in a comprehensive manner simultaneously affecting teachers' education, recruitment, deployment, and retention.

Despite the widespread recognition that teachers are key to improving educational quality, many recurring problems affecting the teacher's work—especially the work of teachers in peripheral areas—have not been dealt with effectively. (Avalos and Haddad, 1981; Fuller, 1986; Lockheed and Verspoor, 1991; Moore-Johnson, 1990; Rosenholtz, 1989; USAID, 1990; Williams, 1979.) Efforts directed at improving the quality of education in peripheral-area schools have, for the most part, seen teachers as no more than mere recipients of national or state mandates placing them at the margin of policy-making and implementation. (Moore-Johnson, 1990; Schiefelbein, 1992; Shaeffer, 1990; Vera, 1990.) The failure to include teachers in policy dialogues, planning, and implementation has meant that many policies have failed to adequately address teachers concerns and needs. (Darling-Hammond, 1984.) Whereas at one time teachers may simply have had to put up with poor conditions and little power, economic changes in most countries have created conditions where current and prospective teachers have more occupational choices. The creation of new and varied job options for upwardly mobile youth means that fewer potential teachers of high ability are entering the profession; those who do frequently drop out after a few years or gravitate to the most desirable teaching locations. Teachers leaving posts in peripheral areas or dropping out of the profession cite professional as well as social concerns for their decisions . (Farres and Noriega, 1993; Kozol, 1991; Moore-Johnson, 1990; Murnane, Singer, Willet, Kemple, and Randall, 1991; Zeichner, 1993.) The mounting challenge for policymakers concerned with the quality of education in the periphery is to attract qualified teachers or individuals, particularly those from the peripheral areas themselves, who have the potential to become effective teachers, and provide the needed support for them to remain at schools and locations where life itself is a challenge.

The chapter begins with the assumption that policies for teachers in the periphery have to take seriously the issue of *teacher choice*. The inclusion of teachers in the policy dialogue and in their own professional development processes seems essential to understanding and addressing teachers' needs and concerns. This perspective is congruent with advances in theories of teacher socialization, which move away from deterministic views of teacher development towards a view of teachers as creators and subjects of new socially constructed teaching realities. (Zeichner and Gore, 1990.) Similarly new ways of thinking about teacher development, derived from constructivism and theories of cognitive psychology (Piaget, 1962, 1968), argue that improvements in teaching may be better achieved by focusing on teachers' cognitive and thought processes rather than on performance, and that this change needs to be socially constructed with and by teachers. (Buchmann, 1986, 1990; Cochran, DeRuiter, and King, 1993; Prawat, 1992; Richardson, 1990; Schon, 1987.)

The main concern of the chapter is to review policies and policy recommendations which address serious issues related to teachers and teaching in the periphery. The literature reviewed here includes, with few exceptions, work published in the English language in the last two decades. The material selected emphasizes the situation of teachers in less industrialized countries, but some studies from more industrialized countries such as the United States have also been included as a way to explore issues and policy solutions across a wide range of social and economic development contexts. A comprehensive contextual analysis, indicating the various adaptations that might be called for given particular enviromental conditions, is beyond the scope of this chapter.

This review thus addresses the following three questions: What are the major issues affecting teachers working—or having the potential to work—in the periphery? What policies have been developed to address these issues? What are some of the contextual factors likely to affect success in implementing such policies in different kinds of localities?

POLICIES ADDRESSING RECURRENT ISSUES CONFRONTING TEACHERS IN THE PERIPHERY

Conceptual Framework

One important point of clarification at the outset is our definition of periphery. *Periphery* is often viewed in relation to the *center*. The dictionary defines center as "a point, a pivot, an axis, around which anything rotates or revolves," and also "the source of an influence, action, force." (Random House, 1987: 335.) Conversely, periphery is defined as "the external boundary of any surface or area, the edge or outskirts, as of a city or urban area"; but also "concerned with relatively minor, irrelevant or superficial aspects of the subject in question." (Random House, 1987: 1441.) As these definitions imply, individuals located "at the center" are more likely to be the source of power and action, around whom resources, people, and other elements in a society revolve and who are, for the most part, far removed from the periphery. In turn, individuals and events at the periphery are often perceived by individuals at the center (and often by themselves as well) as relatively minor or irrelevant compared to those at the center. The meaning behind these concepts is familiar to both rich and poor countries; for whereas poor countries may very well be seen as peripheral themselves in relation to rich countries, both have peripheries within themselves.

The term "periphery" can also be used to refer to a place. In this sense peripheral areas are usually located in rural or remote areas of a country. Conditions in such areas, such as slow transportation and difficult access to communication, lack of resources, and neglect or exploitation by the center, combine to place these regions at the periphery of educational and other social services. Challenges for teachers in these areas are many. They may have to walk several miles to school, reside in rural or remote areas away from their own families, and live as outsiders in their school's community. Whether or not they have had professional training, teachers are often poorly prepared to teach in such areas and lack sources of professional support or development. Because of lack of preparation or knowledge about the community in which they work, teachers may also have difficulty addressing the learning needs of their students. Moreover, rural or remote status is often accompanied by low salaries, scant recognition, and poor possibilities for promotion.

Other peripheries also exist. These include groups living in large urban areas whose marginality is determined by their history of low access to educational and job opportunities, and who generally live in poverty. Examples can be found in cities such as New York City or Los Angeles in the U.S. and Mexico City or Monterrey in Mexico. Schools serving these populations also lack resources to properly address their students' needs. Their teachers frequently have to confront problems of violence, drug addiction, child abuse, dysfunctional families, and various kinds of learning disabilities. In every case, teachers of peripheral populations are peripheral themselves. Although peripheral teachers in remote areas and the central cities of various countries confront very different social and occupational realities, they all must deal with the common fact of working under extreme conditions.

There are at least two perspectives that could serve as a point of departure for analyzing the policy issues concerning teachers in the periphery. The first represents the needs of the employers of teachers, usually the state through a specific branch of the Ministry of Education, or in less centralized countries through school districts, and the second, the needs of the teachers themselves.

The perspective most often found in the literature on teacher policy relates to the needs of the state as teacher employers with respect to the following kinds of issues: (a) attracting qualified and competent individuals from peripheral areas into teaching, or *recruitment* issues; (b) preparing and continually educating teachers in the development of appropriate knowledge, skills, and dispositions, or *teacher education* issues; (c) assigning or allocating teachers, once certified, to positions in peripheral areas, or *deployment* issues, and (d) keeping well-qualified and competent teachers in their assigned or chosen schools as well as in the profession, or *retention* issues. These needs get phrased somewhat differently by central and local authorities, but regardless of their central or local character, they still originate from one side of the work equation.

The second perspective represented by the needs of teachers is also important, but is often overlooked. Whereas it is true that teachers have traditionally complied with their assignments to marginal areas, especially in more centralized and less industrialized countries, with governments/ employers mostly following a coercive model, more recently teachers have begun to exercise their own choices, based on personal and professional needs and concerns. Teacher needs and concerns could be categorized as follows: (a) the need for sufficient economic rewards to cover actual and opportunity costs, or *economic considerations*; (b) the need for supporting structures that will facilitate teachers' success once in the school, or *organizational support*; (c) the need for adequate professional preparation and continued opportunities to develop professionally, or *professional development*; and (d) the need to achieve and maintain an adequate social life and social standing in the community or *social considerations*. The lack of consistency between the needs of the school system and the needs that teachers consider in making choices about work in the periphery has important policy implications, suggesting the need for a new policy-analysis framework.

A more effective framework for thinking about teacher policies would start with teacher needs, in much the same way that Elmore (1995)—when talking about change in school organizations—focuses first on change in practice, and then on the creation of structures in support of such changes. A new analytical framework for teacher policy would consider the state's concern for teacher recruitment, education, deployment and retention only in light of predetermined teacher needs and concerns. Table 6.1 demonstrates such a juxtaposition: the states needs being displayed in the rows and the teacher needs and concerns shown in the columns. The content in the cells are the issues that must be addressed when each of the state's concerns are confronted with teacher needs and concerns; for example, the teacher's economic needs in relation to recruitment, education, deployment, and retention.

The chapter sections which follow review the literature concerning the issues generated by the above analytical framework. After the issues are spelled out, I will then review the policy initiatives which have been used or recommended in address-ing the issues. The sections will be organized according to the categories of teacher needs displayed in the matrix columns, namely: (a) economic considerations; (b) or-ganizational support; (c) professional development; and (d) social considerations.

Table 6.1. Matrix of Policy Issues for Teachers in the Periphery

Teacher Needs /Policy Area	Economic Considerations	Organizational Support	Professional Development	Social Considerations
Teacher Recruitment	Low teacher salary vis-à-vis comparable occupations	Negative image of working conditions	Costs of teacher education often prohibitive	Declining image of social status of teaching profession
Teacher Education	Relatively high cost of teacher education (preservice and inservice)	Preserve education creates unrealistic image of conditions in periphery	Access to teacher education programs difficult Content of teacher education programs (pre- and inservice) largely irrelevant to teachers needs	Problems of separation from spouse /family during long campus-based educ. activities
Teacher Deployment	Low pay and benefits relative to local cost of living Frequent use of non-certified, nonlicensed teachers	Negative mental image of conditions in periphery among potential recruits Lack of candidate input concerning placement	Realization that professional development possibilities at the location are limited	Lack of appropriate housing Concerns about health; educational services Frequent forced separation from spouse

Table 6.1
Continued

Teacher Retention			
Relatively poor opportunities for promotion and salary increase	Poor school conditions (lack of learning materials and facilities)	Few opportunities for teacher upgrading/promotion compared to urban areas	Desire to be near relatives
Little opportunity for secondary employment	Breakdown of distribution systems that provide new materials and inputs	Undifferentiated career path	Cultural distance and social adjustment difficulties
Pay frequently delayed	Little teacher involvement in decision-making	Promotion opportunities constrained by poor record keeping and recording	Poor sense of security (being and feeling safe)
Relatively little job security	Feelings of professional isolation/being ignored by managers	Conditions for new teacher roles rarely met in the periphery	Heavy demands from community for a variety of services

Economic Considerations
Policies addressing peripheral teachers' economic needs and concerns are based on the assumption that extrinsic rewards and incentives, such as salary and benefits, increased job status, and job security, are important factors that can be manipulated in order to attract, deploy, educate, and retain effective teachers. According to some authors, policies that address teachers' economic needs and concerns positively affect the quality and quantity of a teaching force. (Dove, 1986; Thompson, 1990.)

The Issues
A number of issues (see Table 6.1) need to be considered when developing policies to address teachers' economic concerns in the periphery, for instance, (a) low pay and benefits in relation to high cost of living; (b) low teacher salaries vis-à-vis comparable occupations; (c) high cost of professional preparation compared to alternatives; (d) deployment of noncertified, nonlicensed teachers; (e) relatively poor opportunities for promotion and salary increase; (f) little opportunity for secondary employment; (g) frequently delayed pay; and (h) relatively poor job security.

Traditionally, peripheral areas have paid their teachers relatively poorly. (Miller, 1991.) This is especially the case in federal systems, where pay scales may vary greatly from location to location. For example, in Brazil the average salary of teachers in the progressive state of São Paulo was six times higher than that in the states of Maranhão and Piauí. (Hurst and Rust, 1990).

In an effort to avoid such inequities, more centralized educational systems like that of Indonesia have developed uniform pay scales. (IEES, 1986.) But even when salaries are set at the national level, teachers in the periphery may be at a great disadvantage because of the high cost of living there, and because teachers in peripheral schools often fail to qualify as civil servants. (Tibi, 1990; World Bank, 1991b.) There is also evidence that teachers' earnings fall below those for civil servants in other government sectors (World Bank, 1989), and private-sector employees of comparable education. (Hurst and Rust, 1990; Sykes, 1983.)

Finding it difficult to make ends meet on a teacher's regular salary, many teachers in developing countries find it necessary to take up additional employment. (Dove, 1982a) In Indonesia, it is estimated that urban teachers' secondary employment (usually as private-school teachers or tutors) provides a supplement equal to about 50 percent of civil-service salary and benefits. (World Bank, 1989.) Unfortunately from the teachers point of view, supplemental income from teaching is rarely possible in the periphery, where the government school is likely to be the only educational institution around; the best hope for additional earnings there comes from farming or product marketing (activities generally restricted to those who have land or capital).

While making ends meet is a challenge, the very process of becoming a teacher is often financially prohibitive, especially for those who originate from peripheral areas and are therefore more likely to seek work and to remain there. Indonesia again provides a case in point. As of 1990, the government required all new teachers to be educated at an institution of higher education, whereas before they could be certified at a local "normal" or teacher-training secondary school. Since most institutions of higher education were located in metropolitan areas, where fees and costs of rent and travel were high, many potential teachers from peripheral areas gave up hope of becoming certified to teach. (Nielsen and Somerset, 1992.)

Those who obtain teaching jobs in the periphery also find the possibilities for salary increases in the periphery to be relatively weak, a result of either the teacher's lack of initial certification or her/his poor access to inservice teacher-education and promotion opportunities. In remote or difficult areas, the hiring of individuals with little or no formal preparation may be a community's only way of keeping the village school going, but the costs are high in terms of the teacher's future prospects. Increasingly, educators and researchers are calling for appropriate school-based or distance teacher-education possibilities for teachers in peripheral areas in association with salary increments and compensations commensurate to the difficulty of their special assignments. (Tibi, 1990; World Bank, 1992a.)

As mentioned above, peripheral teachers are also often in a tenuous position with respect to job security. For example, teachers hired by the federation, as in Brazil, or by provincial/local governments, as in China, are in a better situation than those hired by the community or the locality, as is often done in peripheral areas. More specifically in China, *gonban* teachers are official employees of the provincial/local governments with corresponding salary and benefits averaging about 100-110 yuan per month. *Minban* teachers, who are not considered government employees because they are directly hired by the local community, receive only subsidies from the government (not a salary), which average about 40 yuan per month, and have no benefits. Although the community gives subsidies to *minban* teachers, this amount varies according to the level of wealth of the community and averages only about 30 yuan per month. In addition, *gonban* teachers' residence status is urban (with all the benefits associated with it, such as urban schools for their children, food subsidies, and easy access to other resources), whereas *minban* teachers generally have a rural residence status in difficult areas. (World Bank, 1991b.)

Similarly in Brazil, teachers recruited by the federation receive contracts as permanent staff, while the state-hired teacher receives temporary contracts; teachers hired by municipalities work without contract, receive nominal remuneration for their work, and have no legal protection. (Tibi, 1990: 5.) The lack of job security for teachers working in the periphery, especially if they have not been formally hired and offered a permanent contract, may increase the degree to which teachers leave the field or stop working in peripheral areas. (Tibi, 1990.)

In summary, a number of important economic considerations, such as salary levels, cost of living, costs of professional preparation, opportunities for promotion and salary increase, opportunities for supplementary income, and job security seem to influence teachers' decisions with respect to recruitment, education, deployment and retention.

Policy Initiatives

Researchers and teacher advocates have argued that addressing teachers' economic needs and concerns will significantly impact teacher recruitment, education, deployment, and retention in peripheral areas. Many have recommended addressing economic considerations in a systemic way, calling for more coherence in incentives for teacher recruitment, education, and professional support. (Thompson, 1990.)

Salary differentials have been successfully used as incentives for accepting difficult assignments in center-city schools in industrialized countries, (Bruno and Negrete, 1983); similar programs have been instituted for remote areas schools in some developing countries. (IEES, 1986; Tibi, 1990.) Tibi (1990) cites Morocco as a country where assignment to a difficult area brings a salary increment of 8 to 10 percent according to seniority and qualifications. Incentives may also include housing or housing allowances, as in the case of Sri Lanka (Baker, 1988; Tatto, Nielsen, Cummings, Kularatna, and Dharmadasa, 1991) or in Senegal (Tibi, 1990). In addition, Tibi (1990) documents the use of an overtime system in French-speaking African countries as a way to insure additional pay to teachers for extra work. This strategy, he argues, has helped solve the undersupply of secondary teachers, especially in science subjects. In Indonesia, a "functional credit system" has been instituted which provides extra credits towards promotion to teachers working in remote areas. (IEES, 1990.) And in China, "hardship" pay is now being given to certified teachers who agree to work in the periphery.

In some places, teachers who are civil servants have benefitted from automatic promotion regulations. For example, in Indonesia an appointed teacher has the right to be promoted every four years. (IEES, 1986.) Despite the good intentions of this system, it is still often flawed in its application to teachers in the periphery, since principals and supervisors are often delinquent in completing the paperwork that makes it possible. (IEES, 1986.)

There are also promising instances of central government collaboration with local educational authorities and community groups in support of teacher salaries and benefits. (Tibi, 1990; World Bank, 1991a.) Recent studies suggest that the perspective of the teacher is crucial in the formulation of policies of this sort, and that community support is often an effective means of improving the teachers' economic well-being. (World Bank, 1991a.)

Incentive policies such as merit pay in the U.S. and certain aspects of Indonesia's functional credit system have been used as strategies to stimulate better performance and to encourage teachers to stay in peripheral schools. (IEES, 1990; Murnane, Singer, Willet, Kemple, and Randall, 1991). But although merit pay is a widely proposed policy, it has several critics who argue, based on empirical data, that giving monetary rewards to teachers for improved performance as measured by preestablished external criteria produces negative effects on teacher morale and tends to fragment rather than unify teachers in schools where it has been implemented. (For an excellent discussion on the limitations of merit pay in the U.S., see Murnane and Cohen , 1986; Moore-Johnson, 1990.)

It is also sobering to realize that policies for improving the job security and job status of teachers have met with mixed results in Brazil. Although in some cases a number of teachers have benefitted from these initiatives, in others it has made it difficult to achieve the goal of staffing peripheral schools. According to Tibi, "the aspirations engendered by this [enhanced] status and by the continual increase in levels of education and [preparation] of new teachers has ... caused the assignment and maintaining in post of teachers in rural areas to be more difficult, given the living and working conditions there." (Tibi, 1990: 5.)

Earning a credential while on the job in peripheral schools is a strategy that has been used in various countries to improve the academic standing of teachers and thus their salaries levels. (Hawley, 1986; Tatto, et al., 1991.) Sri Lanka has been experimenting with different ways of providing teacher certification to village teachers. Two kinds of inservice programs have been used, one which supports a teacher's leave for full-time study towards a teacher certificate, and the other which provides a system of distance education enabling teachers to earn the certificate while on the job. For future teachers, Sri Lanka has created new residential colleges of education where qualified youth study to become teachers at the government's expense, earning a relatively high-status teaching diploma, but also the obligation to teach in rural schools for at least three years. (Tatto et al, 1991.)

In summary, attention to teachers' economic needs and concerns has been found to influence prospective and experienced teachers' choice to teach in peripheral schools. A combination of strategies such as differential pay for "hardship" postings, automatic salary increases, opportunities for advancement within reasonable time periods, credit systems based on hours of teaching in difficult/remote schools, and government-community collaboration in supporting teacher welfare seem promising innovations to address the economic concerns of teachers. This review reveals that teacher policies which have addressed such issues have brought about improvements in the economic status of teachers working in the periphery. This does not mean that such policies will work in all contexts; in each case, new economic packages need to be evaluated in terms of their economic feasibility and possible unintended effects before implementation. (Tsang, 1988.)

Organizational Support
Policies addressing organizational-support needs of teachers assume that the workplace has powerful socializing and motivational effects and that the perception teachers hold about their expected workplace at the recruitment and deployment stages will greatly contribute to whether or not they will choose to work and stay in a school in the periphery. Similarly, these policies assume that the effectiveness and success of teachers depend, at least in part, on the organizational support they receive at the school, which in turn will affect their satisfaction and morale, and their willingness to persevere in the periphery.

The Issues
Although teacher policy has largely ignored the interrelation that exists between what the teacher does and the context where they do it (Fuller, 1991; Thompson, 1990), studies related to organizational-support concerns of teachers have gained importance in recent years. School working conditions contribute to teacher commitment levels and perseverance in a challenging placement. (Baker, 1988; Darling-Hammond, 1984; Dove, 1982a; Hurst and Rust, 1990; Moore-Johnson, 1990.) In both less and more industrialized countries, poor levels of organizational support have been found to be a powerful reason for qualified individuals not taking a position or leaving it prematurely. Teachers who encounter inadequate resources, children not ready to learn, and professional isolation during their first years of teaching are particularly vulnerable. (Baker, 1988; Dove, 1982a; Hurst and Rust, 1990; Moore-Johnson, 1990.)

Conversely, supportive conditions of employment directly affect teacher performance and ability to reach pupils, which in turn positively affect the length of their commitment to a post or to the profession. (Hurst and Rust, 1990; Lortie, 1975; Mitchell, Ortiz, and Mitchell, 1987; Moore-Johnson, 1990; Rosenholtz, 1989.) Nevertheless, attention to organizational environment of schools in the periphery, and alternatives for improved professional support, needs more extensive and serious study, especially in less industrialized countries. (Hurst and Rust, 1990.)

A teacher's mental image of working conditions can also be a great incentive or inhibitor for work in the periphery. Teachers can form negative images of peripheral-area schools in a variety of ways. One is through their preservice education, which may lead them to expect work in an idealized setting. (Fuller, 1991.) The other is a consequence of their lack of input into their school-placement decision, such that they may be coerced to work in a setting and culture vastly different from those of their home area. Moreover, they may perceive the inadequacy of their preservice education for the kind of assignment available; for example, one entailing multigrade teaching and scant support from peers and supervisors. Finally, they may discover that the kind of inservice provided by the district, if any, is entirely irrelevant to their needs. (Thompson, 1990; World Bank, 1991a.)

The irrelevance of their teacher-education curriculum, the inadequacy of their teacher preparation, and the lack of support for coping with the difficulties of peripheral schools is often exacerbated by the poor allocation and use of instructional and material resources. (Raudenbush and Bhumirat, 1991; Fuller and Heyneman, 1989.) In a number of countries, such as Mexico, the provision of free textbooks has been a crucial factor in improving pupil access to education as well as teacher effectiveness. (Departamento de Investigaciones Educativas del Centro de Investigación y de Estudios Avanzados, 1990.) Sri Lanka took similar steps when in 1980 the state promulgated a policy of free textbooks for all children in grades one to ten. Such policies, considered milestones for education in the disadvantaged areas of both countries, were, however, severely hampered by inefficiencies in the countries' distribution systems. (Baker, 1988; World Bank, 1991a.) Similarly, a school meal program, another important initiative in Sri Lanka, has recently lost support from the center with negative consequences for children and education in remote areas. (Caldwell, 1986.)

The organizational support teachers receive in peripheral schools seems to be strongly influenced by a country's financing and governance systems. Cummings and Riddell (1992) have argued that those who pay for education control it. According to them, this is an essential feature that varies across systems. In decentralized systems the financing and control of education are locally managed, and parity and uniformity are more difficult to achieve. In more hierarchical systems the financing and control of education tend to be centrally managed, resulting in greater equity in funding and higher uniformity. Schools in remote or disadvantaged situations often find themselves in a situation of both top-down control *and* inadequate financing with few possibilities for improvement. Expectations of central mandates seem to preclude taking local initiative to solve problems or pursuing strategies to increase organizational support. The case of *minban* teachers in China mentioned above is applicable here as well. Schools in remote or rural areas are mostly dependent on *minban* teachers for their children's education. Although the local communities are allowed to hire these teachers, the government controls teacher salaries, benefits, living conditions, and placement, a situation that exacerbates these teachers' already unequal conditions.

Direct community involvement in schooling has been seen as a means of providing support to isolated teachers in many locations. However, some experiences, such as that in Sri Lanka's Small School Development Program, implemented with the support of UNICEF in the mid-1970s, show that such programs are difficult to sustain over time. When external funding for the program was discontinued, the program died, and its advantages to the teacher were lost. (Baker, 1988.) Also, parental support and community involvement have been constrained by bureaucratic structures and regulations, which have limited the extent to which nonprofessionals can be involved in decisionmaking and school dynamics. (Epstein and Dauber, 1991; Lareau, 1987.)

In summary, teachers' unfavorable perceptions of the workplace; lack of input regarding placement and lack of familiarity with the community; weak administrative support, isolation, poor facilities and materials; low student and parental motivation; and constraints on direct community support of the teacher have been found to negatively influence teacher recruitment, education, deployment, and retention in the periphery.

Policy Initiatives
Recent studies of the conditions of employment and the impact of organizational factors on teachers' success have prompted the development of promising new teacher-support strategies. These strategies basically entail changes in the balance between central and local control of organizational supports to teaching in peripheral areas.

For one thing, negative images of teaching jobs in peripheral schools can be altered during the recruitment and deployment stages by making sure that as many prospective teachers as possible originate from the peripheral areas in question. Such teacher recruits will have grown up in peripheral schools. In Tanzania for instance, schools have created community-school councils whose task is to recruit and select potential teachers to work in the schools' communities. (Dove, 1982b.) This strategy has the advantage of allowing schools to recruit and place teachers locally (rather than coerce teachers through a national placement system), creating ownership and commitment from and to the teachers who will be working in these schools.

The managerial guidance and support that can be provided to teachers through principals, head teachers, or supervisors at the school level is another important strategy. It is widely recognized that a well-qualified and competent principal can greatly improve the quality of education provided in the school and enhance teachers' effectiveness in the classroom. (Cummings, Suparman, and Thoyib, 1992; Kyle, 1990; McLaughlin, Pfeiffer, Swanson-Owens, and Yee, 1985; Raudenbush Suwanna, Kamali, and Taoklam, 1991.) In Thailand, for instance, Raudenbush, et al. (1991), report on a study where the principal received education on school administration, staff supervision, budgeting, planning, and other tasks. This program was successful in achieving the intended effects of improving teaching quality in the schools studied. The crucial feature of this program was the view that principals could organize effective on-the-job education for their teaching staff. This same model has been used in instructional programs for principals in Haiti, Indonesia, and Sri Lanka. (Nielsen and Tatto, 1993; Tatto, et al., 1991; USAID, 1990.) As the support of the principal leads to improved classroom teaching and more staff satisfaction on the job, teacher attrition is likely to decrease.

Participatory guidance and support networks among teachers and school administrators have also been frequently used as ways to develop a supportive environment. Examples of this approach can be seen in Sri Lanka under the recent teacher-education reforms. For example, teachers who participate in Sri Lanka's Distance Education program are introduced by teacher educators to the art of working and learning collaboratively, practices which have had a positive impact on teachers' performance and student achievement. (Tatto, et al., 1991.) School clusters or local teacher working groups have also been found to be effective teacher support systems in Sri Lanka. (Cummings, Gunawardena, and Williams, 1992), Thailand (Wheeler, Chuaratanaphong, Chinnapat, Eamsukkawat, Shinatrakool, Sirijirakal, Pumsa-ard, Sookpokakit, and Kunarak, 1991), and Indonesia (Hawes, 1982). Similarly, in highly industrialized countries such as the U.S., the concept of the "professional development school" has led to the development of supportive learning environments, often in challenging school settings, where new teachers are encouraged and supported in using innovative instructional approaches and reflection on their practice. (Holmes Group, 1990.)

In another vein, innovative programs like Colombia's *Escuela Nueva* have recently encouraged more teacher participation in the development of curricula for both the schools and inservice teacher education. Such measures can lead to a strong sense of teacher solidarity and program ownership. (Colbert and Arboleda, 1990.) *Escuela Nueva,* as well as numerous other programs, have also mobilized community resources and efforts in support of the schoolteacher. (Calkins, 1986a; Comer, 1986; Cummings, Gunawardena, and Williams, 1992; Epstein and Dauber, 1991; Schiefelbein, 1992; Tatto and Velez, in press; Tsang and Wheeler, forthcoming; see also chapters 3 and 8 of this volume.) When such programs lead to special recognition of the teacher by students, parents, and/or the community, another form of organizational support emerges, one which often makes the difference in a teacher's decision to stay with a difficult assignment. (Mitchell et al., 1987.)

Recurrent problems of inadequate resource distribution have prompted some governments to turn increasingly to systems of decentralized resource management. For example, China's free-textbook program relies on local firms to publish and distribute textbooks. (USAID, 1990.) In Mexico, textbook distribution is now managed locally. (Farres and Noriega, 1993.) Although local management strategies tend to be more efficient than centrally managed ones, especially in large, complex countries, they may also exacerbate disparities in quality, since richer communities can generally provide higher quality resources than poorer ones. In the above study on China (USAID, 1990), it was found that textbooks produced in nonmetropolitan areas were of poor quality, lasting sometimes less than a school year. Despite such weaknesses, local management of certain resources has often been found to be a support to the teacher working in relatively remote or disadvantaged schools. (Dove, 1982a, 1982b.)

Professional Development

A focus on professional development is based on the widely shared notions that if teachers have opportunities to grow, they teach better; if they teach better, their students perform better; if students perform better, teachers feel greater job satisfaction; and if teachers feel greater job satisfaction, they are more likely to stay on the job and in the profession. (Dove, 1982a; Mitchell, et al., 1987; Moore-Johnson, 1990; Rosenholtz, 1989;Murnane, et al., 1991.) Although the definition and scope of teacher development is continually changing (Holmes Group, 1986, 1995), the current review will focus on three facets, namely teacher education, teacher career development, and new teacher roles.

The Issues

TEACHER EDUCATION. In most countries, quantitative expansion of public educational has accelerated in recent decades (chapter 1), and with it the establishment of schools in previously unserved areas such as remote villages and urban squatter settlements. In many cases the establishment of schools has outstripped a country's ability to turn out qualified teachers: hence, many communities, particularly those in the periphery, have had to settle for un- or underqualified teachers. Even in countries where teacher supply is plentiful, such as present-day Indonesia, it is difficult to entice qualified teachers to take up assignments in peripheral areas. (Nielsen and Somerset, 1992.) Thus, teachers working in the periphery are often the least qualified to teach.

This situation is not simply a matter of supply and demand. In certain parts of the world, for example, former British colonies, preservice teacher education has not been a high priority, based on the now-vanishing notion that a good mastery of the subject matter was sufficient prerequisite for teaching. (Dharmadasa, 1988.) The legacy of that notion is that in many former British colonies (Sri Lanka, Belize, and many East African countries) the proportion of untrained teachers is still relatively high, especially among those working in peripheral areas. (Nielsen, 1992; see also chapter 7.)

Countries are addressing these issues by stepping up preservice teacher-education programs or providing on-the-job certification opportunities (see below, under Inservice Education), but access to them is still difficult for those most likely to accept and remain in positions in the periphery, namely, those whose origins are there. The reasons for this are simple: the few potential candidates who are out there rarely have access to information about programs, and even fewer can afford post-secondary education. Even if they had information and resources, they often do not meet the educational requirements—such as test scores—needed for admission into the teacher-education program.

But even for those who are able to enter and complete preservice teacher education, their initial professional development needs will rarely have been provided for, since most teacher education is oriented towards the mainstream schools. Very few preservice teacher-education programs pay any attention to the context of teaching in the periphery: the language of instruction required, cultural norms and values of the communities, the organizational context of the school (e.g., the frequent need to use multigrade teaching—see chapter 8), learning resources that are available, and the living and working conditions related to the assignment. (Dove, 1982a, 1986; Farres and Noriega, 1993; Fierro, 1991; McDiarmid, 1990; World Bank, 1991a; and Zeichner, 1993.) Moreover, given the urban location of most institutions of teacher education, few programs will have been able to provide students with student-teaching opportunities in the periphery. As a consequence, many new teachers, even the certified ones, arrive on the job unprepared for the kind of work they will be called upon to do. (Miller, 1989, 1991.)

Education for professional development implies not only *preservice* but also *inservice* educational opportunities. There are many varieties of inservice teacher education: some lead to initial or new levels of certification, others do not; some take years to complete, others only a few days or hours; some are imposed from the top, others spring from teacher initiatives. Teachers in the periphery are generally disadvantaged with respect to inservice education of any variety. As with preservice education, the problem is both *access* and *relevance.* Inservice programs for initial certification are largely inaccessible to those in the periphery unless they are offered through distance education (see discussion in the Policy Initiatives section that follows). Programs for more advanced certification are even less accessible, since they are more often campus-based. Even the noncertification short courses and workshops are less accessible to teachers in the periphery, due to travel and financial constraints. The key to such a situation might be locally developed, school-based training, but even this is difficult, since it requires a critical mass of motivated and knowledgeable teachers.

Even given access to inservice education, both long- and short-term, the professional-development needs of teachers in the periphery may go largely unmet if the content of such education is irrelevant to the problems these teachers face. (Dove, 1982a, 1986; Farres and Noriega, 1993; Fierro, 1991; Moore-Johnson, 1990; World Bank, 1991a.) If, for instance, the latest round of centrally developed inservice is in support of computer literacy, and the school in the periphery is still lacking textbooks, electricity or even a building, then access to inservice education is almost meaningless. Teachers in the periphery clearly need some mechanism for articulating and addressing their unique professional development concerns.

CAREER DEVELOPMENT. In both the industrialized and developing world, teachers generally face a relatively undifferentiated career structure. Consequently, there are very few career incentives, aside from leaving classroom teaching for administrative positions, for encouraging good teachers with high aspirations to stay in the profession. (Darling-Hammond, 1984; Dove, 1986; Holmes Group, 1986; World Bank, 1991a.) This is particularly the case in the periphery, where there may only be a handful of teachers, of whom one may also serve as head teacher. The problem in the periphery goes beyond the flatness of the career path, however; opportunities available elsewhere may not occur in the periphery simply because appropriate administrative machinery may not operate there. In this sense, problems of career advancement in the periphery are linked to those of salary increments discussed in the section on economic considerations. Teachers in the periphery are often passed over for both promotion and salary increments because of their remoteness from centers of record-keeping and decision making.

NEW TEACHER ROLES. Throughout the world, new definitions of teacher professionalism are inviting teachers to take more responsibility for defining what and how to teach. In assuming these new roles, teachers are entering spheres of activity traditionally reserved for school administrators and curriculum designers. (Cohen, McLaughlin, and Talbert, 1993; Elmore, 1990; Schiefelbein, 1992; Tatto and Velez, in press.) Teacher participation in school decision making, and in school and curriculum restructuring, however, is in itself a difficult proposition for teachers, even for those having ample preparation and support. (Buchmann, 1990; Lampert, 1991.) First, teachers need to be prepared to make decisions through teacher-education experiences that are contextually relevant. Second, the structure and management of the school need to be arranged to support professional development. Third, teachers need to have support from their peers, their students, their students' parents, and from the community. Fourth, an appropriate reward and incentive system accompanied by a reasonable salary structure is required (as mentioned above) to provide teachers with the economic stability needed to dedicate their time and energies to develop professionally and to arrive at decisions that will benefit their school. (Holmes Group, 1990; World Bank, 1991a.) Such exacting conditions are almost never fully met in the periphery.

Policy Initiatives
The creation of effective preservice programs for teachers who may be assigned to work in peripheral areas has been a challenging task throughout the world. Recent research studies indicate that certain preservice strategies can be useful and relevant as long as a number of conditions are met, among which are a current curriculum based on recent research on teaching and learning, opportunities to practice what one learns while in the teacher-education program, continuous mentoring, peer support and guidance, and—especially important for those teachers who will be working in the periphery—structured mentoring during the first year of teaching provided by a "mentor" teacher or a trained and supportive principal. (Wilcox, Schram, Lappan, and Lanier, 1991; see also NCRTL, 1991; Tatto, Nielsen, et al., 1991.) In less industrialized countries—especially those with a large rural population such as Sri Lanka, Thailand, or Indonesia—an essential ingredient of successful preservice programs is instruction of teachers in the development of productive relationships with neighboring schools, with parents, and with students who may be quite different from the trainees themselves in social class, gender and/or ethnic background. This aspect has been less stressed in industrialized countries such as the U.S., where until recently it was rare to find teacher-education programs that would address issues related to teacher-parent-student communication, or methods for teaching diverse, multi-age/multi-ability groupings. (Davies, 1989; Flaxman and Riehl, 1987.) Efforts to prepare novice teachers for classroom conditions in the periphery are still rare;

thus, it is encouraging to see countries like Belize and Mexico now offering a "module" on multigrade teaching to teacher-trainees who plan to return to a remote village setting. (Nielsen, 1992; Tatto and Velez, in press.)

Access to teacher education by potential teacher candidates originating in the periphery is still a problem everywhere, but some countries like Indonesia and Pakistan are taking affirmative steps to make it possible. The Indonesian Ministry of Education recently developed a program for identifying remote areas where teacher recruitment is especially difficult and providing scholarship support, dormitory space, and special tutoring for local secondary-school graduates who decide to pursue teacher education. (World Bank, 1992.) In Pakistan, local secondary-school graduates have been hired for teaching jobs in the mountainous regions of Northwest Frontier Province without prior teacher education and then provided field-based teacher education at the schools where they will be teaching (see also field-based inservice teacher education below). The novice teachers work in pairs under the supervision of the school's principal, considered a "master teacher," and develop teaching skills by observing and commenting on each other's lessons. (Chowdhri and Abbass, 1987; Farooq, 1988.)

Concerning inservice teacher education, numerous examples of site-based approaches have been documented. Examples from Mexico (Tatto and Velez, in press) and Colombia's *Escuela Nueva* Program (see Schiefelbein, 1992), have shown how staff-development activities focused on the problems of a particular context can facilitate the adoption of innovation practices and the development of strong learning communities in schools.

Systems which encourage local groups of teachers to implement and sometimes even design their own inservice education activities have been proliferating lately, opening new ways of making inservice education more relevant to teachers' needs. (Booker and Riedl, 1987; Paine and Ma, 1991; Tangyong, Wahyudi, Gardner, and Hawes, 1989; World Bank, 1992.) Increasingly, such initiatives are being recognized and supported as serious attempts to deal with issues that have gone unaddressed by traditional staff-development programs. In fact, research has demonstrated that some of the most important innovations in the education of peripheral populations, such as the Freinet, Freire, and Don Milanis methods, have been initiated in the periphery itself. (Canevero, 1984.)

Field-based teacher education often involves more than educating teachers; it often leads to school renewal or transformation. (Dove, 1982a; Chowdhri and Abbass, 1987; Schiefelbein, 1992.) It includes elements of teamwork in which teachers, principals, and teacher educators working as a team in the school become the center of the learning experience. Field-based teacher education has the advantage of bringing together the elements—teachers, principals, teacher educators, the school community, and parents—essential to the coherent formation of new approaches to schooling and adds contextual meaning to teachers' experiences. In addition to teamwork, community participation in teacher preparation and local recruitment serves a dual purpose, that of facilitating a sense of ownership in the process, and that of educating the community about its schools, the curriculum, and the characteristics of its school children. In addition, locally recruited teachers may develop a special role as mediators between the mainstream culture of the school and the local culture of the pupils. An example of such programs are the Compensatory Education Project in Malaysia which attempted to improve the educational opportunities for the children of the country's rubber estates. This scheme heavily involved parents and was distinguished by its "flexibility and responsiveness to the needs of parents as they educate themselves to educate their children." (Dove, 1982a: 24.)

An initiative based on a somewhat different premise, the Nigerian Primary Education Improvement Project, used mobile teacher educators to successfully train teachers, individually and in groups, in new curricular and instructional methods. This project is an example of a successful partnership between a university, a country's Ministry of Education, and an international agency. It is also an example of a centrally controlled initiative gradually transformed to suit local conditions. (Dove, 1982a: 21.) These experiences call attention to the need to rethink the traditional approaches that have been used to improve the quality of education through inservice programs in rural/remote areas, emphasizing a reliance on resources rarely utilized in a full and collaborative manner: partnerships between central and local groups— including personnel from schools and higher education institutions, development agencies, and the community, especially the families of children attending the school.

Another example of field-oriented teacher is the on-the-job-training received by teachers from the principal in Thailand. (Raudenbush, Suwanna, Kamali, and Taoklam, 1991.) This scheme has been implemented successfully because the principals have received specialized instruction to improve their skills in supervising classroom teaching. The above study found clear evidence of a link between the intensity of internal teacher supervision by the principal and student academic achievement.

Particularly suited for teachers in difficult-to-reach peripheral areas are the various distance education approaches which have been developed in various parts of the world. In a recent global review, Nielsen (1991) showed that by the mid-1980s distance teacher education (DE) programs had been established in more than 40 countries, nearly half of which are in Africa. Of the 15 inservice education projects for which evaluation data were available, nine were found to be relatively effective (in comparison to conventional programs) and seven were judged to be *cost-effective.* Another positive aspect of such programs is their outreach to the periphery—"the fact that DE has made training available to those who, because of isolation or lack of funds, would not otherwise have received any." (Nielsen, 1991: 133.) Moreover, such programs appear to have reduced the mobility and attrition rates of participating teachers. (Nielsen, 1991.)

Another case in point is the distance education programs for initial certification of teachers in Sri Lanka. (Tatto and Kularatna, 1993.) This program allows teachers to receive inservice education while they teach at their own schools, increasing the likelihood that they will apply what they learn. Although this program demands a great deal of discipline and time from teachers, it offers several advantages. For example, teachers can study at their own pace; also, because the program content was determined by a teacher needs assessment, teachers use it to discuss with peers and tutors the dilemmas they confront daily and get help in formulating solutions. Furthermore, the state does not need to supply substitute teachers or risk the possibility that some students would go without teachers for a time. Our evaluation of the program, like those of other DE programs, showed that distance-education strategies are useful and relevant to teachers as long as a number of conditions are met: an up-to-date current curriculum based on recent research on learning; carefully designed, high-quality self-study materials; opportunities to practice what one learns while enrolled in a teacher-education program; frequent mentoring and face-to-face meetings with program tutors; and peer support and guidance. (Biniakunu, 1982; Gana, 1984; Gardner, 1990; Hansen, 1987; Hawkridge, Nkinyangi, Kinyanjui and Orivel, 1982; Henderson, 1978; Ligons, 1990; Lookheed and Verspoor, 1991; Mahlck and Temu, 1989; Nielsen and Tatto, 1993.)

There have been relatively few instances of teacher professional development being encouraged by a more *differentiated career structure*. However, over the past decade in the United States, the Holmes Group (1986) has attempted to address this issue by advocating a three-step career ladder including *instructors* (novice teachers), *professional teachers*, and *career professionals*. Teachers would move up this ladder by earning higher level credentials *and* by demonstrating their professional competence. A number of revised teacher-compensation structures, based on demonstrated competence, group-based performance, and professional advancement, have been implemented in the U.S. in places such as Kentucky, South Carolina, Colorado, and Dallas. (Kelley and Odden, 1995.) Similar ideas are being tried out in other countries. (Dove, 1986.) For instance, in Kenya, able and experienced elementary-school teachers can now gain access to leadership positions through pursuing B.Ed and M.Ed degrees. Likewise, since the early 1980s, exceptional primary-school teachers in Bangladesh have been given access to administrative positions at the subdistrict (*upazilla*) level. Even more to the point, recent changes in civil service regulations in Indonesia make it possible for primary-school teachers to be promoted to the highest ranks of the teaching profession (comparable to that of a university professor), as long as they accumulate a required number of "credit points" through continuous education, professional activities (including the delivery of papers), and teaching service. In other words, teachers can develop professionally without having to give up their commitment to teaching. Working in the periphery can be a plus in that system, since teachers receive extra-credit points for doing so; but it can also be a minus, since record keeping and supervision are poor and access to courses and professional meetings is limited. It is hoped that this situation will change in the future as more functions of the civil service and Ministry of Education are shifted to the provincial and district levels. (IEES, 1990.)

Policy initiatives addressing professional development which take into consideration the *new roles of teachers* are numerous. Many of the school-based initiatives mentioned above have this quality, in the sense that they focus on preparing teachers for curriculum and decision-making roles, and frequently shift the responsibility for designing and managing staff-development activities to the teachers themselves. The professional-development activities within the *Escuela*

Nueva program in Colombia, briefly described above, provides a good example of this. (Schiefelbein, 1992.)

In sum, new policy initiatives addressing teacher professional development in the periphery have proceeded along a number of innovative tracks, including the use of field-based and distance-education systems for initial teacher certification; increased reliance on school-level inservice programs, planned either by the hierarchy or the teachers themselves, and run either by school principals or relatively autonomous groups of teachers; schemes to build partnerships between the school and its community on the one hand and the university community on the other; new career-development systems for encouraging teacher competence and professional growth; and systems empowering teachers to become involved in curriculum design and school-level decision making.

Social Considerations

Social considerations related to teaching in the periphery include factors such as the social status of teaching (in general and in the community in question); the teacher's ability to relate to the local culture; and the availability of social amenities, such as safe, affordable housing, health and educational facilities for self and family, and entertainment opportunities. Teacher recruitment, education, deployment and retention policies which do not take these factors into consideration can be expected to produce disappointing results.

The Issues

The teacher-policy literature pays relatively little attention to social considerations, an indicator of the low priority traditionally given to the difficult adjustments required of teachers in peripheral areas. For example, the literature on teacher-recruitment policy has emphasized the use of economic incentives for teaching in the periphery to the neglect of factors such as the teacher's need for social affiliation, security (being and feeling safe), housing, independence and privacy, and the need to understand and be accepted by the community. Only recently have social considerations been addressed in theory and research. (Dove, 1982b; Moore-Johnson, 1990; Warwick and Jatoi, 1991.)

It is widely recognized that declining image and social status of the teaching profession has discouraged many competent individuals from entering the profession. (Farres and Noriega, 1993; Kerr, 1983; Sykes, 1983.) Similarly, challenging social conditions faced by teachers in the periphery, such as cultural distance between the teacher and the community, and concerns about personal safety, lessen the pool of willing candidates. (Kozol, 1991; Farres and Noriega, 1993.) Furthermore, forced separation from husband or wife often becomes a problem in the periphery, either because one spouse maintains residence in town or because the teacher must leave for long periods of teacher education. (Tatto, et al., 1993; Warwick and Jatoi, 1991.)

Social adjustment difficulties are also a factor in teacher turnover in the periphery. A survey in China in the early 1990s covering 2,000 school teachers in a rural district showed that among those who wanted to leave their posts, 80 percent cited "marriage difficulties" (presumably either finding appropriate mates or convincing a spouse to accompany the teacher to the rural area). (People's

Education, 1990.) In Pakistan, the possibility of separation from a spouse living in town has been shown to be a serious deterrant to recruitment, deployment, and retention in the periphery (Warwick and Jatoi, 1991.) Dove (1982b) reports on a survey of teachers in Cameroon in which the highest proportion (about 20 percent) confessed to leaving their job in a remote or difficult school because of a need to live near relatives; the next-highest proportion cited health reasons. In this same study it was evident that many teachers not only had to adjust to the demands of living in a remote area without their families, but they also had to meet the disparate needs of community members or risk isolation or rejection. About 50 percent of the teachers surveyed said that community members frequently asked them to formulate and write letters, and close to 41 percent said that the community often asked for loans of cash or goods and other types of support. Other requests included having to host school-age children in the teacher's home, providing counseling, supplying medicines, assisting residents in finding jobs, and paying tuition fees.

Because communities in the periphery often lack basic social services, village schools (and this means teachers) are often called upon to fill the gap. Although it is possible to educate the community about the range of responsibilities that a school is expected to fulfill, constant rejection of community requests by teachers may only alienate the community and further isolate teachers.

In summary, general issues in this area are the declining prestige and social status of the teaching profession, the separation from family and community during training and/or assignment to peripheral regions; the lack of familiarity or compatibility with the sociocultural environment; and concerns about housing, personal safety, and the availability of social services.

Policy Initiatives

Recent policy initiatives seem to signal an increase in emphasis given to the social dimension of teaching in the periphery. Concerning social status, for example, certain rural communities in China are now creating special occasions for honoring and rewarding their teachers. (Paine, 1991; Paine and Ma, 1991.) In Indonesia, village teachers, who have obtained teacher certification through distance education, are reporting increases in social status and prestige. (Nielsen, 1991.) Another aspect of social status, namely social isolation, has received attention in Nepal, where an integrated program of support has been developed which aims to overcome teacher isolation through the use of supportive supervision systems, community involvement, and peer support systems. (World Bank, 1992.)

Little has been written about problems related to cultural distance between the teacher and the community. Preservice courses can presumably include briefings about cultural adjustment and ways to avoid culture shock and communication problems. Nevertheless, it seems the best way to assure good cultural adjustment is to create programs that recruit and train locals to be teachers, so that they can teach in their own communities. In Bangladesh, government policy is to recruit teachers at the subdistrict level and to post them as close to their homes as possible. (Dove, 1986.) Recent reforms in teacher education in Indonesia similarly include provisions for "selective recruitment" of youth from "remote areas" into teacher education, accompanied, when needed, by scholarships, dormitory accommodations, and special tutoring. (World Bank, 1992b.) Sri Lanka's Colleges of Education have related goals of bringing talented youth into the teaching profession and supporting them in their subsequent assignments in rural schools. (Tatto, et al., 1991.)

Attention to teachers' social amenities seems to have been confined almost entirely to the provision of teacher housing. For example, programs launched by the Malaysian government in the 1980s to expand educational provision in the country's peripheral areas included teacher housing as part of the school complex. (Dove, 1986.) Similarly, Indonesia's highly successful INPRES program for universalizing primary education contained provisions for teacher housing in remote areas. (IEES, 1990.) Other programs cover moving costs to the remote area schools and subsidized travel for home visits. (Lockheed and Verspoor, 1991; Tibi, 1990; Warwick and Jatoi, 1991.) To ease marital stress connected with remote-area postings in places like Pakistan, researchers have recommended deployment strategies that would keep husbands and wives together. (Warwick and Jatoi, 1991.) And in another vein, distance education is now being used for teacher "upgrading" in peripheral areas so that teachers do not have to leave home for extended periods of time in order to earn basic or advanced qualifications. (Tatto and Kularatna, 1993; Nielsen, 1991.)

In summary, the social needs of teachers have often been overlooked in the development of teacher policies for recruitment, education, deployment, and retention, but are gradually being addressed as governments begin to attend to the quality of teachers' lives in the periphery.

SUMMARY: THE INTERSECTION BETWEEN POLICY DOMAINS AND TEACHER NEEDS

The thesis of this paper has been that issues concerning the recruitment, education, deployment, and retention of teachers working in peripheral areas can only be effectively resolved when the recurrent needs and concerns of teachers are addressed in a comprehensive manner. Based on the growing awareness that teachers can and should exercise *choice* in matters related to their postings and conditions of employment, our attempt has been to reconcile the needs of the state with the needs of an empowered teaching force. Table 6.2 shows how the various kinds of teacher needs can be addressed in the development of policies in the four areas of recruitment, education, deployment, and retention. Many of the items in the table represent elements of policy which are already in place in various locations; others are still at the recommendation stage. More research and development is needed to further test the effectiveness of these policy ideas across a variety of contexts in peripheral areas around the world.

Table 6.2. Policies Addressing Teachers' Needs and Concerns in Relation to Working in Peripheral Areas

Teacher Needs /Policy Area	Economic Considerations	Organizational Support	Professional Development	Social Considerations
Teacher Recruitment	• Put basic teacher salaries in periphery at parity with urban areas • Provide salary differentials and/or hardship pay for teaching in difficult areas • Provide incentives to high-ability local youth to become teachers in their own communities	• Development of community-school councils for the local recruitment of teacher candidates	• Provide subsidized preservice teacher education for local teacher- education recruits (scholarships, special tutoring, etc.) • Develop programs for school-based education/certification of locally recruited teachers	• Develop programs to increase teachers' social status and recognition • Recruit local students who are already familiar with language and culture
Teacher Education	• Subsidize preservice teacher education for teacher recruits from peripheral areas • Subsidize teacher enrollment in courses for earning/upgrading credentials • Associate teacher education with credentials, pay raises, promotion, and job security • Subsidize costs of inservice teacher education	• Empower and train school principals as instructional leaders/ supervisors • Enroll teachers as a group in distance-education programs so they can support one another	• Make sure that the content of preservice teacher education covers problems of teaching in peripheral areas; relevant language instruction; lessons on school-community relations • Hold some student- teaching activities in peripheral schools or in conditions simulating those found in schools in the periphery	• Use distance/extension education programs so that teachers can upgrade credentials without too much disruption to family life

Table 6.2 Continued

Teacher Deployment	• Offer extra credit towards promotion for teaching in peripheral areas	• Use school-community councils for selection of teacher candidates; could also have monitoring, follow-up and orienting roles for new teachers • Create organizational mechanisms to assure that teachers recruited and trained for work in the periphery are indeed placed there	• Provide special preparation for teaching in the periphery prior to teachers taking up assignments (including training in multigrade teaching and working under difficult conditions)	• Develop means of overcoming the image of social isolation • Develop strategies to support deployment of husband/wife teams • Offer subsidized housing as part of teaching contract • Cover moving costs to remote locations
Teacher Retention	• Payment of overtime for extra work/preparation • Improved management of automatic promotion systems (eliminate paperwork bottlenecks) • Community contributions towards teacher welfare/earnings	• Organize school clusters and/or teacher working groups for peer support and group problem-solving • Empower teachers as co-developers of school curriculum and inservice education programs • Solicit community for teacher aids and guest instructors • Promote special recognition of teachers by community • Use decentralized systems of resource (e.g., textbooks) provision and distribution	• Provide access to teacher education/teacher upgrading courses (through distance or extension education) • Make inservice teacher education relevant to teacher needs in the periphery • Involve teachers/teacher groups in the planning and implementation of their own inservice education	• Maintain housing subsidies • Cover costs of occasional "home visits" for those not originating in school vicinity • Provide assistance for health care and education of family members

Teacher Recruitment

As highlighted in Table 6.2, policies for teacher recruitment for peripheral areas which take into consideration the needs and concerns of teachers will at least put basic teacher salaries and benefits at parity with those in the urban and mainstream rural areas. Beyond that they will provide salary differentials and/or hardship pay for work in the periphery, recognizing the many ways in which living and working there are more expensive and demanding. Anticipating teacher allocation and retention issues, the education system should also establish "selective recruitment" activities and incentives to attract high-ability local youth into the teaching field. Such recruitment might be done through some sort of school-community council, which would contribute to a sense of community commitment to and support of the teachers recruited.

Recruitment of local youth for teaching in the community would also be facilitated by the offer of subsidized teacher-education opportunities (scholarships, dormitory space, special tutoring, etc.). Where teacher-education centers are in metropolitan areas far removed by distance and culture from the peripheral area for which teachers are to be recruited, school-based teacher education and certification programs might be called for. Programs facilitating the recruitment of locals will minimize cultural estrangement that might be felt by recruits if they come from vastly different cultural areas. Whether recruits are local or not, they all still need the boost in social status that would come from programs of community recognition and support.

Teacher Education

Policies for teacher education related to teaching in the periphery will also be enhanced by considering teacher needs and concerns. As mentioned before, economic barriers to teacher education can be overcome by providing scholarships and other kinds of financial support to those who are most suited for teaching in schools in the periphery. In addition, given the fact that teachers there have little opportunity to supplement their incomes with outside work, it would be advisable to subsidize the teacher's participation in courses for earning or upgrading teaching credentials. At the central policy level, it is crucial that teachers' efforts to obtain initial or higher credentials are met with assurances of pay raises, promotion, and better job security. Local districts or the community would also do well to financially support short-term, targeted inservice teacher-education activities. In addition, school principals might be trained and empowered to conduct staff-development activities at the school level. For extended courses offered through distance or extension education, teachers would do well to enroll as groups or partners so they can support one another in their studies.

Concerning the content of teacher education, both pre- and inservice, the needs of teachers in the periphery will only be adequately served if the curriculum relates to the location's particular problems and situations: local curricular content; local languages; the frequent need for multigrade teaching; ways of involving the community; surviving with substandard material and equipment. The ideal would be if some practice-teaching could be done in schools in the periphery, or if not possible, at least under conditions simulating such schools. Inservice education activities should not only be relevant to teachers' professional-development needs but also organized in such a way that teachers do not have to leave their families for extended periods of time, prospects presented by distance-education, or school- (or school cluster-) based programs. Finally, teacher education must adapt to the changing roles of teachers, prompted by educational reform initiatives.

Teacher Deployment

Teacher deployment in this review is sometimes difficult to distinguish from teacher recruitment. As the terms are used in this chapter, recruitment involves attracting candidates to the profession while deployment basically concerns "placing" teachers in particular positions. However, this distinction is often blurred in that deployment can also be seen as recruitment at the local level. Policies and programs for teacher deployment are often complex and bureaucratic. I have further complicated the picture by adding the element of teacher *choice*. Deployment policies which address teacher needs and concerns are those in which teachers are inclined to *choose* teaching assignments in the periphery. The first policy element in our matrix which would serve this purpose is the offer of "extra credit" towards promotion for teaching in a school in the periphery. From the organizational support point of view, teachers may also be more motivated to take up such positions if they are selected by local school-community councils, which would continue in support roles after initial deployment. In addition, teachers could be expected to be more willing to take up positions in the periphery if their fears and misconceptions were alleviated by orientation sessions, conducted, preferably, by those having experience and a fondness for teaching in such settings. On the social front, teachers would also be reassured if there were some promise of social support from supervisors, fellow teachers, and the community. In addition, potential recruits who are married would certainly find the assignment more attractive if work opportunities could also be found for their spouse (perhaps in a co-teacher role). Finally, teachers would be more inclined to accept a deployment possibility in the periphery if housing were made available and if the government agreed to cover moving and transportation costs.

Teacher Retention

Teacher retention is the key to building effective educational programs in the periphery and the realm in which teacher needs and concerns are perhaps the most crucial. As illustrated in Table 6.2, addressing the teacher's economic needs and concerns leads to policies which grant overtime pay or similar rewards for the frequent extra work involved (e.g., from managing large numbers of students, or multiple grades, or service beyond the regular call of duty). In addition, teachers in the periphery need to be covered by conventional automatic promotion systems and not overlooked due to paperwork breakdowns. Additionally, community contributions to their livelihood and welfare would also be a plus, since most are unable to earn the kind of additional income that their counterparts in urban areas can.

Professional-support concerns are particularly relevant to teacher retention; since, like other professionals, teachers are motivated by a sense of accomplishment and satisfaction. Collegiality or peer support is widely regarded as crucial to school-improvement efforts; in the periphery this has been developed through the organization of school clusters and/or teacher working groups. Such groups can function in support of group problem-solving and school innovation, and as a means of empowering teachers as co-developers of school curriculum and inservice education programs. Community support can also encourage teachers to remain on the job in the periphery, particularly where the community helps bear the burden by providing tutors, guest instructors, programs of teacher recognition, and even a viable school building. Of course, teaching can still be unrewarding if essential teaching materials (e.g., textbooks and study guides) are missing; resourceful teachers working together can fill in some of the gaps, but local systems of resource provision and distribution have been found to be effective in overcoming the bottlenecks and failures of centralized distribution systems.

From the professional development point of view, teachers can be encouraged to remain in difficult positions if they receive at least some access to upgrading opportunities available to teachers in the mainstream. Given their remoteness from institutions of teacher education, this generally can only be accomplished through distance or extension education. Furthermore, to have the desired effect on teacher morale and perseverance, the content of inservice-education programs should be aligned with the conditions and needs of teachers in the periphery; nondegree programs should be largely designed and implemented by the teachers themselves. In relation to the teachers' social needs, it appears that most teachers need assurances of continued housing support; for those not originating in vicinity of the school, travel subsidies to cover the costs of a "home visit" are desirable. Finally, it is crucial that teachers be assured of assistance with respect to the health care and educational requirements of their dependents.

CONTEXTUAL FACTORS INFLUENCING POLICY DECISIONS

So far I have reviewed in a general way how teachers' needs and concerns can be brought to bear on policies of recruitment, deployment, education, and retention for teachers in the periphery. The discussion has been confined to decision making within the context of the school systems in various countries. A fuller picture would view school systems themselves within wider contexts, the most important of which being the national (or even global) political-economic environment. The final section of this chapter briefly discusses the policy significance of the following contextual factors from the political-economic realm: (a) centralized versus decentralized governance structures; (b) basic changes in the purposes of schooling; (c) changes in national economies and economic priorities; and (d) the position of privilege for the dominant culture.

Centralized Versus Decentralized Governance Structures

Early discussions of this dichotomy seemed to favor decentralized structures as a means of bringing teachers' needs and concerns to bear on teacher policy. More recent formulations now point out that centrally initiated measures can lead to substantial benefits in the periphery as long as there is involvement of the field staff (principals and teachers) in the formation and implementation of the measures at the local (school) level. (Korten, 1980). Schwille and Wheeler (1992) discuss the variable role of the state in policy formulation and implementation. They caution against thinking about centralization and decentralization as an "either/or proposition" and further state that "too much emphasis on one or the other may miss both the realities of how a system works and of constructive options for improving the ability of the State to influence the direction of educational change." (Schwille and Wheeler, 1992: 225.)

A number of less industrialized countries—and often as a result of colonization—have developed complex but efficient lines of command constituting tightly structured hierarchies. These arrangements have allowed policy mandates to reach the lower levels of command, assuring full national coverage. While in the past, central control may have stifled creativity and allowed for little diversification of teacher policy vis-à-vis perceived needs of teachers and the population they teach (Dove, 1986), recently the same structure has also been used to stimulate change at the local levels through central mandates to implement innovative teacher policy aimed at restructuring and improving the quality of schools. In Mexico's PARE project (Tatto and Velez, in press) and Colombia's *Escuela Nueva* (Schiefelbein, 1992), innovations succeeded through the combination of central mandates and local implementation initiatives, supported by such development agencies as the World Bank, UNESCO, USAID, and Interamerican Development Bank (IDB).

These and similar findings in other locations have encouraged policymakers to look for teacher input at the national/district/province and school levels, increasing the likelihood of teachers' participation in their own process of change. (Booker and Riedl, 1987; Haas, 1990; Hansen, 1987; Kyle, 1990; Orvik, 1970; Randell, 1979; Shaeffer, 1990; Sturman, 1982; UNESCO, 1989; Vera, 1990.) The literature on teacher change, however, suggests that without a specific philosophy guiding educational reform with the concurrent development of shared norms and understandings where all the parties enter into dialogue about change, neither the level nor the degree of participation in policy implementation guarantee success. (Feiman-Nemser and Parker, 1993; McCarthey, 1992; Mosenthal and Ball, 1992; NCRTL, 1991; Schiefelbein, 1992; Tatto, in press; and Tatto and Velez, in press.)

Basic Changes in the Purposes of Schooling
Changes in teacher policy are associated with transformations in traditional notions of curriculum and instruction, themselves rooted in basic changes in the purposes of education. Whereas curriculum and instruction in the traditional school served to "transmit" knowledge and skills, more recent models have viewed the purpose of schooling as the development of conceptual understanding in students through a curriculum that is "socially constructed" by teachers and students. (Cohen, et al., 1993; Prawat, 1992; Schiefelbein, 1992; and Tatto and Velez, in press.)

Transmission models have dominated schooling in the peripheral areas of both more and less industrialized countries, supporting the view of schooling as a means to socialize masses into particular ways of thinking. (Puri, 1992.) More conceptually oriented models based on constructivism view schooling as a means for individual liberation and political and social development. Models based on this view have been successfully implemented in peripheral areas of Colombia and Mexico (as shown by

Schiefelbein, 1992; and Tatto and Velez, in press), as well as in peripheral areas of the United States. (Calkins, 1986a, 1986b; Mosenthal and Ball, 1992.) They suggest a new agenda for the future in other locations.

Changes in National Economies and Economic Priorities
Delegates to the World Conference on Education for All from relatively poor countries spoke of stagnant or declining growth in their national economies and more specifically of financial crises in the education sector, even to the extent that current expenditure levels cannot keep pace with those of the past (UNDP, UNESCO, UNICEF, and World Bank, 1990b). The conference *Background Document* also revealed absolute declines in budgets for education in many countries. (UNDP, UNESCO, UNICEF, and World Bank, 1990a.) Such conditions were symptomatic of the worldwide economic recession of that period, but also reflected financial conditions beyond individual countries' control, such as the mounting budget deficit in the United States, and conditions of financial austerity and cost cutting dictated by international lenders such as the International Monetary Fund (IMF) and/or the World Bank. (Carnoy, 1992; Reimers, 1991). Cuts in resources allocated to education in general have often meant devastating reductions in funds for addressing a whole range of teachers' concerns. (Carnoy, 1992). For example, the reduction of funds available for monetary incentives for teaching in the periphery can hamper recruitment and deployment efforts. (McGinn and Borden, 1995). Depressed teacher salaries also increase the opportunity costs of teaching, which can undercut teacher retention . If the national economy is depressed to the extent that high under- or unemployment rates prevail, opportunity costs may not be a factor in teachers' leaving the profession, but they do contribute to the creation of an underpaid and relatively captive teaching force. (Carnoy, 1992; Miller, 1992). If teachers' salaries do not keep up with inflation, as in certain Latin American and Caribbean countries, teachers may end up effectively "financing" education. (Carnoy, 1992; Miller, 1992; Reimers, 1991.) Finally, because of budget constraints, teacher preparation and other professional support measures may suffer. (Reimers, 1991.)

One of the responses to the Education for All Conference has been a temporary spike in the amount of funding allocated by governments and development agencies to basic education for peripheral groups. Although many such educational "packages" have included important provisions for teachers, the low expenditure level allocated to teacher concerns relative to the high costs associated with mass education, the low level of funding for innovations in curriculum and instructional systems (e.g., multigrade teaching), and the weak political momentum typically associated with teacher welfare all combine to bring about teacher policies which are often ad hoc, hurriedly developed, and easily terminated in the same manner.

But some exceptions should be noted. The World Bank and the Mexican government have, for instance, put together a package that combines teacher development with a career ladder, incentives, and increased salaries including plans for long-term teacher education based on a constructivist philosophy and curriculum. Although it is still too early to talk about long-lasting results, the package has reached a large number of teachers in Mexico and has increased motivation to work on professional-development activities and the restructuring of school governance. (Tatto and Velez, in press.) The *Escuela Nueva* program in Colombia, created through collaboration between the Colombian government and UNESCO, USAID, IDB, the World Bank, plus local businesses, has achieved a remarkable degree of success in improving the conditions and quality of teaching, and for the first time in Colombian educational history, teachers have been compensated for their efforts in restructuring education. (Schiefelbein, 1992.) Thus, even in times of tight money, good programs can find local and international agency support for shaping supportive teacher policies.

Position of Privilege for the Dominant Culture

In most countries where peripheral groups are scattered across rural and urban areas, dominant cultural privileges continue to prevail over equity concerns. With a few recent exceptions (Ginsburg and Lindsay, 1995; Reimers, 1991), the influence of the values of the dominant culture on teacher policy has rarely been discussed. Policies for the improvement of teaching continue to be mostly identified with mainstream institutions/schools serving those of the dominant culture. (Reimers, 1991.)

For example, high-quality teachers and high-quality teaching do exist in both poor and richer countries, but these seem to be located, for the most part, in the countries' affluent communities. Anyon's study (1981) in the U.S. documents that transmission models of teaching occur in working-class schools and, as one moves up the social class continuum, teaching becomes more conceptually oriented. Similarly, the least experienced teachers are the ones who often teach in dysfunctional schools in the inner cities in the U.S. (Kozol, 1991), or are sent to the most remote and poorest areas of a country (McGinn and Borden, 1995); as seniority is gained, teachers move out of peripheral schools. That the best-educated teachers serve the better-off students is not a situation that occurs by chance; it is congruent with the values and priorities of the dominant culture within a given society.

Despite this phenomenon, research on teaching in challenging environments reveals that teachers can make a difference if they are given authority over their teaching, support from their colleagues and supervisors, adequate resources and supplies, and appropriate preparation to deal with the challenges present in these locations. (Calkins, 1986a; 1986b; Dove, 1982a, 1982b; Schiefelbein, 1992; Tatto, et al., 1993.) The problem is that such isolated efforts are rarely developed into sustained programmatic responses. The fact that the education of disadvantaged students by disadvantaged teachers in peripheral situations—leading to serious problems of school drop-out and repetition—continues alongside exciting, world-class educational programs in metropolitan centers, betrays a lack of interest and commitment among the dominant culture policymakers to promote and support equitable educational change. Clearly, teacher policy cannot address the needs and concerns of teachers in the periphery until there are some serious challenges to the self-serving controls imposed by dominant political-cultural groups.

In summary, in regard to teacher-policy design and influence, trends in the literature suggest that: (a) the process of teachers' participation in their own change is more important than the level of the authority structure from which mandates for change originate; (b) true and lasting changes in teacher policy seem to be a subproduct of changes in the purposes of schooling (such as the current change observed from transmission to conceptual teaching-learning models); (c) economic conditions and declining expenditures in education deeply affect the capacity of policy-making to address teacher needs and concerns; and (d) teacher policy per se cannot bring about equality in schooling unless it manages to challenge the dominance of the cultural mainstream.

CONCLUSION

This paper has presented a framework for conceptualizing the ways in which teachers' needs and concerns—economic, organizational, professional, and social—can be brought to bear on the formation and implementation of teacher policies for peripheral-area schools. Such a framework can generate fresh, comprehensive solutions to persistent problems related to teacher recruitment, education, deployment, and retention. Most importantly, it takes into consideration the growing recognition that teachers are not passive instruments of the state but agents who exercise choice on a wide range of issues related to the conditions of their employment.

Constructivist theory is gradually affecting the ways educational reformers look at teachers and the roles teachers play in the change process. Ideas about teachers as technicians are being displaced by constructivist concepts which accord teachers new decision-making roles with respect to educational goals, school renewal, and their own professional development.

Teacher-responsive policies are those that invite individuals to participate in the change process, regardless of whether it is initiated in a centralized or decentralized fashion. Teacher policies which enhance the teacher's willingness to enter and stay with difficult jobs in the periphery are more likely than others to be school-based and include the input and participation of teachers, administrators, and the school's community. Policies implemented/or adapted by the school community with the intention of responding to teachers' concerns (and those of their students) in context are seen as more effective in the long run than those ignoring contextual factors. Moreover, policies that are designed to provide teachers with fair remuneration for their work and that attempt to address the social situation of teachers are seen as having a positive impact on teacher recruitment and retention, regardless of where they originate in the educational structure of authority.

This review has also shown that teacher-responsive polices do not need to be complex or expensive. Effective inservice education for upgrading the credentials of existing teachers can be provided quite inexpensively through means such as Sri Lanka's distance-education program. Furthermore, organizational support at the workplace can be improved through relatively inexpensive measures such as increased community involvement, the creation of school clusters, and the organization of in-school teacher support groups having curricular-oriented work objectives.

Educational systems, either centralized or decentralized, need to effectively involve teachers in the formulation and implementation of policies, and need to develop information systems that will help provide feedback on the effects that specific policies have in a diversity of situations for a diversity of purposes. It is evident from the literature that there are few studies of the implementation of teacher-responsive policies in peripheral areas. National and local-level indicators are needed related to the number and aspirations of secondary-school graduates (potential teacher recruits) in peripherals areas, teacher recruitment and deployment success rates, the qualifications and background of current teachers, the rate of teacher turnover, local cost-of-living indices, student-teacher ratios, learning materials and facilities available in schools, the kind of community support provided, and the nature and duration of teacher education opportunities available. Such information would be helpful in the development of future policies.

Similarly, there has been little evaluation research into the success of policies for improving quality of education through teachers in peripheral areas. Particularly lacking is information regarding the costs associated with various innovations relative to their success. This lack of information makes it difficult to develop cost-effective strategies. Some research sponsored by development agencies such as USAID and the World Bank, such as Basic Research and Implementation in Developing Education Systems Project (BRIDGES), Improving the Efficiency of Educational Systems Project (IEES), Lockheed and Verspoor (1991), and Fuller and Snyder (1991) have begun to fill the gap. The evidence from recent studies carried out by the BRIDGES projects in Sri Lanka and in Thailand, for instance, reveals that carefully designed and consistently implemented teacher strategies such as inservice education (school-based and "distance"), the use of school clusters, and the principal's efforts in instructional management exert important impacts on teacher performance and morale in rural areas. (Cummings, Gunawardena, and Williams, 1992; Tatto, et al., 1993; Raudenbush and Bhumirat, 1991; Raudenbush, Bhumirat, and Kamali, 1991; and Raudenbush, Suwanna, Kamali, and Taoklam, 1991.) Still scarce are good comparative studies on the effect of different teacher-supportive policies on teaching and teacher morale/retention in a variety of settings in the periphery.

The need to better understand the challenges involved in teachers' work in peripheral areas calls for both in-depth studies of an ethnographic nature, as well as large-scale studies with quantifiable indicators of program implementation and teacher outcomes across a wide range of social and economic contexts. To be fruitful, such research will need to be conducted in relation to other aspects of education in the periphery, including school-community relations, the language of instruction, curriculum development and/or redesign, school and classroom management, and new approaches to school and system management.

I thankfully acknowledge the support of William Cummings, David Cohen, and Dean Nielsen in the development of this chapter.

Bibliography

Anyon, J. "Social Class and School Knowledge." *Curriculum Inquiry* 11 (1981): 3-42.

Avalos, B. and W. Haddad. *A Review of Teacher Effectiveness Research in Africa, India, Latin America, Middle East, Malaysia, Philippines and Thailand: Synthesis of Results*. Ottawa, Canada: International Development Research Centre, 1981.

Baker, V. *The Blackboard in the Jungle: Formal Education in Disadvantaged Rural Areas. A Sri Lankan Case*. Netherlands: Iberian, 1988.

Beeby, C.E. *The Quality of Education in Developing Countries*. Cambridge, MA: Harvard University Press, 1966.

Biniakunu, D.D. "Inservice Teacher Training Improves Eighth Graders Reading Ability in Zaire." *Journal of Reading* 25 (7) (1982): 662-665.

Booker, J. M. and R.E. Riedl. "Evaluating the Performance of a Rural Field-Based Teacher Training Program." *Research in Rural Education* 4 (2) (1987): 47-52.

Bruno, J. E., and E. Negrete. "Analysis of Teacher Wage Incentive Programs for Promoting Staff Stability in a Large Urban School District." *The Urban Review*, 15 (3) (1983): 139-149.

Buchmann, M. "Role over Person: Morality and Authenticity in Teaching." *Teachers College Record*, 87 (1986): 529-543.

———. "Beyond the Lonely, Choosing Will: Professional Development in Teacher Thinking." *Teachers College Record*, 91 (1990): 481-508.

Caldwell, J.C. "Routes to Low Mortality in Poor Countries." *Population and Development Review*, 12 (2) (1986): 171-220.

Calkins, L. *The Art of Teaching Writing*. Portsmouth, NH: Heinemann, 1986a.

———. *The Writing Project*. New York: New York City Board of Education, 1986b.

Canevero, A. "Lessons from the Periphery." *Prospects: Quarterly Review of Education*, 14 (3) (1984): 315-30.

Carnoy, M. "Educational Change and Structural Adjustment: A Case Study of Costa Rica." ERIC # ED368046 (Working document), 1992.

Chowdhri, S. and S. Abbass. *Evaluation of Field-Based Teachers' Training Programme in the Northern Areas of Pakistan*. Islambad: National Institute of Psychology, 1987.

Cochran, K.F., J.A. DeRuiter, and R.A. King. "Pedagogical Content Knowing: An Integrative Model for Teacher Preparation." *Journal of Teacher Education*, 44 (1993): 263- 272.

Cohen, D. "Knowledge of Teaching: Plus que ça Change," in P. Jackson ed., *Contributing to Educational Change*. Berkeley, CA: McCutchan, 1988.

Cohen, D., M. McLaughlin, and J. Talbert, eds. *Teaching for understanding: Challenges for policy and practice*. San Francisco, CA: Jossey-Bass, 1993.

Cohen, D. and J. Spillane. "Policy and Practice: The Relations between Governance and Instruction," in G. Grant ed., *Review of Research in Education*. Washington, DC: American Education Research Association, 1992.

Colbert, V. and J. Arboleda. *Universalization of Primary Education in Colombia: The New School Programme*, 19. Paris: UNESCO-UNICEF Cooperative Programme, July 1990.

Comer, J. "Parent Participation in the Schools." *Phi Delta Kappan*, 67, (1986): 442-444.

————. *School Power*. New York: The Free Press, 1981.

Cummings, W.K. and A. Riddell. "Alternative Policies for the Finance, Control, and Delivery of Basic Education." (Unpublished manuscript.) Cambridge, MA: Harvard Institute for International Development, 1992.

Cummings, W.K., G.B. Gunawardena, and J.H. Williams. "Management Reforms and the Improvement of Education." BRIDGES Research Report Series 11. Cambridge, MA: Harvard Institute for International Development, 1992.

Cummings, W.K., M.R. Suparman, and I.M. Thoyib. "The Indonesian School Principal: Broadening Responsibility." Paper prepared for the IEES-EPP Workshop. Yogyakarta, Indonesia, June 28-July 2, 1992.

Darling-Hammond, L. *Beyond the Commission Reports: The Coming Crisis in Teaching*. Santa Monica, CA: Rand, 1984.

Davies, D. "Poor Parents, Teachers, and the Schools. Comments about Practice, Policy and Research." Paper presented at the American Educational Research Association Annual Meeting. San Francisco, CA: March 27-31, 1989.

Departamento de Investigaciones Educativas del Centro de Investigación y de Estudios Avanzados (D.I.E.). *Educación Básica: La Reforma como un Proceso Integral.* (Documents DIE, 18). México, D.F.: Instituto Politécnico Nacional, 1990.

Dharmadasa, K.H. *Review of Literature on Teacher Education in Sri Lanka.* Research Division, National Institute of Education, Government of Sri Lanka, 1988.

Dove, L. "The Deployment and Training of Teachers for Remote Rural Schools in Less-Developed Countries." *International Review of Education.* Hamburg: UNESCO Institute for Education, 1982a.

———. *Lifelong Teacher Education and the Community School.* UIE Monographs No. 10. Hamburg: UNESCO Institute for Education, 1982b.

———. *Teacher and Teacher Education in Developing Countries. Issues in Planning, Management and Training.* Wolfeboro, NH: Croom Helm, 1986.

Elmore, R., ed. *Restructuring Schools: The Next Generation of Educational Reform.* San Francisco, CA: Jossey-Bass, 1990.

———. "Structural Reform and Educational Practice." *Educational Researcher*, 24 (9) (1995): 23-26.

Epstein, J.L. and S.L. Dauber. "School Programs and Teacher Practices of Parent Involvement in Inner-City Elementary and Middle Schools." *The Elementary School Journal* (91) 1991: 289-305.

Farooq, R.A. *Training of Primary School Teachers in Pakistan—Different Models. A Background Paper for BRIDGES Project's Study on Classroom Practice.* Islamabad, Academy of Educational Planning and Management, Ministry of Education, 1988.

Farres, P. and C. Noriega. "Estudio Exploratorio Sobre el Magisterio." (Mimeo.) México, D.F.: Centro de Estudios Educativos, April 1993.

Feiman-Nemser, S. and M. Parker. "Mentoring in Context: A Comparison of Two U.S. Programs for Beginning Teachers. *International Journal of Educational Research*, 19 (8) (1993): 699-718.

Fierro, C. *Ser Maestro Rural. ¿Una Labor Imposible?* México: Secretaría de Educación Pública, Libros del Rincón, 1991.

Flaxman, E. and C. Riehl. "Issues in Improving Urban Schools: Dropout Prevention, Hispanic Secondary Education, and Urban Teaching Careers." ERIC Clearinghouse on Urban Education. New York: Institute for Urban and Minority Education, Teachers College, Columbia University, 1987.

Fuller, B. "Raising School Quality in Developing Countries. What Investments Boost Learning?" (Staff working paper.) Washington, DC: The World Bank, 1986.

————. *Growing Up Modern: The Western State Builds Third World Schools.* New York: Routledge, 1991.

Fuller, B. and C.W. Snyder. "Vocal Teachers, Silent Pupils? Life in Botswana Classrooms." *Comparative Education Review* 35 (2) (1991): 274-294.

Fuller, B. and S. Heyneman. "Third World School Quality. Current Collapse, Future Potential." *Educational Researcher* 18 (2) (1989): 12-19.

Gana, F.Z. "Distance Education: A Nigerian Perspective. Educational Technology to Enhance Learning at a Distance." Paper presented at the Conference of the International Congress of Educational Media. Banff, Canada, 1984.

Gardner, R. "The Cianjur Project" in V. Rust and P. Dalin, eds., *Teachers and Teaching in the Developing World.* New York: Garland, 1990.

Ginsburg, M.B. and B. Lindsay, eds. *The Political Dimensions of Teacher Education: Comparative Perspectives on Policy Formation, Teacher Socialization and Society.* Bristol, PA: The Falmer Press, 1995.

Haas, T. "The Knowledge Bases for Improving Rural Education: Their Needs are Unique," in *The Knowledge Base for Improving Policy and Practice: The Regional Laboratories Experience.* Aurora, CO: Mid-Continent Regional Education Laboratory, 1990.

Hansen, K. *Distance Education and the Small School: Policy Issues.* Portland, OR: Northwest Regional Educational Laboratory Program Report, 1987.

Hawes, H.W.R. *Professional Support for Teachers in Schools: An Indonesian Case Study.* EDC Occasional Papers, No. 3. London: University of London, Institute of Education, 1982.

Hawkridge, D., P. Kinyanjui, J. Nkinyangi, and F. Orivel. In- Service Teacher Education in Kenya, in H. Perraton, ed., *Alternative Routes to Formal Education: Distance Teaching for School Equivalency.* Baltimore: The John Hopkins University Press, 1982.

Hawley, W.D. "Toward a Comprehensive Strategy for Addressing the Teacher Shortage." *Phi Delta Kappan* (June, 1986): 712-718.

Henderson, E. S. *The Evaluation of Inservice Teacher Training.* London: Croom Helm, 1978.

Holmes Group. *Tomorrow's Schools: Principles for the Design of Professional Development Schools*. East Lansing, MI: Holmes Group, 1990.

―――. *Tomorrow's Schools of Education*. East Lansing, MI: Holmes Group, 1995.

―――. *Tomorrow's Teachers: A Report of the Holmes Group*. East Lansing, MI: Holmes Group, 1986.

Hurst, P. and V. Rust. "Working Conditions of Teachers," in V. Rust and P. Dalin, eds., *Teachers and Teaching in the Developing World*. New York: Garland, 1990.

International Development Research Centre. *Teacher Effectiveness: Research in West Africa*. International Development Research Centre Manuscript Reports. Ottawa, Canada, 1981.

Improving the Efficiency of Educational Systems (IEES). *INDONESIA: Education and Human Resources Sector Review*. Jakarta: Ministry of Education and Culture, and Washington, DC: United States Agency for International Development, 1986.

―――. *A Review of Teacher Education Issues in Indonesia*. Tallahassee, FL: College of Education, Florida State University, 1990.

Kelley, C. and A. Odden. "Reinventing Teacher Compensation Systems." Consortium for Policy Research in Education, University of Wisconsin-Madison, September, 1995.

Kelly, G.P. "Educational Alternatives." *Educational Policy* 4, (1990): 69-160.

Kerr, D.H. "Teaching Competence and Teacher Education in the United States," in L. Shulman, L. and G. Sykes, eds., *Handbook of Teaching and Policy*. NY: Longman, 1983.

Korten, D. C. "Community Organization and Rural Development: A Learning Process Approach." *Public Administration Review* 40 (1) 1980: 480-511.

Kozol, J. *Savage Inequalities*. NY: HarperCollins, 1991.

Kyle, N. (1990). "Policy, Politics, Parsimony and Pragmatism: The State and the Rural School in Colonial South Wales." *History of Education*, 19 (1) (1990): 41-54.

Lampert, M. "Looking at Restructuring from within a Restructured Role." *Phi Delta Kappan* 72 (1991): 670-674.

Laureau, A. "Social Class Differences in Family-School Relationships: The Importance of Cultural Capital." *Sociology of Education* 60 (1987): 73-85.

Ligons, C. M. "Inservice Education in Thailand, Key Innovations Since 1980." *BRIDGES Education Development Discussion Paper No. 4*. Cambridge, MA: Harvard Institute for International Development, 1990.

Lockheed, M.E. and A.M. Verspoor. *Improving Primary Education in Developing Countries*. New York: Oxford University Press, 1991.

Lortie, D. *School Teacher: A Sociological Study*. Chicago: University of Chicago Press, 1975.

Mählck, L. and E.B. Temu. *Distance versus College Trained Primary School Teachers: A Case Study from Tanzania*. Paris: International Institute for Educational Planning, 1989.

McCarthey, S.J. "Teachers' Changing Conceptions of Writing Instruction." (Research Report 92-3.) East Lansing, Michigan State University, National Center for Research on Teacher Learning, 1992.

McDiarmid, W. *What to do about Differences? A Study of Multicultural Education for Teacher Trainees in the Los Angeles Unified School District*. (Research Report 90-11.) East Lansing: Michigan State University, National Center for Research on Teacher Learning, 1990.

McGinn, N. and A. Borden. *Framing Questions, Constructing Answers. Linking Research with Education Policy in Developing Countries*. Cambridge, MA: Harvard Institute for International Development, 1995.

McLaughlin, M.W., S. Pfeiffer, D. Swanson-Owens, and S. Yee. "State policy and teaching excellence." (Project report No. 85-A5.) *Institute for Research on Educational Finance and Governance*. Palo Alto, CA: School of Education, Stanford University, 1985.

Miller, B.A. *Distress and Survival: Rural Schools, Education, and the Importance of Community*. Portland, OR: Northwest Regional Laboratory, 1991.

———. *The Multigrade Classroom: A Resource Handbook for Small, Rural Schools*. Portland, OR: Northwest Regional Laboratory, 1989.

Miller, E. "IMF-Related Devastation of Teacher Education in Jamaica." *Social and Economic Studies*, 41 (1992): 153-181.

Mitchell, D., F. Ortiz, and T. Mitchell. *Work Orientation and Job Performance. The Cultural Basis of Teaching Rewards and Incentives*. NY: State University of New York Press, 1987.

Moore-Johnson, S. *Teachers at Work. Achieving Success in Our Schools*. New York: Basic Books, 1990.

Mosenthal, J., and D.L. Ball. "Constructing New Forms of Subject Matter Instruction: Subject Matter Knowledge in Inservice Teacher Education." *Journal of Teacher Education* 43 (1992): 361-371.

Murnane, R. and D. Cohen. "Merit Pay and the Evaluation of the Problem: Why Some Merit Plans Fail and Few Survive." *Harvard Educational Review* 56 (1) (1986): 1-17.

Murnane, R., J. Singer, J. Willet, J. Kemple, and O. Randall. *Who Will Teach? Policies that Matter*. Cambridge, MA: Harvard University, 1991.

National Center for Research on Teacher Learning (NCRTL). *Findings from the Teacher Education and Learning to Teach Study: Final Report of the National Center for Research on Teacher Education* (Special Report 91-6.) East Lansing, Michigan State University, National Center for Research on Teacher Learning, 1991.

Nielsen, H.D. "Using Distance Education to Extend and Improve Teaching in Developing Countries," in *Perspectives on Education for All*. Ottawa, Canada: International Development Research Centre, 1991.

———. "Multigrade Teaching in Belize: Research Data Analysis Workshop." Arlington, VA: Institute for International Research, 1992.

Nielsen, H.D. and P.C.P. Chan. "Development Agency Support for the Improvement of Teaching in Asia," in V.D. Rust and P. Dalin, eds., *Teachers and Teaching in the Developing World*. New York: Garland, 1990.

Nielsen, H.D., and H.C.A. Somerset. *Primary Teachers in Indonesia: Supply, Distribution, and Professional Development*. Jakarta: Ministry of Education and Culture and Washingtion, DC: The World Bank, 1992.

Nielsen, H. D. and M.T. Tatto. "Teacher Upgrading in Sri Lanka and Indonesia," in H. Perraton, ed., *Distance Education for Teacher Training*, New York: Routledge, 1993.

Orvik, J. M. *Teacher Survival in an Extreme Environment*. Alaska Rural School Project, University of Alaska. ERIC Clearinghouse Document ED048972, 1970.

Paine, L. "Chinese Reform of Teaching and Teacher Education." Paper presented at The International Symposium: Educational Reforms and Teacher Education. Lisbon, September 26, 1991.

Paine, L. and L. Ma. "Teachers Working Together: A Dialogue on Organizational and Cultural Perspectives of Chinese Teachers." Paper presented at the Annual Meeting of the American Educational Research Association. Chicago, IL: April 5, 1991.

People's Education. Volume 12, 1990.

Piaget, J. *Play, Dreams, and Imitation*. New York: Norton, 1962.

―――. *Six Psychological Studies*. New York: Vintage Books, 1968.

Prawat, R.S. "Teachers' Beliefs about Teaching and Learning: A Constructivist Perspective." *American Journal of Education* 100 (1992): 354-395.

Puri, P. "Cultural and Intercultural Aspects of Education: A New Responsibility for Teachers. Contribution of Education to Cultural Development." Paper presented at the United Nations Educational, Scientific and Cultural Organization International Conference on Education. Geneva, Switzerland, September, 1992.

Randell, S. K. "Accountability for the Education of Disadvantaged Groups Through the Disadvantaged Schools Program." Paper presented to the Sixth National Conference, Australian Council of Educational Administration. Perth, Australia, 1979.

Random House Dictionary of the English Language. New York: Random House, 1987.

Raudenbush, S. and C. Bhumirat. "The Distribution of Resources for Primary Education and its Consequences for Educational Achievement in Thailand." *International Journal of Educational Research* 17 (2) (1991): 143-164.

Raudenbush, S., C. Bhumirat, and M. Kamali. "Predictors and Consequences of Primary Teachers' Sense of Efficacy and Students' Perceptions of Teaching Quality in Thailand." *International Journal of Educational Research*, 17 (2) (1991): 165-176.

Raudenbush, S., E. D. I. Suwanna, M. Kamali, and W. Taoklam. "On-the-Job Improvements in Teacher Competence: Policy Options and their Effects on Teaching and Learning in Thailand." (Unpublished manuscript.) East Lansing, MI: College of Education, Michigan State University, 1991.

Reimers, F. "The Impact of Economic Stabilization and Adjustment on Education in Latin America." *Comparative Education Review*, 35 (2) (1991): 319-353.

Richardson, V. "Significant and Worthwhile Change in Teaching Practice." *Educational Researcher*, 19 (7) (1990): 10-18.

Rosenholtz, S.J. *Teachers Workplace. The Social Organization of Schools*. New York: Longman, 1989.

Rust, V.D. and P. Dalin. "Preface." *Teachers and Teaching in the Developing World*. New York: Garland, 1990.

Schiefelbein, E. *Redefining Basic Education for Latin America: Lessons to be Learned from the Colombian Escuela Nueva.* Paris: International Institute of Educational Planning, United Nations Educational, Scientific and Cultural Organization, 1992.

Schon, D. *Educating the Reflective Practitioner.* San Francisco, CA: Jossey-Bass, 1987.

Schwille, J. and C. Wheeler. "Variable Role of the State in Education: The Thai Experience." *International Journal of Educational Research*, 17 (2) (1992): 219-226.

Shaeffer, S. "Participatory Approaches to Teacher Training," in V. Rust and P. Dalin, eds., *Teachers and Teaching in the Developing World.* New York: Garland, 1990.

Sturman, A. *Patterns of School Organization: Resources and Responses in Sixteen Schools.* (Staffing and Resources Study Report No. 3.) ACER Research Monograph No. 18. Australian Educational Council. Canberra, 1982.

Sykes, G. "Public Policy and the Problem of Teacher Quality: The Need for Screens and Magnets," in L. Shulman and G. Sykes, eds., *Handbook of Teaching and Policy.* New York: Longman, 1983: 97-125.

Tangyong, A., F. Wahyudi, R. Gardner, and H. Haws. *Quality Through Support for Teachers: A Case Study from Indonesia.* Jakarta: Ministry of Education and Culture and London: Institute of Education, University of London, 1989.

Tatto, M.T. "Examining Values and Beliefs about Teaching Diverse Students: Understanding the Challenges for Teacher Education." *Educational Evaluation and Policy Analysis* (in press).

Tatto, M.T. and N.G. Kularatna. "The Interpersonal Dimension of Distance Education for Teachers: The Case of Sri Lanka, *International Journal of Educational Research,* 19 (8) (1993): 755-778.

Tatto, M.T., H.D Nielsen, W.C. Cummings, N.G. Kularatna, and D.H. Dharmadasa. "Comparing the Effectiveness and Costs of Different Approaches for Educating Primary School Teachers in Sri Lanka." *Teaching and Teacher Education. An International Journal of Research and Studies,* 9 (1) (1993):41-64.

Tatto, M.T., H.D Nielsen, W.C. Cummings, N.G. Kularatna, and D.H. Dharmadasa. "Comparing the Effects and Costs of Different Approaches for Educating Primary School Teachers: The Case of Sri Lanka." *BRIDGES Research Report Series* No. 10. Cambridge, MA: Harvard Institute for International Development, 1991.

Tatto, M.T. and E. Velez. "A Document-Based Assessment of Teacher Education Reform Initiatives: The Case of Mexico," in C.A. Torres and A. Puigros, eds. *Latin America in Comparative Perspective*. Boulder, CO: Westview, (in press).

Thompson, A.R. "Making the Best Use of Teachers: Deployment Issues," in V. Rust and P. Dalin, eds., *Teachers and Teaching in the Developing World*. New York: Garland, 1990.

Tibi, C. *What Policies for Teachers?* Paris: United Nations Educational, Scientific, and Cultural Organization, 1990.

Tsang, M. C. "Cost Analysis for Educational Policy Making in Developing Countries." *BRIDGES Research Report Series* No. 3. Cambridge, MA: Harvard Institute for International Development, 1988.

Tsang, M.C. and C. W. Wheeler. "Local Initiatives and their Implications for a Multilevel Approach to School Improvement in Thailand," in H. Levin and M. Lockheed eds. *Effective Schools in Developing Countries*. New York: Falmer Press (forthcoming).

UNDP, UNESCO, UNICEF, and World Bank. *Meeting Basic Learning Needs: A Vision for the 1990's*. Jomtien, Thailand, March, 1990a.

UNDP, UNESCO, UNICEF, and World Bank. *World Declaration on Education for All and Framework for Action to Meet Basic Learning Needs*. Jomtien, Thailand, March 5-9, 1990b.

UNESCO. "Difficult Educational Contexts." *Proceedings of the UNESCO Workshop on the Training of Primary Education Personnel Working in Difficult Educational Contexts* (2nd. Northern Territory, Australia, August 14-19, 1988). Bangkok, Thailand: UNESCO Principal Regional Office for Asia and the Pacific, 1989.

USAID. "Lessons Learned in Basic Education in the Developing World: An A.I.D. Workshop." Washington, DC: The Office of Education Bureau for Science and Technology, United States Agency for International Development. February 15-16, 1990.

Vera, R. "Educators Workshops in Chile: Participative Professional Development," in V. Rust and P. Dalin, eds., *Teachers and Teaching in the Developing World*. New York: Garland, 1990.

Verspoor, A.M. and J.L. Leno. "Improving Teaching: A Key to Successful Educational Change. Lessons from the World Bank Experience." Paper presented at the Annual International Movement Towards Educational Change Seminar. Bali, Indonesia, Nov. 1986.

Warwick, D. P. and H. Jatoi. *Teacher Gender and Student Achievement in Pakistan.* (Unpublished manuscript.) Cambridge, MA: Harvard Institute for International Development , 1991.

Wheeler, C., J. Chuaratanaphong, B. Chinnapat, S. Eamsukkawat, R. Shinatrakool, V. Sirijirakal, S. Pumsa-ard, B. Sookpokakit, and P. Kunarak. "School Clusters in Thailand: A Management Strategy for Improving Primary School Quality." *International Journal of Educational Research*, (17) 2 (1991): 199-216.

Wilcox, S.K., P. Schram, G. Lappan, and P. Lanier. *The Role of a Learning Community in Changing Preservice Teachers' Knowledge and Beliefs about Mathematics Education.* (Research Report 91-1.) East Lansing: Michigan State University, National Center for Research on Teacher Learning, 1991.

Williams, P. *Planning Teacher Demand and Supply. Fundamentals of Educational Planning.* Paris: UNESCO-IIEP, 1979.

World Bank. *Education in Sub-Saharan Africa. Policies for Adjustment, Revitalization and Expansion. A World Bank Policy Study.* Washington, DC: The International Bank for Reconstruction and Development, 1988.

————. *Basic Education in Mexico: Trends, Issues, and Policy Recommendations.* (Report No. 8930-ME.) Washington, DC: Human Resources Operations Division, Country Department II. Latin America and the Caribbean Regional Office, 1991a.

————. *China Provincial Education Planning and Finance.* (Sector Study Report No. 8657-CHA, Volume 1.) Washington, DC: Environment, Human Resources and Urban Development Operations Division China and Mongolia Department, 1991b.

————. *INDONESIA: Basic Education Study.* (Mimeo.) Washington, DC: The World Bank, 1989.

————. *INDONESIA: Primary School Teacher Development Project.* Washington, DC: The World Bank, 1992b.

————. *Informal Review of Basic Education Projects 1980-1990.* (Mimeo.) Washington, DC: The World Bank, 1992.

Zeichner, K.M. *Educating Teachers for Cultural Diversity.* National Center for Research on Teacher Learning Special Report. East Lansing: Michigan State University, 1993.

Zeichner, K.M., and J.M. Gore. "Teacher Socialization" in W.R. Houston, ed., *Handbook of Research on Teacher Education.* New York: Macmillan, 1990.

CHAPTER 7

School and Classroom Organization in the Periphery
The Assets of Multigrade Teaching

S. Dunham Rowley, Jr., and H. Dean Nielsen

INTRODUCTION

Effective education in any country depends on able teachers and school conditions which facilitate learning. Unfortunately, peripheral areas are usually hard-pressed to find able teachers (see chapter 6), and their schools frequently lack even the most basic of organizational features and resources. One organizational feature most teachers have come to expect is a self-contained single-grade classroom. But in many peripheral areas, school population is not large enough to justify one teacher per grade. In these areas teachers must manage two, three, or even all grades at the same time. *Multigrade teaching*, sometimes considered a relic of the past, is, in fact, still widely used throughout the world in both agrarian and industrialized countries.

Often ignored and unacknowledged, this form of school/classroom organization presents educators many challenges as well as opportunities. The challenges are particularly evident in cases where teachers have not been prepared to teach in this kind of setting and are unsupported. To a well-prepared and well-supported teacher, however, multigrade teaching assignments afford opportunities not available in larger schools, particularly for creating relatively enduring student learning communities. Experience shows that when working in multigrade settings, teachers must abandon the *industrial model* of education that almost all grew up in, with its age-graded, batch- processed classes, and adopt a *family model* of organization in which students and "significant others" interact in less age-specific ways. Under such a transformation, the conditions of the small, multigrade teaching school can be seen not as constraints but as *assets*.

Moreover, since such schools, covering the entire basic school curriculum, can be set up in the remotest villages, multigrade teaching provides school access to previously unserved populations, including a group parents were often reluctant to send to school, their daughters. Providing both boys and girls in the periphery with *access to quality* is one of the main charges of the "Education for All" movement, and is the ultimate goal of the multigrade teaching strategies that we will review here.

HISTORICAL PERSPECTIVE

The premise that one teacher is responsible for teaching a group of age-specific students with a graded curriculum is a fairly recent innovation in education. Preindustrial or agrarian schools, as described by LeVine and White (1986) were developed from and exemplify the cultural contexts of their settings. They tended to be religious and centered on the hierarchical relationship between teacher and pupil; to emphasize the mastery of sacred texts; to respect the local age-sex values of the agrarian societies; and to be organized around a looser, more variable standard of learning (p.76). Even though such schools were disengaged from economic activity, they were organized to preserve the social order and often met as mixed-age groups, such as boys in a Koranic School under the leadership of an imam.

The European eighteenth-century one-room school adapted itself from the agrarian models by engaging a full-time teacher who used individual and tutorial methods to instruct a group of 10 to 30 pupils ranging in age from 6 to 14 years. (Cremin, 1961.) On the frontier of the United States, one-room schools established in the early 1800s followed the eighteenth-century European model education. (Fuller, 1982.) These schools were almost always taught by one teacher and became the standard of American education until the consolidation movement displaced and discredited them in the early twentieth century. Horace Mann sounded the death-knell of the one-room school after he visited Prussia in 1843 and reported that:

> the first element of superiority in a Prussian school . . . consists in the proper classification of the scholars. In all places where the numbers are sufficiently large to allow it, the children are divided according to ages and attainments, and a single teacher has the charge only of a single class . . . .There is no obstacle whatever . . . to the introduction at once of this mode of dividing and classifying scholars in all our large towns. (Cited in Pratt, 1986: 287.)

Pratt (1986) states that within a decade, Mann's ideas were being widely accepted by administrators who saw in them a parallel to successful manufacturing principles. Population growth, improved transportation, and the legislative process forced schools to sort students into single-grade classrooms, grouped by age and presumed ability. Comparative studies were initiated to disprove the educational viability of one-room schools so that the process of consolidation could proceed unimpeded and with scientific legitimacy. (Foote, 1923; Morrison, 1922.)

The historical trends that were a part of industrialization encouraged the thinking that schools should be set up like factories. The colonial and metropolitan powers standardized the organization of schools around the single-grade format and created the bias that such classrooms were better than any other alternative. Sharing this viewpoint, communities with small schools and multigrade classrooms became concerned that their schools might not be the real thing while parents worried about inferior instruction. Parents and community leaders have until today sought assurances that children will not be academically disadvantaged by not attending a conventionally organized, modern school.

PREVALENCE OF MULTIGRADE TEACHING

The prevalence of multigrade teaching (MGT) in primary schools throughout the world is unknown, but is undoubtedly greater than is commonly recognized. A UNESCO conference on multigrade teaching in the Asia-Pacific region revealed the practice of multigrade teaching in large numbers of schools in China (about 420,000), India (about 327,000) and Indonesia (around 20,000). In less populous areas in the region, the prevalence of multigrade teaching is also quite high: in the Philippines about 8 percent of all schools are multigraded, whereas in the Northern Territory of Australia the proportion is around 40 percent. (UNESCO, 1989.)

The industrialized world also supports a plethora of MGT approaches, some even of the one-room school variety. Marshall (1985) indicates that about one quarter of Scotland's primary schools have fewer than fifty students; eighty percent of Portuguese children go to schools with no more than two classrooms; and there are 11,000 one-teacher rural schools in France. Currently in the United States there are only about 800 one-teacher schools, but as late as 1918 there were close to 300,000.

A recent sample survey of primary schools in Pakistan reveals that 58 percent of primary-school teachers teach more than one grade of students. (Warwick, Reimers and McGinn, 1989.) Rising population in many countries has increased the demand for primary-school education, and put a strain on government policies for universal primary education. Pakistan's recent Five Year Plan committed its government to providing a minimum of three teachers and two classrooms to every primary school. (Government of Pakistan, 1988.) However, this plan was never implemented. A severe teacher shortage meant that a large number of rural schools had to ask teachers to manage three or more grades each.

In spite of the overwhelming need for more and higher quality primary education and the projected dependence on multigrade classrooms to provide it, many school systems have neither research plans nor designated strategies for multigrade teaching. (UNESCO, 1989.) Governments are under pressure to improve quality in primary education because progress toward educational goals is now a matter of global scrutiny (UNDP, UNESCO, UNICEF, and World Bank, 1990) and also because many countries cannot afford to maintain classrooms of repeating students while large segments of student-age populations remain unserved.

Yet in country after country, school systems plan, train their teachers, and organize their curriculum around the single-teacher, single-grade classroom approach. Moreover, few governments have recognized the fact that multigrade teaching may, in fact, be their most effective approach to education under certain circumstances.

A brief reference to the literature will reveal the benefits (and drawbacks) of multigrade teaching, and the relatively high levels of achievement multigrade teaching can produce if managed effectively.

ADVANTAGES AND DISADVANTAGES OF MULTIGRADE TEACHING

In review of multigrade teaching for the World Bank, Thomas and Shaw (1992) reported the following as advantages and disadvantages of multigrade teaching:

Advantages	Disadvantages
• efficient in providing basic education in thinly populated areas	• students may receive less individual attention, and must often work independently
• efficient means of utilizing scarce educational inputs, such as trained teachers, classrooms, and materials	• student achievement may fall if programs are not supported by the required resources and teachers are not properly trained
• students can attain higher achievement levels than single-grade students, especially in math, language, and sciences	• demands on teachers' time and organizational capabilities are high; they need special training and materials to perform their jobs effectively
• maintaining rural schools is important in building village identity and cultural life	
• can benefit girls by expanding available school spaces and by helping to ensure that schools are located closer to home	
• students "learn to learn" and "learn to teach" through independent inquiry and peer tutoring	
• students and teachers develop a strong relationship over time	
• students benefit from the unique multi-age and peer socialization patterns	
• the stigma associated with repetition is removed.	

The advantages to multigrade teaching make it well worth examining as an alternative to the conventional school. In addition, there is growing evidence that multigrade teaching can produce positive student outcomes.

MULTIGRADE TEACHING AND STUDENT OUTCOMES

In a pathbreaking review of studies reporting outcomes of multigrade teaching, Miller (1989) provides a picture of the relative effectiveness of multigrade teaching. Since the 21 studies which he reviewed were mainly from North America and Australia, the results cannot necessarily be applied to multigrade teaching as conducted in poorer, less industrialized countries. However, since most of the studies cover rural or remote areas in the countries mentioned, they do provide some notion of what might be occurring in peripheral areas of other countries.

Academic Achievement

Thirteen of the studies reviewed by Miller covered academic achievement of students in multigrade teaching situations compared to those in conventional classrooms. According to Miller:

> The studies indicate that there is little or no difference in student achievement in the single or multigrade classroom. Two studies (Knight, 1938; Chace, 1961) found that multigrade students performed consistently higher in mathematics, reading and language than did single-grade students. However, the differences were not statistically significant. In eight studies (Drier, 1949; Adams, 1953; Way, 1969; Harvey, 1974; Adair, 1978; MacDonald & Wuster, 1974; Lincoln, 1981; Pratt & Treacy, 1986) researchers found no difference between student performance in the multigrade or single-grade classroom. Only in the studies that reported mixed results do we find significant differences. (Miller, 1989: 6.)

The message of these studies is clear. Multigrade teaching does not put students at an academic disadvantage, at least in relatively prosperous countries. Such results have been recently confirmed for a less developed country as well. Psacharopoulos, Rojas, and Velez (1993) found that schooling in Colombia's innovative *Escuela Nueva* had significant and positive effects on a wide variety of student outcomes, even when student and family background, and school input variables were controlled.

Affective Outcomes

The nine studies reviewed by Miller covering affective outcomes showed more affirmative results in favor of multigrade teaching. The nine studies covered 23 separate measures of student attitudes: 65 percent favored the multigrade classroom at a significant level; 13 percent showed a trend favoring multigrade classrooms; 22 percent revealed no differences between the two types of classrooms; only one of the 65 measures favored the single-grade classroom. As a whole, the studies showed that students attending multigrade classrooms have significantly more positive attitudes towards themselves and their schools. A trend towards more positive social relationships was also noted.

The study of *Escuela Nueva* noted above did not confirm higher self-esteem for the students of this multigrade teaching system, but it did discover that repetition and school drop-out was lower for *Escuela Nueva* students than for those in comparable conventional schools. (Psacharopoulos et al., 1993.)

In sum, it appears that there is something about multigrade teaching which produces students who achieve as well or better than conventional school students and whose attitudes towards themselves and school is generally better. Unfortunately, few of the studies reviewed made detailed analysis of the features of multigrade teaching which have contributed to these outcomes. In some ways, the results seem to be counter-intuitive, since multigrade teaching often occurs under circumstances thought to be disadvantageous. But this may simply be a conceptual problem. Those features that may seem disadvantageous within the *industrial model* of education—small buildings, sparse facilities, isolated teachers, a small and diverse student body, an intrusive community—can, within a "family" model of education, be seen as *assets*. The main purpose of this chapter is to show how different aspects of life in peripheral areas can be used as assets in multigrade teaching. It will focus on four basic features of the educational mix in peripheral areas, namely: (a) classroom conditions, (b) teachers, (c) students, and (d) the community. We will attempt to show how it is that these features can be organized in such a way as to provide multigrade students with education that is comparable, if not , in many ways, superior, to that in mainstream schools.

CLASSROOM CONDITIONS

Space
Multigrade teaching and small school size generally go hand in hand. Governments feel justified in allocating fewer than a "full" complement of teachers to schools where student numbers are well below the standard for a "regular" class. In places like Indonesia, such schools are actually designated "small schools." They are defined as having 60 or fewer students and no more than three classroom teachers. Small schools of this sort are also generally given small buildings. In Indonesia, the standard building for a small school has three classrooms, but many have fewer. In Belize, where one-third of the nation's teachers manage two grades or more, one-room schools are very common, comprising about 50 percent of all schools where multigrade teaching is done.[1]

Given these constraints, it might seem strange to list space as a possible asset. Common sense might suggest the opposite, as captured in the common late-nineteenth-century criticism of one-room schools in the U.S. as being crowded, untidy, and noisy. (Fuller, 1982.) Rarely were such criticisms based on fact, however; and a revival in interest in the one-room school has begun to yield some surprising findings about space and its use in multigrade teaching. The review will focus on three issues: (a) crowding; (b) shared space; and (c) community space.

Crowding
In many countries, the notion that small schools managed by multigrade teaching are crowded is not born out in fact. The standard definition in Indonesia for its MGT schools (three teachers and classrooms for 60 students) yields a comfortable student-teacher ratio of 20. Although this ratio is not achieved in all cases, since many hardship posts fail to recruit their prescribed numbers of teachers or lose teachers

during the year due to resignation or transfer, the numbers of students per classroom is still quite comfortable. In Belize, where, as mentioned above, 50 percent of the MGT schools are the one-room variety, the average space per child in MGT schools is about twice the national standard (28 square feet compared to the standard 15 feet). Again, this does not mean that all schools are uncrowded. Of the 70 schools that entered into the Belize analysis, 14 (20 percent) provided less than the standard amount of space per student. But even in this case, the exception proves the rule: *in multigrade teaching, small does not necessarily mean crowded.*

Shared Space

Those who characterized small as noisy might have been right if only the decibel level was at stake. When various small groups of students are actively working on different tasks in the same classroom, the volume is likely to rise, but the content is usually lesson-oriented, not mere noise. The use of *shared space* by different grade levels can be distracting to be sure, but, as Fuller (1982) points out, this has often had beneficial side effects. Old-timers who attended one-room schools tell of overhearing lessons covered by other groups and finding it both a good review and preview. By the time they got to the upper grades, many of them already knew what to expect. According to Reck (1988), this is also a feature of the small Catholic school of today.

Other aspects of shared space is the chance to see posted work of students from other grades, another kind of preview not possible with self-contained, single-grade classrooms, and greater opportunities to interact socially across grade levels. The latter phenomenon is a good illustration of the family concept, as Reck states: "The mix of varied ages—especially in classrooms where several grades work together— more closely approximates the natural mix of different ages in their families and communities which promoted their rapid learning as pre-schoolers." (Reck, 1988: 13.) Such a mix also increases the likelihood of students finding social matches, precocious lower graders being able to associate with older students and immature upper graders being able to befriend younger students, both without stigma. It is such a mix that, among other things, as Miller (1989) has pointed out, leads to positive attitudes of MGT students towards school, themselves as learners, and other students.

Community Space

All schools serve communities of various kinds, but the small school in sparsely populated areas often fills a space of immense social and symbolic value. Miller (1991) shows how the community school can be the key to the survival of marginal, economically threatened communities. Monk and Haller (1986) view the school as one, if not the only viable institution for some localities, providing a "stable pattern in the web of social life that binds individuals together." This is also reflected in Bray's (1987) concept of the small school as the focal point of some communities. He quotes the Welsh writer Roy Nash (1980) as saying: "although church and chapel have far more influence in the Welsh countryside than they have in urban areas, and clearly help to integrate the community and give it a sense of identity, attendance is declining and they no longer hold the central position that they had only 30 or 40 years ago. The place of the school as a focal point is therefore possibly of greater importance today than at any time previously."

The image of the lively Friday night school "spelling bee" and its capacity to capture the attention and passions of the entire community, painted by Fuller (1982) about life in late-nineteenth-century rural America, is still alive in small rural villages in the American West, the Philippines, and Belize, among other places.

Time

Time is a resource which is theoretically available to all schools in the same amounts. However, the way in which time is managed varies enormously across schools and classrooms, and these variations of "time on task" are strongly linked to differences in educational outcomes. The management of time is one of the factors which distinguishes the family model of MGT from the more conventional industrial model. In the industrial model, time is unrelentingly linear. Children are sorted into grades according to age and passed to the next level en masse at the beginning of the next year. School calendars set by central offices apply to all schools of a state or district, no matter what their circumstances. Curriculum is organized according to fixed sequences and taught in small segments, each subject being covered during 40- to 50- minute periods in the daily schedule. Bells or buzzers ring in order to signal the beginning and end of each period and children who are late are penalized for tardiness. The standardization of textbooks and lesson plans leads to considerable uniformity within the system. It has been said that in France the inspectorate took pride in knowing that at a certain hour of the day, all students in the same grade nationwide would be studying the same lesson.

In the family model, time is not quite so linear. Students of different ages are often combined in the study of the same material, even though they may not receive it in the same *sequence* in relation to other subjects in the field (see the discussion of science and social studies below). Nongraded schools avoid classifying students according to age altogether, using instead the student's readiness for certain content; others let students proceed at their own pace, according to the *mastery learning* model. A broader view of time is also a feature of the family model: a *lifelong learning* perspective, which encourages adult members of the community to use the school as a learning center.

This discussion sees time as an asset in MGT in terms of: (a) magnitude; (b) management; (c) and extra effort.

Magnitude of Time

The conventional schools all present a façade of efficiency by following the industrial model of grading and scheduling, but in reality this efficiency is often subverted by weaknesses in implementation. For example, Shaeffer's (1979) observations in Javanese villages showed that, despite a federally mandated timetable, schools often ended the school day early, in some cases providing only one and a half hours of instruction a day to first graders, and about three hours to fourth graders. Teachers often ended their instructional day early in order to report to their second (moonlighting) teaching job at a private school. In chapter 2 above, Nielsen presented information on time use in two "conventional schools" in remote Indonesian villages. In Central Kalimantan, a single teacher managed five age-graded classes by meeting each in turn throughout the day, meaning that each class only receives about an hour's worth of supervised instruction a day. On a small island in North Sumatra, three teachers taught two classes each by having them come in different shifts, one in the early morning, the other late. The teachers put in the conventional five-hour days, but each group of students met for only two and a half hours. It is hard to imagine students making any great strides in learning with only one to three hours of instruction.

When MGT is implemented as envisioned here, teachers keep students on task during a full school day. In most cases the groups supervised by a single teacher are kept within the teacher's line of vision; they are kept busy either by combined whole-class lessons, small-group work, peer- or cross-age tutoring, self-guided instruction, or the use of guest teachers (volunteers) from the community. With more time on task comes higher levels of achievement.

Management of Time

Good time management is crucial to effective multigrade teaching, but this does not imply the same linear programming as used in the conventional schools. For example, some versions of MGT (*Escuela Nueva* in Colombia; *Sekolah Kecil* [Small Schools] in Indonesia) employ certain forms of mastery learning, where students work through self-study materials at their own pace. In addition, many schools employ a circular approach to subject matter sequencing, especially in the subjects which are not skills-based, such as social studies, science and literature. For example, a teacher in charge of grades four through six may decide to combine the grades for social studies, giving world history one year, national history the next, and local history the third. Only one grade, say the sixth graders, would be taking the courses in this sequence, however, the others would have a sequence of either nation-local-world, or local-world-national. As long as one course is not designed to be built upon the other, this should not cause difficulty to any learner.

Another concept related to time management is that of *wastage*, defined as student drop-out, repeating and absenteeism. Wastage is a serious problem in most peripheral areas, given the fact that the curriculum is often largely irrelevant to students' lives; the language of instruction is often a second language; cycles of work (harvesting and planting) are often in conflict with the school year; there is little chance for students to receive direct help from their parents; and rigid scheduling and sequencing often catch students in a downward spiral of failure and loss of self-confidence. Studies in peripheral areas of poor countries in various parts of the world reveal high drop-out rates in grade one (e.g., 35 percent in Colombia; Psacharopoulos, et al., 1993), and at the end of the cycle (e.g., in India 60 percent drop out after grade five; UNESCO, 1987). According to UNESCO (1987) some countries also report that up to 40 percent of school children are habitual absentees from school.

Time management under MGT helps students deal with some of the causes of wastage: in ungraded or multigraded classrooms the stigma attached to working "below grade level" disappears. Also, timing is flexible enough that students are able to stop out and reenter with relative ease. In addition, assuming that the teacher has organized the day well, students are kept motivated and actively on task throughout the school day. Finally, the family atmosphere of the school creates a relatively informal, supportive learning environment.

There have been few formal studies of wastage in relation to the implementation of multigrade teaching. An exception is the study mentioned above by Psacharopoulos, et al. (1993) of the *Escuela Nueva* movement in Colombia. This study shows significant differences between *Escuela Nueva* grade-five students and comparable conventional-school students on both repeating and propensity to drop out, both in favor of *Escuela Nueva*. There has been no comparable study of student absenteeism.

A final concept of time has a long horizon: namely lifelong learning. MGT schools are organized to engage the entire community in the learning enterprise, primarily as resources for teaching and student support. But as people contribute to the school, they also grow intellectually and thus become learners. Village schools which serve the broader purposes related to community survival also have explicit roles of engaging youth and adults in exploring solutions to community problems. Time management becomes an asset as it transcends the normal boundaries of a person's season for learning.

The management of time in MGT teaching, the use of non-conventional approaches to scheduling, sequencing, and student-progress assessment, and the encouragement of lifelong learning, can be seen as an asset, both in terms of increased opportunities to learn and decreased educational wastage.

Time Demands

This discussion of time management within MGT would not be complete without a reference to time demands. The effective use of time in MGT is itself a product of extra time devoted to planning by the teachers and the community. Daily preparation for classes involving three or more separate learning activities by groups and individuals at different levels is unquestionably more demanding of the teacher's time than planning for a single-grade classroom. Add to that the necessary interaction and service to the community, most of which is after school hours, and the result is a work load which is far above average. Village schools everywhere boast amazingly creative and committed individuals who take on such loads as a matter of course, but in fairness to teachers, there should be extra incentives and rewards for those who expend the extra time demanded by good multigrade teaching. In other words, the asset of good time management in MGT should be paid for.

THE TEACHER

The teacher is obviously an asset to the MGT school; in fact, in poorer countries where books, materials, and access to electronic media are limited, the importance of the teacher overwhelms everything else. Yet, given the difficulty in recruiting and retaining teachers in peripheral areas, teachers working in MGT schools are generally young, poorly trained, and inexperienced. Even this fact can be turned into an asset, however, as shown in the following covering: (a) teacher background; (b) teacher resourcefulness; and (c) teacher influence.

Teacher Background

According to Dove (1985) and Matthes and Carlson (1987), teachers shy away from peripheral assignments in the first place largely because their family, social, economic, and professional aspirations are incompatible with conditions in peripheral communities. Those taking jobs in small community schools generally see this as an entry point into the profession and a stepping stone to more desirable postings. Where fully-trained teachers are scarce, MGT schools may have a choice of nontrained teachers or none at all.

Our analysis of the population of MG teachers in Belize revealed that almost 70 percent were untrained (lacking a teacher-education certificate), well below the national average. Grade-level breakdowns further revealed that 84 percent of those working with lower grades were untrained, whereas only 50 percent of those working with upper grades were not trained. Clearly, the youngest learners had access to the least-prepared teachers.

Our data also revealed high rates of teacher turnover. Of the 174 teachers surveyed, 42 percent had been at their current school for one year or less. Moreover, over half had spent no more than two years teaching in a MGT school. Since teachers come into MGT unprepared and thus must learn on the job, it would be desirable for them to stay in one place long enough to learn the complexities of MG teaching; obviously this isn't happening for most teachers.

Nevertheless, it does happen for some, and those are often individuals who originate in peripheral areas. One of the striking findings of our Belize study is that nearly *one quarter* of the MG teachers surveyed were teaching in the elementary schools they attended as children. It is unlikely that this finding can be replicated in other countries; however, it reveals an important lesson. The average length of time teaching in the current school for these *hometown* teachers was 5.9 years, compared to 3.1 years for the overall sample. Moreover, 72 percent were involved in extracurricular activities (largely PTA and sports) compared to the overall average of 54 percent. Thus, the hometown teachers were much more likely than the total pool to represent the kind of assets required for effective MGT, individuals maintaining residence at a school long enough to learn its complex routines and involved enough in the community to create good school-community relations.

Ironically, it may have been the recruitment system (seen as deficient by many) that allowed these teaching assets to enter the profession in the first place. If the system had insisted on trained teachers, few of the home-grown teachers would have been appointed; in fact, few of the village schools would have survived. Recruiting untrained teachers allowed the system to find individuals willing to work and stay in difficult conditions and thus to keep village schools going. This does not mean that teachers of MGT should remain untrained. A program now underway in Belize will provide opportunities for inservice training to the untrained teachers, using a combination of distance and residential training similar to that used in other countries. (Nielsen, 1991.)

A further irony is the fact that countries which have emphasized formal credentials often fail to avail themselves of this kind of asset. For example, Indonesia now produces more than enough trained teachers for all of its elementary schools. It thus uses a competitive examination for screening candidates. Although there are many candidates from the villages where vacancies exist, these hometown teachers rarely survive the competition with their urban counterparts. The latter accept teaching appointments in the village long enough to arrange a transfer to town; the local candidates often return to their villages unemployed or drift to town for marginal employment. (See Nielsen and Somerset, 1992.)

Temperament and Resourcefulness

Throughout the world, teachers drawn into multigrade teaching have been essentially left to their own devices. Some find this distressing and intolerable; hence, the high turnover; other seem to thrive. In our MG teacher survey in Belize about the same number were "very positive" about multigrade teaching as were "very negative."

The overall tendency leans in the positive direction, the modal response being "somewhat positive." Differences among districts were minor. Those who were at the extremes, both positive and negative, had some pointed comments to make, as follows:

Positive

"Great! It's a lot of hard work, but the personal satisfaction is unequaled. You learn the true meaning of patience, creativity and innovation. I would not change it for any other."

"I feel grateful because I have to work very hard and that is the way I like it, and the students cooperate with me."

"For me it is very rewarding, because you get more experience in handling more than one class, and if you have more than one class it is better, because you can interrelate (combine) different groups within the class."

"It is really hard, but if you put your whole mind and soul into it, you'll see the fruit of it. It keeps both teacher and children fully occupied."

Negative

"Does not lend itself to sufficient class grouping and individual helping. Very tiresome and frustrating."

"I frankly believe it is too punishing for the teachers. Also, the children get less time of the teacher, e.g., 45 minutes of Math has to be divided by three classes. That is 15 minutes of Math. Not enough. With two classes that are of the same stage better can be done."

"Discouraging, unfair, tiresome, and unrewarding."

"It is very difficult to attend and teach more than one class, cause lots of problems do arise, for example, misbehavior, lack of learning, lack of patience."

Teachers, like other professionals, react differently to the same kinds of circumstances. What some find tiresome and frustrating, others find challenging and rewarding. These and similar findings by other investigators (Barker, 1986; Miller, 1989) suggest that although teachers can be trained and supported in the complex and difficult tasks of multigrade teaching, the capacity of a teacher to thrive in this kind of setting is in large measure a consequence of individual *temperament*. As Barker remarks: ". . . the assignment to teach in a one-teacher school may be the most demanding of all positions in the profession, but for those who love young people and enjoy teaching, it could well be the most rewarding." (Barker, 1986: 150.)

The "coping strategies" of multigrade teachers are varied and creative. In most countries they receive little explicit training for MGT, and few guidelines and special resources are provided. In poor countries in particular, the multigrade-teaching resources that are taken for granted in wealthier countries, such as educational radio and TV, computer media programs, and self-instructional packages, are rarely available. What remains is the teachers' *resourcefulness*. Given the wide variation in community conditions, even a motivated, locally recruited teacher will need to develop her/his own "coping strategies" in order to flourish in the periphery. The following are two kinds of coping strategies observed among highly successful MG teachers in Belize, one emphasizing "trial and error," the other "community mobilization." Both strategies reveal a reflective approach to teaching which adapts methods to conditions and responds to student outcomes. Teachers relying on this kind of resourcefulness are employing "action research" without even knowing it.

Trial and Error

At times, I had to make use of the brightest student in the class who finished first, to help a class in spelling or in reading, or telling a story to the infants. This gave me a chance to take a particular class in subjects taken separately in respective classes, like oral reading. For some time this strategy worked fairly well, until it came to my notice that some topics in Social Studies and Science were common to both Middle and Upper Divisions. By taking both divisions together in these subjects, I was able to economize time and effort. Religion, singing and literature were also used to the same advantage. However, the VI Class of two students, preparing for the Primary School Leaving Certificate, was not receiving the appropriate preparation. So here was another problem to solve. . . . A way to solve this problem was to take this Std VI Class half-an-hour after school. This extra voluntary work had to be done for the benefit of the students. . . . (*Santiago S. Garcia, Jr., Principal, Santa Cruz Government School, Orange Walk District*)

A technique that I developed by trial and error that seemed to work well in multigrade is, for example, using work cards. In Std I and II classes, I used to say that the cards would be too hard for Std I and too easy for Std II, but I discovered that the cards suit both classes, because the younger ones will learn [new lessons] from them and the older ones will be reinforcing previous lessons; so both classes benefited from the cards. (*Eleanor Usher, Teacher, Christ the King Anglican School, Stann Creek District*)

Community Mobilization

For my internship I was sent to San Jose Nuevo School. Again, I was principal. I got acquainted with the parents and Village Councillors. In this school I noticed that the children were very undernourished. I encouraged my staff to give the children the skimmed milk that CARE used to provide. I invited the Health Nurse to give them lectures on nutrition and intestinal worms. I then raised funds to purchase cod-liver oil capsules and some vitamins for them. With the parents' approval I did these activities and with their cooperation the school acquired a half an acre plot of land. CARE supplied the school with various vegetable seeds and with other local seeds such as peanuts, hot pepper and okra, the garden was packed. I also encouraged the upper classes to join the 4H movement. As 4Her's, they chose whatever animal project they desired. Some went into piggery, poultry, raising of rabbits and black-belly sheep. CARE and 4H officers helped with a water pump and pipes to bring water from a distant pond to irrigate the plants. After a few weeks and months, the children have learned to eat radishes, cucumbers, and other vegetables. The children become so interested that learning was fun. They became strong and healthy and were able to learn. At present, if you take a walk to San Jose Nuevo, you will see herds of black-belly sheep. (*Adopha Cal Garcia, Teacher, Orange Walk District*)

Teacher Influence

In the family setting of multigrade teaching, individual teachers are likely to have a much stronger influence on the students than in the milieu of the conventional schools. Whereas in the conventional school, teachers only work with a stable group of students during one academic year, in the MGT setting teachers work with the same students during at least two years, and often during the entire elementary-school cycle. In small schools where the principal also teaches, students also have a strong, multiyear relationship with the principal. Besides being more enduring, student-teacher relations in MGT schools are also qualitatively different as compared to single-grade schools, as portrayed by Reck in her book about small Catholic schools:

> Not only do teachers know each student, but students know the principal and each teacher. They find no maze of bureaucracy; rather, they regularly relate with the key people in the school, totally at ease talking with adults—a rare phenomenon in many larger settings. Students interact more frequently and more informally with their teachers than in the larger school. Observations show that parents also feel very free to ask for help when a staff member is available. (Reck, 1988: 18.)

The influence of teachers on students in MGT schools thus can go deeper than in conventional schools, creating the potential for not only greater intellectual development but also to improved social skills and character development. In this sense the MG teacher becomes an asset for the entire community.

THE STUDENT

In the conventional school based on the factory model, students are treated as passive inputs, to which "value is added" during successive levels of "processing." In the MGT schools students are not only objects but also subjects, contributing to the teaching process and other aspects of school operation. Those who know social conditions in the periphery recognize that children generally take on important family responsibilities at an early age, such as doing household chores, working in fields or in product marketing, looking after livestock, taking care of younger siblings, and so forth. (UNESCO, 1987.) The self-reliance and competence that even the youngest students in the periphery bring to school is itself an asset. Unfortunately, this fact is often missed by urban-oriented teachers and school managers, who tend to focus on more conventional assets such as "reading readiness" and thus undervalue the resources that a child brings to school, even to the point of "deskilling" the child. (UNESCO, 1987.)

In the classroom, the child's self-reliance and competence can be built upon in two ways: (a) to create self-directed learners, and (b) to develop peer tutors. In addition, in many MGT settings students are involved in school-level decision making, school operations, and school upkeep.

Self-Directed Learners

Reck attributes the positive learning outcomes in small Catholic schools largely to the schools' expectation that students will be responsible for their own learning:

> In multigrade situations, students must work without direct teacher assistance for a significant part of the school day. As a result, students have more frequent opportunities to follow directions, to complete a task by themselves, to work for sustained periods without interruptions. These youngsters are more likely to develop the ability to concentrate and work independently. Moreover, they have regular opportunities to learn that they are able to meet challenges if they keep working. (Reck, 1988: 16.)

Miller echoes this emphasis on self-directed learning, demonstrating how the student's ability to learn on her/his own becomes a particular asset to the multigrade classroom:

> In the multigrade classroom, self-management activities tend to be of first concern to the teacher. Students who can manage their time, follow schedules, find needed resources, and stay on task until assignments are completed facilitate the teacher's ability to manage the diverse levels found in the classroom. Successful multigrade teachers create environments that encourage these skills. (Miller, 1989: 230.)

These two proponents of multigrade teaching both based their optimism on data from relatively well-endowed schools in the sparsely populated areas of industrialized countries. In such schools, self-direction is facilitated by an abundance of educational resources, including electronic media and commercial self-instructional packages. For example, Reck's list of available resources in small Catholic MGT schools in the U.S. includes:

- film projectors and films/film strips
- videocassette recorder and videotapes
- audiocassette recorder and audiotapes
- record player and records
- computer and computer software
- self-correcting classroom kits
- flash cards
- games
- commercially prepared spirit masters
- idea/activity books
- Cuisenaire rods or other math-manipulation materials
- ideas for possible field trips
- other community resources (Reck, 1988: 71)[2]

This is in stark contrast with the resource base of MGT schools in poorer, agrarian countries. Our data from Belize reveals that fewer than 10 percent of students had access to their own science and social-studies textbooks. Also, a school in Indonesia visited by one of the authors (see Nielsen, chapter 2) had not taught science for several years since it had never received the "new" science textbooks. The school systems in many such countries have worked on ways to get around such constraints. In the 1970s and early 1980s, six countries adopted the IMPACT system (Instruction Managed by Parents, Community and Teachers), which included a substantial self-instructional component. (Cummings, 1986.) Based on a programmed-learning model, this project broke the curriculum in the basic subject areas into small segments which were then provided to students in self-instructional modules. Students were allowed to move through the materials at their own pace irrespective of their grade levels. Although all countries showed good learning outcomes using such an approach, none of them were able to get the system adopted for widespread use in rural schools, in part because of the large numbers and expense of the learning modules (over 200 titles in Indonesia, for example). (Nielsen and Cummings, 1985.) In addition, recent years have seen the model of highly structured programmed learning go out of fashion.

Other less ambitious systems of self-instruction seem to have faired better. Colombia's *Escuela Nueva* program (Psacharopoulos, et al., 1993; Schiefelbein, 1992), to be described in more detail later on, provides study corners for focusing on different subjects such as science, math, and social studies. Here students can pursue self-directed learning through the help of study guides, created by the teachers. In Belize, where textbook distribution in sporadic, 75 percent of teachers create their own individualized study materials, most common of which are games, flash cards, and puzzles. Thirty percent of the teachers in the Belize study also used study corners. The main subjects for self-directed learning, both with teacher-made materials and in study corners, were math and language arts, subjects which are hierarchically organized such that a student must master, often through drill and repetition, one level before moving to the next. In that country, other subjects, such as science and social studies, were more often covered by the teacher using combined age-groupings.

The crucial point here is that even where resources are limited, self-directed learning can still become an asset in MGT, largely due to the resourcefulness of the teachers.

Peer Tutors

As mentioned above, many students from the peripheral areas of low-income countries enter elementary school already experienced in caring for younger siblings. To them, helping younger students comes automatically. In fact, according to Miller (1989), much peer tutoring is automatic and "incidental." In cases where ages and grades are mixed, younger students learn from older by observing, overhearing, and asking for help. Although such tutoring is an asset to the school, research evidence on its impact is nonexistent; however, substantial documentation exists in support of structured tutoring. (Miller, 1989.) In a World Bank report, Thomas and Shaw report that:

> Having students serve as teachers within and across grade levels can be a very effective tool for learning, and is an essential part of multigrade teaching . . . .Peer tutoring benefits both tutors and learners, and serves as a powerful tool for extending the influence of the teacher in the classroom. Tutoring programs help to re-enforce and encourage a deeper understanding of subject matter, to create positive attitudes towards subjects, and to foster a productive learning environment. Structured tutoring may be looked at as a logical extension of the natural process by which students already learn from one another. (Thomas and Shaw, 1992: 15.)

These reports confirm findings of a meta-analysis of 65 studies of peer tutoring reported several years earlier by Cohen, Kulik and Kulik (1982), which showed significant positive effects of tutoring on the academic performance and attitudes of both the students tutored and the tutors. Much like the above, they found that both structured and unstructured programs produced measurable effects, "but the structured programs were indeed stronger."

Miller (1989) documents the following seven uses of peer tutoring in MG classrooms:

- Drill each other—spelling, math, etc.
- Help other students develop a skill that the tutor possesses
- Build self-esteem of the tutor
- Peer modeling—pushups, song, dancing, etc. (skills)
- Ask a student to explain a concept in "kid language"

- Let a student (or students) teach a chapter in social studies
- Help each other with study skills and researching.

These kinds of tasks can be done anywhere without the help of special learning materials or training. In fact, in Belize over 50 percent of the MG teachers reported the use of peer tutoring. Most instances were cross-age tutoring, involving the use of fifth and sixth graders in helping grades one through three. However, there were also many cases of same-age tutoring, mostly involving fast students helping the slower ones with spelling or arithmetic. Like self-instruction, most of the tutoring was in the skills areas of math and language.

More complex schemes of peer tutoring, such as the "programmed teaching" in the IMPACT projects (Cummings, 1986), involving elaborate patterns of stimulus and response, seem to have suffocated under their own weight. (Nielsen and Cummings, 1985.) It is now clear that simply having the listening ear of older students is an immense help to young readers. In this and many other ways, peer tutors become significant assets in multigrade teaching schools.

Contributors to School Decision-Making, Operations, and Upkeep
Multigrade teaching schools often ask students to be responsible for certain decision making and operational tasks. For example, in the *Escuela Nueva*, youth in student government roles contribute significantly to school goal-setting and planning. (Psacharopoulos, et al., 1993; Schiefelbein, 1992.) Similarly, Reck (1988) notes that small Catholic schools in the U.S. often involve students in school operations such as caring for playground/PE equipment, taking and reporting the lunch/school milk count, operating audio-visual equipment for classes or small groups, or cleaning up the classroom. With respect to school upkeep, one of the chapter authors recalls observing Indonesian primary-school children arrive at school in the early morning in their smart, red-and-white uniforms carrying brooms and plastic buckets, and then proceed, without any teacher direction, to sweep and scrub the school playground and walkways. To these students, school upkeep was a routine, and perfectly natural function.

Such student contributions represent clear assets to the school, and might even be considered a form of student exploitation were it not for the fact that students often learn and grow from performing such tasks, increasing their sense of responsibility and school "ownership."

THE COMMUNITY
The community itself—parents, civic leaders, local merchants or business, the surrounding population of the school—can become a rich asset to the multigrade-teaching school if school personnel know how to work with it effectively. This is not to say that MGT schools are unique in this respect: conventional schools often can and do take advantage of community resources. It does appear that MGT schools are particularly well positioned to take advantage of such resources. For example, at those MGT schools in which service is the social focal point of their communities, community members are likely to congregate at the school often—during and outside of school hours—and develop a first-hand idea of the kind of resources that teachers

need. Reck (1988) suggests that the staffing gaps at MGT schools, particularly in specialty areas such as art, music, sports, and religion, will be clearly visible to community members and leaders. Even when the MGT school does not serve as a community center, smaller schools are likely to be more open and accessible to parents and others than more formal, bureaucratized schools of the mainstream, which often intimidate parents with their aura of professionalism.

This is not to say that parents and communities adjacent to MGT schools in peripheral areas *should* provide a higher proportion of the school resources than they do in more conventional schools in the mainstream. Such a stipulation would be a form of regressive taxation: poorer communities having to contribute more for public services than more prosperous ones. However, spontaneous contributions do frequently occur and effective MG teachers have often found ways to build constructive relationships with community members which benefit both them and the schools. Three ways in which the community can become an asset to the MGT school are by: (a) contributing to school curriculum; (b) providing volunteer teachers; and (c) contributing other services and resources.

Contributing to School Curriculum

Our frequently cited MGT model, *Escuela Nueva* of Colombia, makes special effort to integrate local community themes into the curriculum by involving students *and their parents* in such activities as: "mapping" the school surroundings, constructing family records, creating a county monograph and developing a local agricultural calendar. (Psacharopoulos, et al., 1993.) In compiling these materials, children are using both their parents and the community-at-large as sources of information; once compiled, this information becomes school-based reference material that can be used by the students, teachers, community members, and even community-development agencies. (Schiefelbein, 1992.)

A less formal example of using this kind of community asset, one from Belize, was mentioned above in relation to teacher "coping strategies." In this case, the school principal sought help from the community in creating and nurturing a school garden and livestock project. Community members donated seeds, farm animals, labor, and expertise, and the school staff developed ways of using the garden to teach concepts in science, arithmetic, social studies, vocational skills, and other subjects.

Providing Volunteer Teachers

The use of "voluntary teachers" from the community has been seen as a positive asset in multigrade teaching by various observers. (Lungwangwa, 1989; Miller, 1989; Reck, 1988; Thomas and Shaw, 1992; UNESCO, 1981.) Thomas and Shaw suggest that using parents as teachers' aides and local school graduates as volunteer teaching assistants in MGT schools can "help to breakdown barriers between school and the community . . . .Where parents not only visit the school, but often participate in the social and learning activities, mistrust of the school is often eliminated." (Thomas and Shaw, 1992: 23.) They also cite the benefits of such an arrangement to the school; for example, lightening the workload of the MG teachers, and providing them time to work with remedial groups or individuals. Similarly, Reck (1988) points out how the use of volunteer teachers extends the capacity of the school to teach specialty subjects such as the local language, physical education, art, and gardening skills. Her list of possible fields for voluntary contributions to small Catholic schools in America is impressive:

- Playground and cafeteria/lunchroom supervisor
- Computer supervision and assistance
- Art lessons
- Music sessions
- Physical-education classes
- Service as "room mothers"
- Assistance with seasonal dramatic programs
- Listening to reading
- Leadership of Great Books program
- Driving students to field trips
- Assistance with spelling units
- Testing individuals or small groups
- Conducting mini-courses, e.g.,
    -demonstrating national [or local] customs
    -teaching skills of gardening
    -reading stories of the saints
    -conducting story hours for younger students
- Supervising one grade of a combined classroom during library work
- Filling in when no substitute can be found
- Supervising during a videotape or film
- Following other directions from the teacher
- Helping with the lunch program—baking rolls, making cookies.

Many of these roles assume a rather high level of education and commitment on the part of parents. For communities where parents may be barely literate or even illiterate there are still many possibilities. For one thing, not all volunteers need to be parents. Some of the most effective are older siblings who have already finished their secondary schooling and have returned to the village but are marginally employed. Others may be employees of local government offices or development agencies. A list of actual community contributions and contributors to MGT in a relatively poor country, Belize, is as follows:

Kind of Contributor	Kind of Contribution
• Parents	• Give classes in arts, crafts, sewing
	• Teach classes
• High School graduates	• Teach classes in art and music
• Artists and musicians	• Give science lessons
• Red cross staff member	• Lead activities in health and
• Community Health Workers/ Public Health Officers	nutrition
	• Give talks on local government;
• Mayor; Chair of Village Council	answer questions
• Peace Corp Volunteer	• Lead health and science activities; help with English and language arts

Clearly from the above list, MGT programs attract a variety of voluntary teachers—parents, older siblings, community workers, civil leaders, and international volunteers—in a variety of teaching roles, from total classroom management to answering questions about local government. For small schools in peripheral areas these represent substantial assets.

Contributing Other Services and Resources

Contributions other than those for instruction are also often mentioned. These could be financial contributions (as in Indonesia for hiring "guru honor"), contributions of time and labor (e.g., for school construction or maintenance), and contributions of materials and equipment, such as school furniture. The list by Reck (1988) above includes a number of these kinds of contributions, from maintaining computers to making cookies. Miller's (1991) list includes such items as "provides sources of information regarding culture and values"; "serves as advocate for the school, teachers and programs"; and "serves as an advisor or decision-maker, serving on committees." The latter mode of service is well illustrated in the *Escuela Nueva* program, where, as mentioned above, parents are involved in school-level decision-making. The list in Belize includes the less grandiose item of "cleaning the school." Finally, everyone's list, implicitly or explicitly, also includes parents in their role as monitors of their children's school progress and homework. Once again, such a role is assumed in any kind of school, but with small community schools the opportunities for informal contact between teacher and parents is relatively high, as are the opportunities for informal consultations about student progress.

In the foregoing, we have demonstrated how communities can become rich assets to the MGT school in peripheral areas, by contributing curricular material, volunteer teachers, and other resources. These resources are frequently raised by parents and community members on their own initiative, but more often than not are marshaled by effective, community-oriented school leaders and teachers. As mentioned in our section on teachers, resourceful teachers, particularly those who grew up in small, village schools, can be quite effective at reaching out to and involving the community in the school and its educational mission.

ESCUELA NUEVA: A MULTIGRADE TEACHING SUCCESS STORY

Like other chapters in this volume, which provide case studies of successful innovation in the periphery, this chapter concludes with a full description of *Escuela Nueva* (The New School or EN), as a way of pulling together the various features which have already been mentioned in various sections of this chapter. An even fuller description of this case can be found in Schiefelbein (1992).

After nearly twenty years of development and programmatic evolution, beginning in the mid-1970s, the *Escuela Nueva* has defined its goals for basic learning as follows: reading with understanding, communicating in writing, valuing good citizenship and being able to learn from one's surroundings. Schiefelbein (1992) claims that with 20,000 schools, the *Escuela Nueva* has found solutions for typical multigrade classroom conditions by creatively overcoming problems of space, time, curriculum and specialized teaching practices. The *Escuela Nueva* was created so that pupils could learn at their own pace, and designed in such a way that teachers would not be overwhelmed by planning and organizational demands that would tax even the most highly disciplined teacher.

For example, conditions of space, time, and teaching practices are fully integrated with the curriculum, which has been designed to maximize student learning time either in a whole-class setting or with self- or group-instruction. Learning corners that focus on thematic areas such as language or science are established in the classroom. Space, therefore, is a fundamental yet flexible educational asset for classroom instruction. Seating arrangements can be changed easily and quickly for either task-driven, small-group discussions or for whole-group activities. Moreover, in *Escuela Nueva*, learning activities extend beyond the classroom into the community itself, where pupils may spend considerable time, for example, constructing a map of the village, or taking field trips, and where they interview parents and community members to record and analyze key historical and economic data about the area.

After extensive revision, the architects of *Escuela Nueva* designed a modular curriculum which allows pupils to progress at their own pace. Completing discrete units of instruction reinforces feelings of success for the student in school and permits him or her to participate in crucial family activities when agricultural labor is needed. The curriculum uses many self-instructional approaches, and when problems arise, older pupils can give assistance with guidance from the teacher.

Instead of the teacher being the *source* of knowledge for the students, the curriculum serves as the guide to discovery and inquiry by the students. The teacher's role in *Escuela Nueva* is to act as a facilitator, a motivator and a quality-control expert as pupils complete their curriculum modules. The teacher is also responsible for creating a learning environment that tolerates different points of view and encourages pupils of different abilities and ages to learn together and to assert themselves in a working group.

To focus attention on curricular themes that apply to all grade levels, the teacher will set up activity centers in corners of the classroom, where students can pursue learning tasks in science, language, or reading. These activity centers can be used by the teacher to keep some groups occupied on specific tasks while attending to the instructional needs of other groups. Special learning projects are also regularly set up by the teacher to be pursued at a designated corner, and the results are displayed on the wall of the classroom.

After an initial short-term training period in the basic techniques of *Escuela Nueva*, new teachers continue their training through periodic and regular meetings at designated "resource centers." EN trainers or head teachers help the newer, less experienced teachers share experiences and solve problems. The approach for teachers learning this new set of practices is predicated on the same principles used in the classroom with students: teachers must discover their own ways of handling problems and maximizing opportunities for learning among diverse student groups. However, the discovery process for practitioners is facilitated and enriched by teachers who have had experience using the approach.

Schiefelbein asserts that the inputs required to launch *Escuela Nueva* are more numerous and more expensive than in traditional primary-school settings. The curricular modular materials, books and other supplies, and a minimum of classroom furniture are basic requirements. Many of the materials needed for instruction can be collected from the community in the form of tin cans, waste paper, and the like. The increased costs at the beginning can be more than offset by the subsequent cost reductions associated with lower rates of student repetition and drop-out. (Psacharopoulos, et al., 1993.)

Attempts to launch the *Escuela Nueva* on a broader scale within Colombia and in other countries have begun, but results are mixed and preliminary. In Colombia, first-year drop-outs are still high, and achievement test scores do not reveal significant differences between these schools and the traditional rural schools. However, unlike other reforms that sought to make substantial qualitative improvements in primary education (Shaeffer, 1990), the *Escuela Nueva* project lacked the disorienting effects of multiple foreign donors, abrupt political changes at national and regional levels, and uneven commitment and funding from the government in the earlier phases of its development. The decentralized nature of Colombia's education system, which accords self-governing autonomy to the districts for educational management, is a factor which may have encouraged EN's early successes but may also hamper its efforts to implement the project at the national level. (Hanson, 1986.)

SUMMARY

In this review of multigrade teaching we have tried to shed new light on this surprisingly prevalent form of education. First, we have demonstrated how this is an instructional system with ancient roots, which has been supplanted over the past century by the modern school based on the industrial model of organization. Despite these modernizing tendencies throughout the world, multigrade classrooms are still surprisingly prevalent in today's world, operating in as many as 50 percent of schools in some countries. Although this fact is generally more by default than by design, educators are now beginning to wake up to the benefits of multigrade teaching, especially (but not exclusively) for schools in sparsely populated peripheral areas. Whereas at one time educational planners viewed multigrade teaching as a stop-gap measure to be endured until a legitimate "graded" school could be set up, they are now beginning to recognize that multigrade teaching may be better adapted to certain conditions than conventional schooling. Particularly attractive to them is the fact that students exposed to good multigrade teaching appear to develop more positive attitudes towards themselves, the school and others than those from single-grade classrooms, and also tend to drop out and repeat less. At the same time, multigrade teaching seems to produce achievement comparable to that of conventional schools and costs no more. We suggest that the effective use of multigrade teaching depends on a mind-set change. Instead of viewing the conditions surrounding multigrade teaching as disadvantages, this new mind-set sees them as assets. Using this mind-set, we described the assets for education in *school conditions*, the *teachers*, the *students* and the *community*. Multigrade teaching often takes place in small school buildings having one or few rooms and, at least in the developing countries, modest resources. We demonstrated how children can actually benefit from being in close proximity to those working at different levels of the curriculum; we saw a shortage of commercial learning materials as an invitation to local resourcefulness and exploration of the surrounding environment.

With respect to the teacher, we found that multigrade teaching allows for relatively long and enduring relationships to form between teacher and student, and there are documented cases of extraordinary teacher resourcefulness and dedication. High teacher turnover is a problem in multigrade teaching schools, but those who stay with it—often the hometown teachers—find particular satisfaction in the kind of influence they can have on both students and the community.

Students in the industrial-model schools are essentially taken as raw material to be processes and shaped; in the family-style multigrade teaching school they are considered to be teaching resources. Their contribution to teaching includes various modes of self-instruction and tutoring; in addition, they are frequently involved in school decision-making, operations, and upkeep.

Finally, various forms of community support are used as assets in the effective MGT schools. The limited range of teacher competencies often requires the school to look to the community—parents, siblings, craftsmen/women, public agency workers—for help with specialty subjects like the local language, art, music, sports, health and nutrition, and vocational/skills education. In addition, there is a tendency for close-knit communities to be involved in school decision-making and to volunteer other resources such as tutoring, parent organizations, materials and equipment, and school upkeep. In communities where the school functions as a social focal point, such assets are often provided spontaneously and not as a form of local taxation.

RECOMMENDATIONS

In order for multigrade teaching to play its positive role in the periphery, numerous adjustments in policy and practice are called for. We recommend the following:

1. A mind-set change is needed such that multigrade teaching is accepted as a legitimate form of education in public schools, and not a temporary aberration. With such a mind-set change, the conditions of multigrade teaching can begin to be seen as assets and not as factors to be changed.

2. The benefits and contributions of multigrade teaching should be recognized. In particular, MG teachers who have often spent years in isolation and forced to rely on their own resourcefulness, should be recognized for their extraordinary efforts and contributions.

3. The home-grown methods and coping strategies that good MG teachers have developed over the years should be studied and documented such that they can be available to other teachers and teacher educators as exemplary practice.

4. Multigrade teaching should be officially recognized as a legitimate form of education so schools using the approach can be allocated appropriate resources and be covered by appropriate regulations. This does not imply the development of a "standard MGT model," since that would subvert the ideal of local problem-solving and adaptation, but at least it would mean providing the legal basis for elements such as peer instruction and use of community volunteers in the classroom.

5. Where multigrade teaching is practiced and legitimated, teacher education, pre- and in-service, should be modified accordingly. This means preparing teachers for work in multigrade teaching settings and mounting refresher/inservice courses in order to assist practicing teachers in overcoming the barriers they encounter. Following the lead of certain programs in Australia, some teacher candidates could be assigned to do their student teaching in MGT schools.

6. Multigrade teaching should be managed by school system administrators in a systemic manner. This implies more than acceptance of a particular form of classroom organization and instructional approach. It also implies adjustment of policies in areas such as:

- teacher recruitment, deployment and training (recruiting locals and placing them in familiar settings after appropriate preparation);
- school language policies (allowing instruction in the local language, using volunteer teachers if necessary);
- curriculum and materials design (using more integrated approaches; substituting self-instructional or locally constructed materials for conventional texts);
- school-governance procedures (involving both the community and the students in schoolwide decision-making); and
- school financing plans (providing block grants to allow flexibility in resource allocation; use of community resources).

The survival of multigrade teaching as a strategy for extending high-quality education to those in the periphery depends in a very real sense on the development of such linkages across components of the educational system. It is a central message of this chapter and of this book.

Endnotes

1. Data on multigrade teaching in Belize was collected by the second author during 1991-92 under the Learning Technologies Project funded by the U.S. Agency for International Development and managed by Educational Development Center of Newton, Mass. The data analyses have not yet been released in published form, so much of the information about multigrade teaching in Belize is being published here for the first time. A more complete version of the findings can be found in an unpublished manuscript by H. Dean Nielsen, entitled "Multigrade Teaching in Belize: Current Practice, Teacher Attitudes, and Student Achievement" (Institute for International Research, 1992).

2. Today this list would almost certainly include a telephone and modem attached to a computer for use in Internet communications.

Bibliography

Adair, James H. "An Attitude and Achievement Comparison between Kindergarten and First Grade Children in Multi and Single Grade Classes." *Dissertation Abstracts International* 39 (1978): 659A-660A.

Adams, Joseph J. "Achievement and Social Adjustment of Pupils in Combination Class Enrolling Pupils of More Than One Grade Level." *Journal of Educational Research*, v 47 (1953):151-155.

Barker, Bruce O. "Where Two or Three Are Gathered Together: A Profile of the One-Teacher Schools." *Texas Tech. Journal of Education*, v 13, n 1 (1986).

Bray, Mark. *Are Small Schools the Answer? Cost-Effective Strategies for Rural School Provision.* Commonwealth Secretariat, University of Hong Kong, 1987.

Chace, Earl S. *An Analysis of Some Effects of Multiple Grade Grouping in an Elementary School.* Unpublished doctoral dissertation. University of Tennessee, 1961.

Cohen, Peter, James A. Kulik, and Chen-Lin C. Kulik. "Educational Outcomes of Tutoring: A Meta-Analysis of Findings." *American Educational Research Journal* (1982): 237-247.

Cremin, L.A. *The Transformation of the School: Progressivism in American Education 1867-1957.* New York: Vintage Books, 1961.

Cummings, William K. *Low-Cost Primary Education: Implementing an Innovation in Six Nations.* Ottawa, Canada: International Development Research Centre, 1986.

Dove, Linda A. "The Development and Training of Teachers for Remote Rural Schools in Less Developed Countries: Aids to Programming UNICEF Assistance to Education." New York: Unit for Cooperation with UNICEF and WFP, 1985.

Drier, William H.. "The Differential Achievement of Rural Graded and Ungraded School Pupils." *Journal of Educational Research,* v 43 (1949): 175-185.

Foote, John M. "A Comparative Study of Instruction in Consolidated and One-Teacher Schools." *The Journal of Rural Education*, v 2, n 8 (1923).

Fuller, Wayne, E. *The Old Country School: The Story of Rural Education in the Middle West.* Chicago, IL: University of Chicago Press, 1982.

Government of Pakistan, Planning Commission. *The 7th Five-Year Plan, 1988-1993, and Perspective Plan 1988-2003,* v II, 1988.

Hanson, M. *Educational Reform and Administrative Development: the Cases of Colombia and Venezuela*. Stanford, CA: Hoover Institution Press, 1986.

Harvey, Sidney B. "A Comparison of Kindergarten Children in Multigrade and Traditional Settings on Self-Concept, Socio-Emotional Development, Readiness Development, and Achievement." Unpublished doctoral dissertation. Virginia Polytechnic Institute and State University, 1974.

Knight, Elton E. "A Study of Double Grades in New Haven City Schools." *Journal of Experimental Education*, v 7 (1938): 11-18.

LeVine, Robert A. and Merry I. White. *Human Conditions: The Cultural Basis of Educational Development*. New York: Routledge and Kegan Paul, 1986.

Lincoln, Robert D. *The Effect of Single-Grade and Multi-Grade Primary School Classroom on Reading Achievement of Children*. Unpublished doctoral dissertation. University of Connecticut, 1981.

Lungwangwa, G. *Multigrade Schools in Zambian Primary Education: A Report on the Pilot Schools in Mkushi District*. Stockholm: Swedish International Development Authority, Educational Division, 1989.

MacDonald P.A. and S.R. Wurster. *Multiple Grade Primary Versus Segregated First Grade: Effects on Reading Achievement*. Bethesda, MD. ERIC Document Reproduction Service, No. ED094336, 1974.

Marshall, D.G. "Closing Small Schools: Or When Is Small Too Small?" *Education Canada*, v 25, n 3 (1985).

Matthes, W.A. and Robert V. Carlson. "Why Do Teachers Choose Rural Schools?" *The Education Digest*, v 52 (February, 1987).

Miller, Bruce A. *The Multigrade Classroom: A Resource Handbook for Small, Rural Schools*. Portland, OR: Northwest Regional Educational Laboratory, 1989.

———. *Distress and Survival: Rural Schools, Education, and the Importance of Community*. Portland, OR: Northwest Regional Educational Laboratory, 1991.

Monk, D.H. and E.J. Haller. *Organizational Alternatives for Small Rural Schools: Final Report to the Legislature of the State of New York*. New York: Cornell University, 1986.

Morrison, J. Cayce. "Comparative Study of Instruction in Consolidated and One Room Rural Schools in New York State." *The Journal of Rural Education*, v 1, n 8 (1922).

Nash, Roy. *Schooling in Rural Societies.* London: Metheun, 1980.

Nielsen, H. Dean. "Using Distance Education to Extend and Improve Teaching in Developing Countries." In *Perspectives on Education for All.* Ottawa, Canada: International Development Research Centre, 1991.

Nielsen, H. Dean, and William K. Cummings. "The Impact of IMPACT: A Study of the Dissemination of an Innovation in Six Countries." Mimeo. Ottawa, Canada: International Development Research Centre, 1985.

Nielsen, H. Dean, and H.A. Somerset. *Primary Teachers in Indonesia: Supply, Distribution, and Professional Development.* Washington, DC: The World Bank, 1992.

Pratt, D. "On the Merits of Multiage Classrooms." *Research in Rural Education,* v 3, n 3 (1986).

Psacharopoulos, George, Carlos Rojas, and Eduardo Velez. "Achievement Evaluation of Colombia's *Escuela Nueva.*" *Comparative Education Review,* v 37, n 3 (1993): 263-276.

Reck, C. *The Small Catholic Elementary School: Advantages and Opportunities,* Washington, DC: National Catholic Educational Association, 1988.

Schiefelbein, Ernesto. *Redefining Basic Education for Latin America: Lessons to be Learned from the Colombian Escuela Nueva.* Paris: International Institute for Educational Planning, UNESCO, 1992.

Shaeffer, Sheldon. *Educational Change in Indonesia: A Case Study of Three Innovations.* Ottawa, Canada: International Development Research Centre, 1990.

———. *Schooling in a Developing Society: A Case Study of Primary Education.* Unpublished doctoral dissertation. Stanford, CA: Stanford University, 1979.

Thomas, Christopher and Christopher Shaw . "Issues in the Development of Multigrade Schools." (DRAFT.) Washington, DC: The World Bank, 1992.

UNDP, UNESCO, UNICEF, and World Bank. *World Declaration on Education for All and Framework for Action to Meet Basic Learning Needs.* Jomtien, Thailand, March 5-9, 1990.

UNESCO. *Education of Disadvantaged Groups and Multiple Class Teaching: Studies and Innovative Approaches*. Bangkok: Asian Programme of Educational Innovation for Development (APEID), 1981.

———. *Education in Difficult Contexts: Report of a Technical Working Group Meeting on Training of Primary Education Personnel*. Bangkok: Asian Programme of Educational Innovation for Development (APEID), 1987.

———. *Multigrade Teaching in Single Teacher Primary Schools*. Bangkok: UNESCO Regional Office for Education in Asia and the Pacific, 1989.

Warwick, Donald, F. Reimers and N. McGinn. "Teacher Characteristics and Student Achievement in Math and Science." Papers on Primary Education in Pakistan, Report #5, BRIDGES Casual Papers. Cambridge, MA: Harvard Institute for International Development, 1989.

Way, Joyce. W. *The Effects of Multiage Grouping on Achievement and Self-Concept*. Cortland: State University of New York, Cortland College, Institute for Experimentation in Teacher Education, 1969.

Managing Change

CHAPTER 8

Management Initiatives for Reaching the Periphery

William K. Cummings

The *Background Document* for the World Conference on Education for All (UNDP, UNESCO, UNICEF, and World Bank, 1990a), prepared specifically to identify approaches for reaching the periphery, devotes one-quarter of its text to management strategies that can be executed at the national level.[1] But are the strategies identified in this document sound?

Interestingly, of all the national-level management ideas proposed by the drafters of the *Background Document*, only the proposal to "Strengthen Partnerships" was finally incorporated in the World Declaration (UNDP, UNESCO, UNICEF, and World Bank, 1990b). This suggests considerable ferment concerning "what works" in the improvement of educational management. The fact is, we really are not sure.[2] This chapter seeks to depict that uncertainty by contrasting two management approaches and their implications.[3] With respect to each, we ask the following questions:

- What combinations of school and higher-level management initiatives will be most effective for reaching the periphery?
- What management initiatives will, along with improving access and learning, also promote greater efficiency in the use of scarce resources?

MANAGEMENT MODELS
Management consists of those activities that secure, direct, and energize people and resources for the realization of common values. There are various ways to carry out these activities.

Modern Management
Much of current understanding about management activities derives from an approach that emerged in the nineteenth century as modern states attempted to assert control over large territories and expand their authority. The modern state had a mission, to impose its culture—so often hostile to church, to local values—on as wide an area as possible, neutralizing (or even eliminating) traditional culture. The state was successful to the extent that many people bought into the state's values. In most instances, the state had been established by the bourgeoisie and it served their interests; as the bourgeois class expanded, so did the state's penetration. The state even reached beyond its original base. But at a certain point, the state encountered a

zone of indifference and even of resistance—what James Williams calls a "low demand" setting. At that point, the state's effort to push modern culture slowed. The modern state provided various services, but with the aim of reciprocating loyalty. It sought to be efficient in the provision of these services, which led to a willingness to hold back on effort when faced with obstacles, as in the periphery.

Over the course of the modern period, several styles emerged. For example in Continental Europe and later in Japan and the socialist nations, a centralized approach emerged. In contrast, in England and the United States, authority was located in local governments. (Cummings and Riddell, 1994.) But within the respective levels of authority, there were considerable similarities in the basic principles of management.[4]

The modern model involves a top-down multilevel management structure. While primarily designed for other sectors (notably the military and the capitalist manufacturing sector), this model has been widely adopted in the developing world for the delivery of education. In the educational sector, its objectives can be characterized as follows:

- Management arranges for the construction of schools in as many locations as is feasible.
- Central Management designs the inputs for these schools with particular stress on a centralized, integrated, and highly nationalistic curriculum; and the provision of teachers who believe in the main tenets of this curriculum.
- Management delivers inputs to the schools.
- Management establishes a system of top-down supervision in an effort to insure that the inputs are correctly deployed according to central guidelines.

This modern approach has resulted in much expansion of educational opportunity—but it may have reached its limit. As other chapters of this volume note, management costs are increasing and enrollments are peaking.

The visible indicator of the modern approach's limit is the failure to realize education for all; in most nations, enrollment ratios have plateaued with only three-quarters of the young children in school. Another sign of this failure is the growing level of alienation among those enrolled. The modern management model, while professing to offer equal educational opportunity to all citizens (in France) or subjects (in Prussia) was and is, in fact, geared towards instilling loyalty and docility in the commoner while biasing educational opportunities towards the urban middle class. The modern model is not for the periphery. The main problem is its isolation from the public.

Peripheral Community Model

In contrast to the modern model we will seek, in the second half of this chapter, to outline a new approach for educational management, which we tentatively call the Community-Oriented Model (or Theory C). This approach is advanced specifically for education, though it has wider applications. Theory C, to be outlined here, views communities (the pupils and their parents) as full partners in the educational or human-development endeavor. It proposes a fundamental reordering of existing management systems:

- Management starts with the needs of the periphery rather than the goals of the center.
- It focuses on strengthening value-knowledge rather than producing and distributing products.
- It responds directly and flexibly to different needs rather than by uniform regulation.

Many recent management reforms (and related theories) include elements of Theory C.[5] Here we will examine why Theory C is emerging as the preferred or inevitable management approach, and some of the steps or initiatives that go into institutionalizing this new approach. We will especially focus on the implications of Theory C for access, learning, and efficiency.

THE MODERN APPROACH

The Strategic Role of Management

At the outset, it is essential to recognize that managers have come to occupy a central role in modern educational systems, and thus it can be said they have a strategic role in the current educational quagmire.

In early times, strong rulers or parties—or in corporations, strong owner-rulers—set up the modern organizations. These self-appointed rulers thought of themselves as spokesmen for the people. Management was hired to merely implement the ruler's program.

But over time, management became more professionalized, and thus was able to show greater initiative. Adding to the authority of management were the civil-service reforms that resulted in increased competence in management ranks.

Management continued to be responsible to the official government, whether hereditary or elected. But at least in certain sectors, including education, the government came to defer in an ever-wider range of decisions to the top managers, as they devoted full time to their task and were in command of the requisite information and people.

Management, over time, divided its tasks into subgroups that become the responsibility of distinctive units. In education, the following is a typical list of differentiated tasks that management seeks to realize in order to deliver modern education:

- Fiscal—through taxes, user fees
- Information—through census, registration, surveys
- Professional—through civil service
- Soft technology—through curriculum committees, textbook production
- Physical plant—through school construction service

But with the growth in the scale of education comes the growth of the management bureaucracy, and often an increasing isolation from clients. Thus, the problems in realizing these tasks multiply.

In the realm of education, in the first modern societies this style of management had already reached its limit by the first decade of the twentieth century. But it was diffused more broadly to developing countries so that it still achieved gains into the seventies—before education experienced a global Waterloo.

The Limitations of Modern Management

The indications of modern management's crisis are manifold. Some of the key areas are as follows:

Class Bias of Modern Education

The modern state was typically formed by the rising middle class for their benefit. Thus in education, major stress was placed on secondary and especially higher education to provide access to jobs in the modern sector, in large corporations and the civil service. The major public-educational institutions were typically established in or near large cities, and the schools most successful in sending students to these schools were also primarily urban. In some nations, unit costs for the universities are 80 times greater than for the primary schools.

Critics of this urban bias have proposed a major reallocation of public funding towards basic education, with tertiary education relying more on user fees. (Windham, 1992.) But these proposals have often met with resistance from the established classes. Thus an alternate proposal has been to encourage "Community Support of Schools," assuming that communities will be willing to support schools they control. (Kemmerer, 1990.)

Modern managers seem unwilling to give up a system that directly benefits their own class interests. Where modern management is in place, the only hope for the periphery may be their own initiative outside of the established system.

Lack of Appropriate Knowledge

Modern education is essentially a system of schools, and relies primarily on the components of this system for its information. Schools fill out periodic reports on their needs and on local conditions, which higher levels review as a basis for planning and procurement. In the early stages of the establishment of schools, local governments and communities may also have been sources of information concerning where to establish schools and what needed to be taught. But once some initial decisions were made on school location, these external sources of information were replaced by the internal sources, the schoolmasters and supervisors.

However, the existing separation between information gatherers and final users of services inevitably leads to knowledge gaps. Population shifts can result in some local areas having less demand that originally envisioned, whereas others have more.

In several Central American countries, a different problem has become evident. Education officials make assumptions on the internal efficiency of the system through computation of school reports on drop-out and repetition rates. What the officials fail to take into account is that dropouts from one school often drop back in to another school. Surveys of parents readily reveal a pattern of behavior that officials have, for many decades, ignored. The policy implications are profound, as indicated in the following box:

Box 8.1. Central Statistical Units Often Overestimate Drop-out Rates

Studies conducted in many Third World countries have shown that the information collected by ministries of education from schools regarding student enrollment is fairly reliable. The information on student repetition, however, tends to be less reliable. The reason that repetition rates are not accurate is because many schools do not require the students to show their school certificate when they enroll at the beginning of the academic year. To record the number of repeaters, schools must rely on the teachers' recollection of who was enrolled in each grade during the previous year, or on students' own reporting. Sometimes students do not even know what it means to be a repeater, especially students in lower grades.

Because of the weakness of the repeater data, an alternate means for determining their numbers is to rely on an age/grade formula that relies on standard school statistics. This method was used to design a simulation model for estimating promotion, repetition, and dropout rates in six Central American countries. In all six countries the model produced repetition rates that were higher than the official estimates published by the ministries of education. Correspondingly, the model produced lower drop-out rates. The reliability of this model was confirmed with a field study in Honduras which asked parents about their children's behavior. The magnitude of error in official estimates is substantial. For example, whereas the official estimate was of a 46 percent drop-out rate, the simulation model and the parent survey arrived at an estimated drop-out rate of 11 percent.

The implication of this study is that official policies, heavily directed to reducing drop-out rates, might better be directed to other educational issues.

Source: Ernesto Cuadra, *Indicators of Student Flow Rates in Honduras: An Assessment of an Alternative Methodology*. BRIDGES Research Report Series No. 6 (December 1989).

Fiscal Limits

Perhaps the clearest indication has been the increasing difficulty of obtaining revenues to realize the plans of the modern managers. In lieu of taxing an unwilling public, these managers in recent decades have turned with increasing frequency to deficit funding drawing on loans from commercial and international banks. While the managers expected substantial returns from these investments, they were often disappointed. The extent of this disappointment has been well documented; all too frequently national economies, rather than taking off, went into a tailspin. And governments were saddled with heavy debt servicing burdens that crippled new initiatives.

Under the banner of decentralization, modern managers have sought to shift more of the financial burden to regional and local governments as well as the direct users of public services. But these steps have often encountered resistance. Local groups, accustomed to the former pattern of centralized subsidies, ask why they should be required to pay for something they did not create. Thus, fiscal decentralization has often failed.

Dependence is Fostered

While local communities once provided their own schools, the modern state moved in to offer its own form of education at little or no cost. Over time, local communities came to accept this service as a natural right. Local communities thus abandoned their earlier autonomous efforts to provide educational services. A condition emerged at the grass-roots level of accepting what the center provided rather than considering what was needed. The local community gradually lost its ability to act on its own.

Poor Distribution of Resources

Modern management systems seem to have greater success in distributing hardware (things that can be counted, such as school buildings and furniture) than software (know-how and training). From the point of view of the central office of a modern school system, schools need a range of inputs which include buildings, principals, teachers, books, supplies, etc. In principle it would seem that each of these inputs could be provided in an equally effective way. But among these several inputs, central offices tend to place the highest priority on personnel—because these inputs are also part of the educational system and they have a habit of talking back. The higher priority on personnel means that other inputs are often neglected. Thus schools are more likely to have teachers than books or other instructional aids.

Inequity in Distribution

The modern organization distributes resources through a hierarchical bureaucracy, whose local offices are typically located in regional towns. Inputs move down from the center through these local offices and out to the schools. The members of these local offices have a keen interest in the process of distribution, for it has a direct impact on the quality of their lives. In a context of scarcity or of tardiness in the supply of inputs, these local officials are likely to bias the process of distributions so that their immediate locale reaps the greatest benefits. A recent study of teacher distribution in Indonesia shows an extraordinary inequity in teacher placement, with some rural schools getting only one teacher per one hundred pupils, while some urban schools had one per ten pupils.

Lack of Professionalism

Supervision is presumably a critical element in the provision of inputs and their effective utilization. The modern organization tends to recruit capable people for these supervisory tasks, individuals who have demonstrated a strong record as principals and teachers. But often the tasks assigned the supervisors are poorly defined, and, moreover, the supervisors are not given adequate resources to accomplish these tasks. A common example is school visitation; supervisors may be assigned responsibility for from fifty to one hundred schools over a wide area, but not provided with either transportation or a travel budget. Hence the supervisors can't get around, and even if they can, they find that in the time available they can make no more than superficial contributions. [6]

Box 8.2. Disparities in Teacher Placement by Local Educational Offices in Indonesia

Overall, Indonesia makes generous provision for staffing its primary schools. The national pupil:teacher ratio is 23.24, and the national teacher:class ratio is 1.14.

The problems of primary-teacher provision in Indonesia are essentially problems of distribution rather than of supply. In aggregate there is a plentiful supply of teachers, but many of them are teaching in the wrong places. "Pockets of shortage" frequently exist alongside "pockets of oversupply."

Teacher distribution is executed and hence can be analyzed at four levels: national level to provinces, provinces to regencies (*kabupaten/kotamadya*), regencies to districts (*kecamatan*), and districts to schools. The higher levels are mainly responsible for distribution while decisions on transfers are mainly made at the lower levels.

An Interquartile Ratio was used to determine the equality of distribution at each of these levels. The ratio compares the pupil-teacher ratio of the lower quartile of schools with that of the highest. Perfect equality between quartiles would be an index of 1.0, with higher levels indicating greater inequality. The following are the results by level:

Distribution Level	IQR	(n)
1. National to province	1.35	1
2. Province to regency	1.47	27
3. Regency to district	1.63	256
4. District to school	2.76	36

It is clear that processes at the central levels tend to distribute teachers more evenly than processes at more local levels. In the 36 districts for which data was available, the most favored quartile of pupils have, on average, about two-and-three-quarters more pupils per teacher than the least favored quartile.

Source: H. Dean Nielsen and H.A. Somerset. *Primary Teachers in Indonesia: Supply, Distribution, and Professional Development.* Washington, DC: The World Bank, 1992.

Overload at the Local Level

The school is one outpost of the modern state. But distinct from the modern school system typically managed by a central ministry of education, the state provides a number of other services that have local implications, some virtually duplicating the mission of the school. Among these are local centers for adult education that teach literacy and skills, local health and family planning centers, and local youth programs. In some settings, the diversity of local programs causes confusion. For example, in Indonesia at one point there were four competing programs to teach job skills and crafts to rural people. This overlap in the outputs of the modern state reflects a lack of integration and a high degree of competitiveness to create programs and command budgets at the center. But the local level may not have been consulted in the planning of these programs, resulting in confusion and overload.

These limitations are more extreme in some settings than others. The fiscal difficulties are very evident in the poorer countries. In some of the more developed countries such as the U.S., the fiscal difficulties are more localized, leading to regional disparities. In East Asia, the modern system, being introduced later than in other regions, is still functioning reasonably well. Yet even there, major difficulties are now being encountered in responding to the new challenges of urbanization and technical change.

Reforming Modern Management

The limitations of modern management have long been recognized, and the standard approach has been to propose improvements. A first step towards identifying weaknesses in management systems is a careful "situational analysis" (alternately called a "sector assessment").

Insights from Sector Assessments

The 1988 Liberian Sector Assessment provides a typical example:

> The assessment begins by asserting that "school enrollments in Liberia are dropping, due to a series of economic, fiscal and managerial problems being encountered in the education sector." Specifically, the assessment observes there is "a lack of management capacity at both the school and Ministry level. This is manifest in the lack of data for planning and management of primary education, the lack of communications between schools and the Ministry, and in poor utilization of donor funding and lack of donor coordination." The lack of management capacity is said to be "manifest in the lack of effective supervision of the schools and by the lack of information to support resource allocation, planning and program implementation decisions." The assessment concludes with recommendations for centralizing management, improving the management information system, and management training. (Chapman, 1992.)

Diagnoses of this kind have provided the background for management reforms in various countries. Box 8.3 below provides a thumbnail summary of 14 management reforms that were initiated over the past two decades in a variety of national settings. In the following sections, we would like to look in more detail at several examples.

Box 8.3. Recent Instances of Management Reforms

Bangladesh, 1980s **Supervision** **Lockheed and Verspoor, 1990**
A group of *Upazilla* Education Officers were appointed to intensify supervision through both scheduled training sessions and surprise visits. Teacher absenteeism was significantly reduced.

Colombia, mid-1970s *Escuela Nueva* **Rojas and Castillo, 1975**
The government developed a new multigrade approach to basic education called *Escuela Nueva*, which involved strong participation. A parent committee worked with the student council on joint projects to improve the school and curriculum. *Escuela Nueva* has led to significant increases in access, educational quality, and student self-esteem.

Costa Rica, mid-1970s **Nuclearization** **Olivera, 1983**
To overcome the dismal state of rural schools, networks of five schools were linked to "nuclei" to share a library, teaching aides, workshops, and certain administrative services. Nuclearization helped to empower and motivate teachers, and resulted in a curriculum more relevant to local needs.

India, 1980s **Multilevel Planning** **Mathus, 1983**
With the sixth Five-Year Development Plan (1981-1986), India shifted major responsibilities for the planning and implementation of educational programs to the district level. The shortage of personnel and the separation of educational planning from that of other sectors have prevented the full benefits of this shift from being realized.

Madagascar, late 1970s **Regional Offices** **Razafindrakoto, 1979**
The 1975 Constitution recognized communities as the basic unit of government. Each community was expected to build a primary school and develop syllabi responsive to local needs. With the central government subsidies for school construction, significant increases in primary-school enrollments were achieved.

Malaysia, 1980s **Training** **Lockheed and Verspoor, 1990**
The National Institute of Educational Management was established to improve the planning and management capabilities of school managers. The Institute was able to develop an inexpensive and popular set of courses that attracted far more applicants than originally anticipated.

Mexico, 1980s **Decentralization** **McGinn and Street, 1986**
An official program to transfer control of funds to the state level was found to have little impact on the actual operation of schools. The reform was introduced to strengthen the power of the new government vis-à-vis State educational officers, as a way to circumvent the entrenched bureaucracy.

Box 8.3. Continued

Nigeria, 1980s   **Community Schools**   **Okeye, 1986**
Facing a rising demand for secondary education and declining revenues, the State acceded to community requests to build their own schools. The communities were able to build the schools at low cost through voluntary labor and donated materials. The outcome was a rapid but geographically uneven expansion of secondary education.

Papua New Guinea, late-1970s   **Clusters**   **Bray, 1987**
The primary responsibility for the planning and reconstruction of schools was shifted to the provincial level. Given significant variations in regional resources, this has heightened regional inequalities in access to education, and in quality.

Peru, 1970s   **Microplanning**   **Ruiz-Duran, 1983**
In 1972, Peru was divided into Community Education Nuclei (25 schools per nucleus), where important planning and administrative decisions were to be made. However, lack of power, funds, and appropriate training for staff prevented them from taking on new responsibilities.

Sri Lanka, 1980s   **Clusters Reorganization**   **Bray, 1987**
Clusters of between 10 and 15 schools were established, and cluster principals were appointed to coordinate resource-sharing, joint training, and intermural activities. The change improved student achievement in the weaker schools.

Swaziland, 1980s   **Training**   **UNESCO, 1987**
To improve the performance of a recently privatized system, a program of headmaster training was established to improve school-based skills in financial and resource management, curriculum development, and evaluation.

Tanzania, 1970s   **Integrated Planning**   **Mapuri, 1983**
Integrated planning for all sectors, including education, incorporated inputs from a decentralized administrative structure into local village councils. To help carry out their plans, village councils were given power to raise revenue and recruit personnel. The reform had a positive impact on school enrollments, but suffered from a shortage of capable personnel and administrative ambiguities.

Thailand, 1980s   **Training, EMIS**   **Wheeler et al., 1989**
A selected group of "effective" principals developed an inservice training course for their peers, which involved modules, videos, slides, and practical exercises. Principals who failed a post-training test had to repeat it until they were successful.

Source: William K. Cummings (ed.), "Reaching Peripheral Groups: Community, Language and Teachers in the Context of Development," *Special Studies in Comparative Education, No. 31.* New York: State University of New York at Buffalo, 1993.

Management Information Systems
One of the most consistent themes in modern management reform is to improve the quality of information available to managers. Knowledge gaps, it is argued, lie behind many of the failures of modern education:

> It is only by using resources (both financial and human) more efficiently that educational systems can provide greater opportunities for learning. The only way to evaluate a system's efficiency is by establishing "objectively verifiable indicators" or benchmarks. Objectively verifiable indicators are quantitative measures that indicate the nature of change, its direction, and its extent. A simple example of benchmark data is female enrollment statistics. (Windham, 1991.)

Existing information systems collect information on the inputs to schools, but fail to consider what schools do with these inputs. Thus, MIS reformers propose the collection of new information to focus on process and outputs. An expert group has proposed a three-phase schema for improving management information systems, and has pioneered in reforming MIS in a number of countries. The key indicators of the MIS they recommend are identified in Table 8.1 below.

Accountability
It would be a great mistake to ignore the challenge involved in improving the quality of information available to managers. There have been many attempts, yet remarkably few successes, and invariably these successes required far more effort and time than was originally envisioned. A group under the sponsorship of USAID has been working in Egypt for over ten years, and only recently has begun to see encouraging examples of information-based decisions. Even so, the quality of information collected is still suspect, and the turn-around time from local collection to utilization at the local level is nearly a year; central utilization typically begins a year and a half after collection. (Cassidy,1990.)

However in some systems, considerable strides have been taken to develop information that is both comprehensive and reliable. Thailand provides an interesting example. Relative to most developing societies, Thailand has a large cadre of highly educated and research-oriented officials who have been experimenting with MIS innovations for nearly two decades; moreover, the computer culture has caught on in the broader society so that there are a number of young staff who feel comfortable with the new information technologies.

Concern for the quality of basic education led Jordan's National Centre for Educational Research and Development (NCERD) to create a national system for monitoring and assessing the achievement of fourth-grade pupils. Box 8.4 (following the table) describes this system and reports on some student achievement outcomes and their implications.

Table 8.1. Seven Indicators of Efficiency: Benchmark Data For Three Phases of Development

Efficiency Indicators	Phase I	Phase II (phase I data plus the following)	Phase III (ph. I & II data plus following
1. Student characteristics	• Enrollment by school • Gender ratios • Progression rates (aggregate only)	• Gender data cross-tabulated with size-of-place & region • Ethnic distribution • Detail by level and type of program • Separate repetition and attrition rates • Age distrib.	• Subject or course specialization • Attitudinal and behavioral measures • Time use
2. Teacher and administrator characteristics	• Distribution by qualifications • Student-teacher ratios	• Qualifications and distribution, including specializations • Age and experience • Distribution by location • Students per administrator • Turnover rates and incidence of absenteeism	• Time use • Training needs • Interaction with community • Job satisfaction
3. Curriculum/ educational materials	• Textbook availability • Regional and size- of-place distrib.	• Textbook availability and use • Availability of support materials • Status of curriculum development and dissemination	• Knowledge of curriculum by administrators and teachers • Users' evaluations of curriculum and materials • Evaluation of alternative instructional technologies

4. Facilities/ equipment	• Number of "complete" schools • Students/school • Students/class	• Facilities use by level and program • Equip. availability • Distribution of special-use facilities	• Equipment use • Needs analysis • Maintenance and replacement projections
5. Student achievement	• National exam pass rates • Promotion rates	• Examination scores and pass rates cross-tabulated with student and school characteristics • Attainment distributions by student and school characteristics • Promotion rates by student and school characteristics	• Determinants of educational outputs • Determinants of inequalities • Analysis of high- and low-achieving schools
6. Education and training outcomes	• No data	• Earnings from public employment • Employment (aggregate) by level of education • Tracer studies of secondary-school and higher education graduates	• Net present value estimates by level and type of education • Studies of graduate attitudes and behaviors • Job search rates by level and type of graduate
7. Costs	• Teacher salaries by qualifications • Aggregate budget data • Cost per student by level of education	• Ingredients-approach cost calculated for each level and type of program • Unit and cycle cost for all programs	• Detailed cost-analysis of major programs and alternative technologies • Cost projections by level and type of education

Source: Douglas M. Windham, "Indicators of Educational Efficiency," *Forum for Advancing Basic Education and Literacy,* 1991: 3.

Box 8.4. Assessment of Learning Achievement of Grade Four Students in Jordan

Aware of the importance of monitoring the quality of education, UNICEF and UNESCO launched an initiative to encourage several countries to develop national systems for the monitoring and assessment of learning achievement. Jordan is one of five countries that participated from the beginning, monitoring and assessing the achievement of fourth-grade pupils in order to evaluate learning achievement with respect to the Education for All goals.

Achieving the goals of Education for All requires the fulfillment of two basic conditions:

- The provision of essential educational facilities for all.
- Effective mechanisms to ensure basic educational skills.

For the collection and evaluation of information related to the expansion and reach of the educational system, the National Centre for Educational Research and Development (NCERD), in cooperation with the Ministry of Education, maintains a comprehensive educational database and an Educational Management Information System (EMIS).

The main focus of this monitoring evaluation is the measurement of achievement levels among primary students, with the fourth grade targeted in this particular analysis. The study focuses on both direct (short-term) and indirect (long-term) objectives.

The direct objectives include the following:
- Measuring learning achievement in the: Arabic language, mathematics, science, and life skills.
- Studying the family backgrounds of the students.
- Studying the instructional practices of the teachers.
- Studying school characteristics.
- Studying students' attitudes.

The indirect objectives include the following:

- Building up the national capacity for monitoring educational progress.
- Institutionalizing the evaluation function by establishing a mechanism for monitoring learning achievement at regular intervals.
- Establishing a channel of communication and promoting dialogue between the parties responsible for evaluation research and educational planning.
- Establishing an Educational Management Information System (EMIS).

Box 8.4. Continued

After considering the statistical, financial, and practical aspects, it was decided that a random sample of 245 schools would be adequate for the monitoring exercise. The schools selected were examined to ensure that they adequately represented a broad range with respect to the following areas of interest: school size, location, gender (whether male, female or co-educational), and governorate.

Learning achievement in Jordan had to be measured within the context of the ongoing Education Reform Plan (ERP), which is aimed at raising the quality of basic education. The achievement tests were thus designed, inter alia, to establish current achievement levels among students, with the results serving as the base-line data against which future progress could be measured. Other purposes included comparing the achievements of different groups of students, and studying regional, locational, and gender differences in student achievement.

Results

Arabic. An Arabic language test was administered to 4,908 fourth-grade students in 205 schools, representing all of the educational authorities and governorates in Jordan. The average test score was 54.19 (out of a possible score of 100). The total scores of the upper 10 percent of students ranged from 84 to 100, i.e. from 91 to 100 in reading, from 85.4 to 100 in dictation, and from 82.3 to 100 in grammar.

Results showed that students in the Amman governorate outperformed the students of other governorates, with Kerak scoring lowest. Results also indicated that the performance of female students was higher than that of male students, with total female scores averaging 57 percent against 51 percent for males.

Science. A science test was given to 2,412 fourth-grade students in 205 schools. The total scores averaged about 42 per cent. The performance of the top 10 percent of students ranged from 60 to 100 percent. There were some in the bottom 10 percent who failed to answer any of the test items correctly. Again, the total scores of the female students were significantly higher than those of the males, with females scoring an average of 43 percent, against 40 percent for male students.

Mathematics. This test was administered to 2,428 students in 205 schools. The national average on the test was 30 percent, reflecting low performance overall. The results of male and female students did not show a significant difference.

Life skills. This test was given to 4,776 fourth-grade students in 205 schools. Results indicated that the national average score was 61.2 percent. The test included questions relating to health and nutrition, environment, daily behavior and civic education. Results show that the Amman governorate's performance was much higher than that of students in the other governorates.

Source: Final Report of the "Joint UNICEF-NCERD-UNESCO Regional Seminar on Monitoring Learning Achievement," held in Amman, July 23-26, 1994.

Supervision

Of course, in many educational systems it is difficult to collect and evaluate information on school performance, at least on a nationwide basis. Regions may speak different languages, or the infrastructure for the rapid communication of information may not be in place.

IMPROVING THE QUALITY OF SUPERVISION. Supervisory systems are an alternate means of obtaining information about school performance and encouraging improvements. As noted in Table 8.3 above, many reform efforts have focused on improving the quality of supervision. The following are some principles that can be followed in the reform of supervision:

1. Change the span of control. A major obstacle to the quality of supervision is the heavy load assigned supervisors, and the physical difficulties that stand in the way of their reaching schools. This situation can sometimes be relieved by alterations in the chain of command. For example, until recently in Sri Lanka, supervisors (known as circuit officers) were directly responsible to provincial offices. Beneath a provincial office were about ten circuit officers, and these officers assumed responsibility for 50-80 schools. A recent reform decentralized the provincial offices by transferring many of their functions to more localized divisional offices. The division offices, staffed with up to three supervisors, in turn related to cluster principals (see below). The reform added a level in the organizational hierarchy but reduced the number of units, or span of control, for each level to an average of ten units: ten clusters per division, up to ten divisions per provincial office. This arrangement significantly improved communication.

2. Strengthen horizontal linkages. Supervisors are put in place primarily to maintain vertical linkages. However, many of the best insights about how to run a school or teach a class lie in the schools themselves rather than a central or provincial office. Some schools do much better than others because they are rich in these insights. Another strategy of management reform is to open up horizontal linkages so that the more effective schools have an opportunity to share their wisdom (and other resources) with their neighboring schools. The above-mentioned cluster is a useful mechanism for encouraging these vertical linkages.

3. Train principals to assume greater initiative. Another reform often advocated to improve the modern system is to provide principals with special management courses directed to helping them learn leadership skills as well as techniques for improving the quality and efficiency of school management. Malaysia, for example, has developed an extensive nationwide program which is generally regarded as having a major impact. But these training programs are not guaranteed to have the desired impact if they are not accompanied by other changes which actually empower principals, altering their status from that of last-line implementor of central decisions to first-line innovators of a flexible and responsive system. In the absence of empowering reforms, principals may consider the lessons hollow in that they are at the bottom of a large hierarchy and everything they initiate is ultimately subject to review. If they do well, they will be ignored. If they do poorly, they will be sacked!

4. Some principles of modern management reform. Experience with the reform of modern management suggests several lessons:

- The "center" is, in reality, many centers that may formulate policies independent of each other.
- A bureaucracy's potential for assisting schools may be in inverse relation to the schools' need for that assistance.
- Reforms that require joint action are more likely to encounter difficulties.
- Reform implementation may be thwarted by a personnel policy that encourages the frequent rotation of key personnel.
- Reforms should be thought of as a creative process to be continually monitored and reshaped.
- It may be difficult for principals to accomplish all of the changes in the reform.
- Different contexts may require different reforms.
- Schools have considerable potential for stimulating community involvement.
- It is important to appreciate the diverse communities associated with schools.

Perhaps the most important conclusion is that management reform from above tends to gloss over the gross disparities in local conditions, the capabilities of local schools and communities. It fails to involve communities, and hence does not succeed in capturing the energy available there. In this next section, we introduce a new approach to educational management that overcomes this weakness.

STRENGTHENING PERIPHERAL COMMUNITIES

The modern management approach has simply viewed schools as an outpost of the modern enculturation endeavor, with principals as line subordinates of higher levels in the modern educational bureaucracy, and with teachers below the principals. Parents have been assigned the duty to bring their children to school, leaving them at the gate. In many modern systems, parents are penalized for failure to comply.

There are surely a range of variations to the modern approach. A slight modification is to expand the role of parents through the formation of Parent Teacher Associations, thus allowing parents to be informed witnesses of the educational process. A second possibility is to designate certain parents as trustees with some level of authority over school processes.

A yet more radical approach is to designate the community as the central vehicle for local improvement, and to entrust all authority for education to the local level; with this approach, the center becomes a subordinate partner in education, offering support to local leaders in exchange for local cooperation in promoting a limited range of central objectives such as implementation of a central curriculum or other central programs (such as immunization, public health, vocational skills). In the sections below, we explore some of the implications of this peripheral community approach. We will alternately refer to it as the Theory C or community-oriented approach. The center becomes an advocate and consultant for education, rather than an autocrat. Education thus evolves in correspondence with the imperatives of local or communal values and needs.

New Approaches for the Schools

Community Values/Needs as the Base

The starting point for the peripheral community approach is the natural communities where people reside and develop mutually supportive networks. These communities become the foci for thinking about educational goals and school location.

Egypt's Community Schools provide one illustration of a focus on people in their community settings (see Box. 8.5).

Education as the Backbone of Local Development

Local communities are often flooded with requests to emphasize various development initiatives such as small-scale irrigation, skills programs, family planning, and immunization. School leaders, looking at this plethora of initiatives, can turn their backs, standing firm on their narrow purpose of using the school to promote academic learning; but this would be a mistake. Other local leaders may be more open to certain of these other programs, and may decide to promote one or the other. All of the programs may be good for the local people. But as a practical matter, the local government apparatus is not strong enough to handle them all. To the extent the local government seizes on one program, such as family planning, it is likely to slight others.

The wise educator would seek to position education as the central activity of local communities, rather than face the prospect of neglect as other initiatives capture the imagination of local leaders. Education can be plausibly promoted as the foundation of local development, to the extent the schools are open and prepared to incorporate other development activities such as health clinics, birth-control seminars, experimental farming plots, and skill training into the school's overall program. Each new activity should be viewed as enhancing the school's vitality and usefulness as a knowledge-center and development agency, not as detracting from the school's partial objective of fostering academic learning.

Communities as the Foundation of Effective Education

Perhaps the most consistent finding from several decades of research on school achievement is that the out-of-school effects (that is, the effects of family and community) are far more powerful that the in-school effects. This consistent finding underlines the strategic good sense in basing a strategy for effective education on the values and needs of the community, rather than on those of the central educational authorities.

While it is important to understand the great power of the community over education, it would be a mistake to think that this power is inexorable or unmalleable. Good school management involves building a strong relationship with the community. This relation should be dynamic and reciprocal. Schools have much to offer communities: for example, schools can mobilize children to help communities in projects such as canal repair, cleaning public and religious buildings, and providing services such as music or labor during community festivities. Schools also can reach out to communities through visiting the homes of children who are experiencing academic difficulties or who are frequently absent, so as to discuss new approaches.

Box 8.5. A Review of Egypt's Community Schools

Almost 30 percent of the population in Upper Egypt live in hamlets cut off from the direct services of larger towns. Many have no electricity, and schools and health services are a long walk away. Over half of the boys in these areas walk to the nearest government primary school (at least five kilometers away), while most of the girls do not attend. In 1992, UNICEF began to look for ways of helping the government reach out to the rural areas of Upper Egypt with a quality basic education focusing on girls.

During 1991/1992 a UNICEF team of women trained as community health facilitators, working to gather information on the use of UNICEF-installed water systems and latrines, established that there was a strong local desire for education—even for girls —provided that it could be given within the community itself. Community leaders indicated that they would be able to provide classroom space—a room connected to a mosque, a community center or a renovated house, for example—and/or community self-help to build a classroom on land donated for that purpose. Through discussions with local leaders, families, women and children, a strategy began to develop.

The initial objective of the Community Schools Initiative was to develop a sustainable model for providing quality basic education to boys and girls in the rural communities of Upper Egypt. The project formally began with the signing of a Memorandum of Understanding between UNICEF and the Ministry of Education in April 1992. UNICEF agreed to organize and finance the consultants and technical staff, training, supplementary materials for teachers and children, school furnishings and equipment, and an evaluation of the community school model. The Ministry would pay the teachers, provide guidance on curriculum matters, provide instructional materials, and participate in training and supervision.

Four community schools were opened in October 1992. Preparations had been carried out by the communities, and project participants included the Ministry of Education, the District Council, UNICEF, and local NGOs. As the project grew mainly out of the UNICEF community health education program, a priority consideration was to incorporate health, nutrition, and first-aid concepts into the instructional program, and to ensure that pupils' health needs were met.

The first community schools generated a great deal of enthusiasm and received considerable attention from the local leadership (including the governor), the communities, and the Ministry of Education. The expansion to 25 sites was driven by demand.

A central claim of the program is that the community schools constitute an affordable, sustainable approach to providing quality basic education. Although the costs for instructional materials, training, and supervision are higher than in regular schools, there are no central costs for land, school buildings, or maintenance. It was realized at the outset that the development costs would require a higher level of recurrent and capital expenditure per

Box 8.5. Continued

pupil than would be the case after expansion. At current exchange rates, the annualized per-class cost for community schools is approximately US $4,000, and the per-pupil cost is estimated at US $120 per year. As the program develops and expands, per-pupil expenditures for support staff and facilitators will decline, so that the estimated per-pupil cost will eventually fall to approximately US $90.

Attendance rates are very high—generally 95 to 100 percent—although there are religious holidays or calls for work which have caused higher absence rates. The facilitators and supervisors have worked with the school committees to alter school schedules and provide free days to accommodate these real pressures.

There are two sources of information on the pupils' achievement in the community schools: internal assessments and internal tests, prepared and marked under the supervision of staff from the National Centre for Educational Examinations and Evaluation (NCEEE). These two sources indicate that the pupils in the community schools have performed well; results show that every student in the community school program has satisfactorily completed Grade 1. External evaluators have made the following observations:

- The class facilitators and supervisors exhibit outstanding motivation, as well as an interest in and dedication to their work.
- The instructional design used by facilitators is well understood and implemented.
- The support and participation of the community and parents in school activities is unique.

Although the principal initial objective for the program, as mentioned before, is to provide quality basic education in the rural areas of Upper Egypt, it also seeks to have a positive influence on the process of community development. So far, community leadership in developmental activities is growing. Communities are also taking pride in these schools, contributing land, labor and skills, and also ensuring that children attend. Having realized its potential, policymakers at different levels of government are seeking ways to implement the program on a larger scale. The Ministry of Education has announced plans to establish 3,000 schools to serve small rural communities—particularly to reach girls who are presently not enrolled in school.

The program has clearly made significant gains in developing a viable approach to multi-age and multigrade quality instruction. Yet the work should continue to be viewed as experimental, and should evolve based on ongoing monitoring and reflection.

Source: UNICEF. *A Case Study of the Community Schools Initiative.* Cairo: UNICEF, 1994 (Mimeo).

To the extent that schools help communities, the communities will reciprocate: this may be through financial support, through voluntary labor to improve school buildings and grounds, or even through the provision of specialized support as teachers of certain skills, or as tutors.

All of the success stories in basic education for the periphery, such as *Escuela Nueva*, Zintech, IMPACT and Pamong, involve close and dynamic relations between school and community. (Shaeffer, 1992.)

The Diversity of Communities

Communities differ widely in terms of religious commitments, principal economic activities, size, dispersion, and degree of integration. The modern approach tends to minimize these differences, proposing a standard packet of educational inputs for all communities; except where a community is large, it may receive several of these packets.

The community-oriented approach starts with the community, building on the community's own understanding of its values and needs. Some communities may wish schools to place a strong emphasis on religious education; others may not. Some may require a single school in a central location, while others may wish to devise a different approach to reach a highly dispersed population. By placing educational decisions in the hands of communities, it becomes more possible to devise solutions appropriate to the local context.

Developing a Local Plan

Starting at the community level leads to new questions about the ideal structure of schools appropriate to local circumstances. For many tight-knit communities that reside in a restricted area, the standard multiclass school building may be the answer. In these settings, it is always advisable to achieve agreement on the maximum size for the facility. If the number of children of school-age exceeds two to three hundred, it may be advisable to build new schools.

In other settings where the population is more dispersed, it may be asking too much to rely on a single school. Numerous small schools widely dispersed so as to be close to the actual settlements may work better. These small schools can be fortified with distance-learning technology (interactive radio or even TV) to enhance the quality of instruction in core academic subjects such as arithmetic and language.

Whatever the approach chosen, it should be locally designed to reflect local circumstances. Moreover, to strengthen the effectiveness of each school, it will be helpful if local leaders arrange events to maximize interaction between the respective educational units. These events may range from periodic meetings of teachers to local athletic or cultural events that enable children from the various school sites to meet each other. Ideally, these events will be arranged in such a way as to strengthen community solidarity, rather than to foster divisive competitiveness.

Community-Oriented Education Requires Community-Based Resources

The rapid expansion of modern schools has been achieved because the center has dropped its educational packets on localities. Prior to the central intervention, many localities had their own means for education—though this was often limited in content or scope; but the central intervention often led to an abandonment of local initiative. Communities became dependent on the central solution, even though they often questioned the value of much of its content.

If the community is going to resume command of education, it will have to assume a major portion of the responsibility for supplying schools with needed resources. There is considerable debate about the prospects for local financing of education, particularly at the basic level. The balance of expert opinion is skeptical. Yet there are many instances of local financing on a large scale in the developing world, particularly where schools place significant stress on values education. For example, Indonesia has a large system of religious schools parallel to the state-supported secular schools. So does India, Pakistan, Egypt, many countries in Latin America, and most of the Francophone African countries. Local communities are prepared to support education if it promotes their values.

The community-oriented approach does not assume that basic education should be exclusively based on local funding. But it advocates that local leaders should take the responsibility for establishing the financial framework for schools, based on locally designed plans. A major component of actual financing may come from outside, from the center, which seeks to enter into partnership with the local authorities. However, the local level should be in charge.

This proposal is not advanced simply as a pious platitude. One of the clearest findings from the recent harvest of research on effective schools is that effectiveness is associated with school-based discretion over the use of educational resources. Those closest to the educational process are able to respond. Schools will not get discretion over funds unless some of the funds have been raised directly by the schools.

Low-Demand Communities

It is clear that most schools are fortunate to have parents who agree with the school's externally derived agenda of teaching academic subjects, so the school does not have to exert special efforts to reach the parents. But in some areas, parents may look skeptically on schools (what we referred to in chapter three as areas of "low demand").

The initiatives we have suggested above are unlikely to lead to much improvement in these communities, at least over the short-run. On the other hand, as the leaders of these communities hear more about the value of education in nearby communities, they are likely to shift their priorities and begin to place greater emphasis on education. It is fair to say that it is difficult to find a single community in today's developing world where there is not at least a small cadre who believe in the value of education.

In any case, the community-oriented approach does not depend solely on local initiative. In the next section, we outline a new approach for those in regional and national governments that will increase the likelihood of education reaching these low-demand areas. Partnership is the working principle in these external initiatives, in contrast with the former command principle of the modernizing approach.

Reforming the Center

The community-oriented approach seeks to enhance the role of the periphery in designing and carrying out educational programs. The major reason for proposing this shift is that the prevailing modern approach seems to have reached a limit. But there may be yet other compelling reasons. It can be observed in recent years that the authority of central governments is often challenged, and thus the centers may find it in their own interest to buy goodwill through shifting more authority to lower levels. Also, it would seem that new trends in information provide communities and their local governments with greater potential for assuming a major role in public policy-making.

A New Philosophy for the Center

The starting point for the community-oriented is a fundamental reordering of center thinking. Whereas the center once assumed a paternal attitude that it was the generator of essential value and insight, in the new approach the center needs to accept the principle that local communities have a better understanding of many issues, and particularly concerning the socialization of young people, local communities should be deferred to. The new goal of the center should be to support local actors, while in the process attempting through selected incentives to achieve certain goals that the center especially values—such as the spread of a uniform national culture, the realization of equity, and the development of a sufficient amount of highly developed talent to promote national competitiveness and security. In sum, the center shifts from a focus on control to one of support.

The Center Needs to Identify Its Comparative Advantage

In the modern stage, the center assumed responsibility for delivering a uniform and comprehensive package of educational inputs to schools across the nation. With respect to some inputs, the center was quite successful, often in curriculum design and school construction. Yet it did a slipshod job in other areas, typically the delivery of textbooks and instructional materials. Concerning personnel, the center's record was usually mixed.

As the center adopts the new philosophy, it needs to decide which of these functions is essential for accomplishing its ends, as well as which functions are practical. One recent study, arguing that the best decisions are informed decisions, proposed the following division of authority between central and local actors:

Box 8.6. When Is Centralization Excessive?

Most countries have relatively centralized education systems. A ranking of one hundred national governments with respect to degree of regulation, on a scale in which 1 was equal to total local control and 7 was equal to total national control, produced an overall average of 5.46 for primary education.

These patterns of centralized governance are the product of a long process marked by considerable conflict. Whether centralization is excessive depends on the perspective of the group affected. The centralization of education benefits some groups, while decentralization benefits others.

From a strictly technical perspective, it can be argued that some aspects of governance should be centralized, while others should be decentralized. The most effective system of governance is one that gives those persons with the most information about the particular situation the authority to decide how best to achieve the objectives set at a higher level.

- Teachers are the people who have the most information about the students' progress in learning; they should have the authority to decide which methods to use, and to determine the pace and sequence of the lessons.
- Principals are the people with the most information about conditions within the school as a whole; they should have the authority to decide about matters which affect the whole school.
- Teachers know more about teaching and curriculum, but parents know more about the local values and economic requirements of the community.
- District supervisors or education officers know the most about the overall problems of the district and the resources available for distribution, but school principals have more information about the kind of teachers required in their particular school.
- The central ministry may have more information about the overall requirements for school construction, but district officers will know better where new buildings should be located.

From this perspective, centralization is excessive when decisions are located too far from the source of information. Decentralization, on the other hand, is excessive when decision-makers do not have information about the effects of their actions on others. (See McGinn and Borden, 1992; and Winkler, 1987 for more information.)

Source: McGinn, Noel F. and Allison M. Borden. *Better Education for All: A BRIDGES Manual for Managers and Policy Makers* (Monograph). Cambridge, MA: Harvard Institute for International Development, September 1992.

But it is questionable that the center could achieve the impact it desires simply through restricting its activities to *school construction*. Most central governments would at least seek to have a major hand in curriculum design, since the curriculum is a major vehicle for influencing the values of citizens: what is taught has an obvious impact on what is learned.

In view of the community-oriented approach's concern for local values, the center should not have exclusive control over *curriculum design*. Rather a preferred approach would involve a shared approach with curriculum involving a combination of both national and local components. (See chapter five above.)

The center may wish also to retain selected *training* functions as a way of reinforcing its values; as Peters and Waterman observe in their book, *In Search of Excellence*, large and highly decentralized firms such as IBM achieve a high level of common purpose through frequent meetings and training sessions organized by the center. (Peters and Waterman, 1982.) These meetings enable the center to convey its core values to personnel in charge of regional and other offices.

In other areas, the comparative advantage is not so clear. For example, who should *employ teachers*? Teachers are often the most expensive component of the educational process, and local communities would have difficulty in shouldering this burden. On the other hand, when the center hires teachers as part of a national educational service, the teachers often enjoy transfer rights that enable them to move out of peripheral teaching assignments. Thus the national approach tends to weaken teacher commitment to local communities.

Similarly, who should *print texts*? Most local communities lack the skills to write texts or the technology to print them. While the center has these resources, the texts that often result employ images and language that do not fit local circumstances.

Strengthening Regional Offices

Particularly where nations are very large, one reform which may make some of these answers easier is to consider shifting the locus of many central decisions to regional governments. For example, in Indonesia the total population is approaching 200 million, spread over a vast and diverse archipelago. Hence, the government periodically gives serious attention to dividing the nation into several regions, each with a distinctive and relatively autonomous administrative structure. A reform of this kind was actually carried out in Sri Lanka, resulting in the establishment of ten regional governments, each with primary responsibility for basic education. This reform has brought "central" decision-making much closer to the schools.

Inter-Ministerial Consolidation

In recent years, one of the greatest problems with the center's performance in promoting education has been that the center has spoken with many tongues. In the field of education, the Ministry of Education is always the chief actor. But even within the Ministry there are often several bureaus with considerable autonomy. And sometimes these bureaus promote policies which conflict.

Moreover, it is not uncommon to find several other ministries which either have large educational portfolios or which, for other reasons, seem to undercut the efforts of the Ministry. For example in Indonesia, several ministries have substantial programs that impact on rural villages: the Ministry of Agriculture, the Ministry of Labor, the Office of Manpower, the Ministry of Health, the Family Planning Agency, and the Ministry of Technology. The many and competing arrangements proposed by these diverse ministries sometimes overwhelm the capacity of local areas.

Thailand faced a similar problem before 1980, at which point it took steps to consolidate several of the central ministries. The result was a more decisive central program in the field of education, as well as in other sectors. A number of other nations in recent years have taken modest steps towards consolidation, joining several smaller ministries into a common "Ministry for Human Resources."

Of course, often it is unreasonable to hope for major reforms in the entrenched central ministries. A different strategy is through finance. Often the standard approach is to let each ministry develop and manage its own budget, including those funds intended for local government. An alternate approach is to develop a comprehensive budget incorporating all of the central initiatives, and then to offer these funds in a more consolidated way such as in the form of block grants to the local governments. Ideally, the size of the grants should be determined in such a manner as to provide relatively more to the financially stressed local governments.

In providing the block grants, the center might indicate that the funds are to be used for the implementation of one or more local programs, while ultimately leaving the decisions on which programs a local government might undertake to the local government themselves. Thus a mesh could be achieved between central and local priorities.

Re-Thinking Finance

Possibly the most essential reform for promoting the community-oriented approach is the reform of educational finance. In a well-developed periphery approach, much of the financing for schools would come from those who attend. But due to a long period of central-government monopolization of revenue collection, local traditions of revenue collection have been largely subverted. Moreover, and equally important, the resources available to peripheral locations are usually less than to more central locations. So even as local communities develop greater sophistication in revenue collection, without countervailing financial equity policies, these peripheral areas will generally be at a disadvantage. New approaches to school finance need to be devised.

At the heart of these new approaches should be the philosophy that the center has an obligation to provide partial funding for schools, for the center seeks to achieve several of its goals through the schools—specifically the promotion of national unity, equity, and human development. For this the center should pay.

But how? We suggest the following types of options as an initial basis for discussion; financial specialists will be able to devise more refined alternatives:

a) The basic approach should be direct block grants to local communities or schools, based on a needs-formula.

b) This formula should not be based on a simple count of pupils, but rather should have a strong element of affirmative action to take account of scarce community resources, wide population dispersion, and geographic isolation/ peripherilization.

c) Performance goals may be associated with the block grants, drawing on the specific objectives of the community's plan rather than on a predetermined handbook devised at the center.

d) Local communities which agree to take on a fuller array of educational objectives (e.g., along with basic education, additional programs in public health, family planning, environmental protection, vocational skills) might be entitled to larger grants.

e) The execution of these grants might best be trusted to regional governments.

f) While the block grants may continue to provide a major share of local school financing, built into each community's contract should be a clear commitment to local generation of resources.

Accountability

While the center may shift from comprehensive supply to limited support of local initiatives, it still will be providing substantial resources to local governments. The center thus may wish to establish some mechanism for evaluating the impact of its support. This is particularly likely to be the case if the center provides local support on a specific contract basis where it outlines certain outcomes it seeks in exchange for the interventions it introduces. The establishment of a nationwide evaluation system might also be useful for local governments in determining how well they are doing relative to areas with comparable characteristics. While some accountability efforts may be contemplated, it is unlikely that these will or should have much teeth. They should be used as a basis for encouraging local improvements rather than for punishing shortcomings in realized projected objectives.

The Necessity of an Integrated Package

It is tempting when considering management initiatives to think of piecemeal changes such as altering some central regulations or focusing on "leadership training" at the school level. Much of the recent literature on "school-based management" assumes that changes from below can succeed even if the center remains as it is. Our view is that management improvements are most likely to be realized when they are approached in a comprehensive manner, with complementary changes at all levels.

One of the best examples of a comprehensive attempt to bring about management change in the Third World is Sri Lanka's recent experience. The Sri Lankan system is characterized by a small number of privileged schools of very high quality, an intermediate layer of good schools, and a very large bottom layer of community schools that are often very small and of low quality. The major objective of the reforms was to provide these small schools with more support and more dynamic leadership.

Reforms ranged from a restructuring and downsizing of the central ministry through a strengthening of local educational offices to new training courses for principals and new regulations enabling communities to contribute more resources to their schools. The implementation process proceeded over a period of ten years, during which time parts of the nation were engulfed in a tragic civil war. As with most reforms, not all of the original objectives were realized. But the evidence that is available suggests the reforms resulted in a better system, particularly at the periphery.

Putting the Center Inside the Periphery

In presenting the community-oriented approach, our aim is to outline a new philosophy of development that starts from the bottom. But how to get started? It will be impossible to move towards de-peripheralizing the periphery unless the center gets behind the effort. The center, if it concurs with changes along the lines we have suggested, will have to take major responsibility for the "social marketing" of these changes. The task of social marketing cannot be taken lightly. There are far more failures than successes in decentralization of education. For example, Peru's interesting effort to "nuclearize" schools failed. (Ruiz-Duran, 1983.) Brazil enacted impressive legislation to decentralize educational authority and finance, but the implementation effort was soon stalled. (Plank, 1987.) In sum, the process of realizing the community-oriented approach involves the center in a new role, as consultant and promoter. Chapter 9 outlines our thinking on the steps involved in putting Theory C into practice.

CONCLUSION

Major changes are required if education is going to reach the disadvantaged and peripheralized. While big changes are required, much that is under consideration today is no more than fine-tuning of the existing centralized bureaucracy. We have reviewed several of these conventional initiatives. But we do not think they will make much difference.

Hence, we suggest a radically new approach needs to be considered that puts the periphery first. Ours is not a Robin Hood approach. We do not think the periphery can be improved simply through a massive infusion of central aid. Rather the periphery, in order to move forward, has to rebuild its spirit and local organization, which has largely been subverted by decades of piecemeal central intrusion. Thus we advocate that the periphery, to improve, will have to assume a major part of the responsibility for planning where it wants to go and even for financing the journey. Our suggestion is that the educational institutions should assume the central role in the resurrection of the periphery, so that the future course of development can be integrated from below rather than fractionalized from above. Our argument in this chapter identifies many specific initiatives that might be launched. However, we doubt that true success in de-peripheralizing society will be possible without a comprehensive approach to change, which includes reforms at all levels.

Endnotes

1. These include such activities as assessing needs, defining targets, planning; creating a supportive policy environment; improving managerial, analytical and technological capacities; mobilizing information and communication channels; and building partnerships and mobilizing resources. WCEFA, *Meeting Basic Learning Needs: A Vision for the 1990s*, pp. 79-98.

2. At the outset, we offer a cautionary note. While a big fetish is made about effective management and quite a lot is written, much of this is opinion including many of the prescriptions found in this chapter. The scientific basis for different management theories is weak.

3. Management theory is a fertile field, and we could extend the list almost infinitely. What we seek to do here is to contrast the conventional theories that focus on improving conditions within organizations with a new (and yet inadequately developed) group of theories that focus on improving the conditions of the clients of organizations. The former theories are sometimes given names such as Theory X,Y,Z. So we will give this new group a name, Theory C, to reflect our interest in developing a management approach that helps the peripheral community.

4. The management literature has tended to rephrase these national styles in the abstract language of Theory X (the continental model), Theory Y (the more participatory American model), and Theory Z (the more inclusive and humanistic Japanese model). W. Scott has provided an interesting comparison of these different modern approaches that was neatly summarized in Peters's and Waterman's well-known study "Excellence."

5. For example, excellence, total-quality movement, full-service movement; see T. Sakaiya, *The Value Knowledge Revolution.* Tokyo: Kodansha International, 1991.

6. For a thoughtful report on problems in supervision in remote rural areas, see Raymond F. Lyons, ed., *Problems of Educational Administration in Remote Rural Areas: Report of an Expert Meeting in Kathmandu, Nepal, 7-11 May 1979.* UNESCO: International Institute for Educational Planning, 1980.

Bibliography

Cassidy, Thomas. Unpublished doctoral dissertation. Harvard University, 1990.

Chapman, David. *Facilitator Manual: Formulating Conclusions and Recommendations.* New York: UNICEF, 1992.

Cummings, William K. and Abbey Riddell, "Alternate Policies for the Finance, Control, and Delivery of Basic Education." *International Journal of Educational Research,* v 21, n 8 (1994): 751-776.

Kemmerer, Frances. "An Integrated Approach to Primary Education Incentives," in David W. Chapman and Caorl A. Carrier, eds., *Improving Educational Quality.* New York: Greenwood Press, 1990.

McGinn, Noel F. and Allison M. Borden. *Better Education for All: A BRIDGES Manual for Managers and Policy Makers* (monograph). Cambridge, MA: Harvard Institute for International Development, September, 1992 .

Peters, Thomas J. and Robert H. Waterman. *In Search of Excellence.* New York: Warner, 1982.

Plank, David. "The Expansion of Education: A Brazilian Case Study," *Comparative Education Review*, v 31 (August 1987).

Ruiz-Duran, G. "Experience of Educational Micro-Planning in Peru Through Nuclearization," in *Educational Administration and Multi-Level Plan Implementation: Experience from Developing Countries, IIEP Seminar Papers.* Paris: UNESCO, 1983.

Shaeffer, Sheldon, ed., *Collaborating for Educational Change: The Role of Teachers, Parents, and the Community in School Improvement.* Paris: International Institute for Educational Planning, 1992.

UNDP, UNESCO, UNICEF, and World Bank. *Meeting Basic Learning Needs: A Vision for the 1990's.* Jomtien, Thailand, March 5-9, 1990a.

UNDP, UNESCO, UNICEF, and World Bank. *World Declaration on Education for All and Framework for Action to Meet Basic Learning Needs.* Jomtien, Thailand, March 5-9, 1990b.

Windham, Douglas M. "The Role of Basic Education in Promoting Aggregate Effects and Marginalized Populations, " in David Chapman and Herbert Walberg, *International Perspectives in Educational Productivity.* Greenwich, CT: JAI Press, 1992.

Windham, Douglas M. "Indicators of Educational Efficiency," *Forum for Advancing Basic Education and Literacy* (Sept., 1991).

Winkler, D.R. *Decentralization in Education: An Economic Perspective.* Washington, D.C.: The World Bank, 1987.

CHAPTER 9

Reaching the Periphery
Toward a Community-Oriented Education

H. Dean Nielsen and Zeynep F. Beykont

CONTRIBUTORS TO SCHOOL FAILURE IN THE PERIPHERY

The various chapters in this volume have revealed the contributors to school failure of peripheral groups. Factors examined included scarce material resources; weak school-community relations; misdirected school-language policies; irrelevant curriculum; inappropriate teacher preparation, placement, and support; ill-suited school/classroom organization patterns; and rigid system rules and regulations. In chapter 3 James H. Williams describes how government control of education has generally led to a loss of community initiative and involvement in education. Zeynep F. Beykont, in chapter 4, describes how misdirected language policies ignore the particular expectations of communities and the educational needs of children whose native languages are different from the official language.

Prema Clarke, in chapter 5, illustrates how an irrelevant school curriculum can result in low student and parent motivation and low student-enrollment rates. In chapter 6, Maria Teresa Tatto shows how teacher policies have failed to consider the special needs of teachers working in the periphery and to address their needs for financial security, social adjustment, and professional growth. The chapters by H. Dean Nielsen and S. Dunham Rowley, Jr., and William K. Cummings illustrate structural inflexibilities of the conventional school system, resulting in unsuitable, "industrial-style" approaches to school and classroom organization, and center-based (top-down) and "modern" system management patterns, that are ill-suited to the education of peripheral groups.

None of these constraints operate in isolation: in reality, they are interlinked in a multitude of complex ways, creating formidable barriers to educational improvement. To convey an image of their interactive nature, they can be represented schematically as follows:

Figure 9.1: Contributors to School Failure in the Periphery

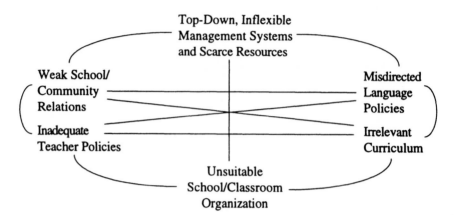

Weak School-Community Relations

In chapter 3 of this volume, Williams notes that "mass education, as currently organized [and implemented down to the village level], places relatively little value on the community, whether as a participant in the education of children, as a legitimate source of knowledge, or as a partner in the management of educational change." The weakness of school-community relations implied here is particularly problematic for peripheral communities. By emphasizing mainstream values exclusively, the school often contributes to the loss of community initiative and input. Furthermore, the school becomes an alien body when members of the community are not engaged (in children's education) in meaningful ways.

According to Williams, communities can be classified as *high* or *low* in their demand for mainstream education. The problem with school-community relations where the community demand for mainstream education is high is that community members, including parents, have no effective means for channeling their support; in situations where the community demand for mainstream education is low, members may not feel inclined to even send their children to school, let alone contribute to school resources and activities. In the former case, the school deprives itself of valuable community resources and support; in the latter, it may deprive itself of a diverse student body due to nonenrollment and drop out (a point also emphasized by Clarke's discussion of education in Tamil Nadu, India, and Beykont's discussion of language policies). In either case, current structures undermine the capacity of the community to contribute to the school and the school to the community.

Misdirected Language Policies

School-language policies, reviewed by Zeynep Beykont in Chapter 4, have profound effects on the education of peripheral language groups whose native languages are different from the language of instruction. From a pedagogical point of view, school-language policies that ignore linguistic needs of peripheral language groups and teach them in mainstream classrooms are myopic. Such policies rarely lead to adequate literacy in the official language, while at the same time deny the opportunity for literacy development in a child's native language. They also depreciate the value of the child's first language and culture, and contribute to the kind of alienation between school and the family/community mentioned above. The effect of the school on students and community is thus "subtractive,"[1] promoting the school language and culture at the expense of the child's own.

As pointed out by Beykont, school-language policy decisions are generally governed by sociopolitical and economic considerations rather than pedagogical ones. Many governments have a vested interest in assimilating peripheral groups into the mainstream as part of a nation-building agenda. School for them becomes a crucial channel through which mainstream values and culture and language are imposed on the community. Other governments may value the linguistic and ethnic diversity and build on it by providing bilingual and bicultural education and developing children's native-language literacy skills in addition to the official-language literacy skills. Still others may deny participation of nondominant language groups in the mainstream by educating them in the native language only.

Peripheral language groups, in turn, have varied responses, aspirations, and expectations regarding their children's education. In some cases, parents in peripheral language groups may desire their children to enter the mainstream as soon as possible by participating in mainstream classrooms and learning the official language. Other groups may see it as the school's role to teach children their home language and culture in addition to the official language and culture. Still others may not be interested in participating in the mainstream culture at all. Where there is a lack of congruence in the educational goals of government and peripheral groups, community support for public education falters and the children caught in the middle rarely do well at school.

Inappropriate Curriculum

Prema Clarke's discussion of curriculum in the state of Tamil Nadu, India (chapter 5), illustrates how formal education is dysfunctional for a large part of the rural Indian population. Still marked by a British colonial past and emphasizing themes such as national unity (defined by the dominant castes) and technological progress and industrialization, the curriculum of the formal school is largely irrelevant to the world of the millions of students in low-caste villages and communities. This phenomenon is particularly evident in official state-school textbooks. In Clarke's view, the center's dominance is conveyed both in the books' content and in their representations of the physical and sociocultural worlds through pictures and illustrations. Also obvious is the total lack of themes and images from the world of poor and low-caste villagers.

Such curricula reinforce the legitimacy of an urban and high-caste ideology and promote a false sense of unity in the extremely diverse nation of India. It fails students in the periphery in two ways: first, it fails to convince the parents of the value of enrolling or keeping their children in school; second, it fails to engage the interest and effort of those children who do enroll. Both contribute to disastrous levels of participation and drop-out in many parts of rural India.

Inadequate Teacher Preparation, Placement, and Support Policies

As outlined in chapter 6 by Maria Teresa Tatto, policies for teachers rarely take into consideration the needs of teachers assigned to remote schools. The state has the legitimate concern to place qualified teachers in classrooms throughout the country, but if in filling this need it overlooks a teacher's concern for financial stability, social adjustment, organizational support, and professional growth, the inevitable problems of teacher dissatisfaction and turnover results.

Concerning financial stability, standard salaries and benefit packages for teachers often overlook the fact that the "cost of living" in peripheral areas is much higher than in central districts, and access to extra income through part-time jobs or tutoring is limited. Moreover, teachers placed in such areas may have difficulty adjusting and being welcomed by the community unless they happen to be local, a possibility that is limited by teacher selection, training, certification, and placement procedures. For example, governments rarely adopt policies in which peripheral communities' gifted youth are encouraged to become teachers and supported in making it through selection, training, and placement processes, despite the fact that doing so would produce teachers much more likely than others to live and remain in the community, and serve its school children with commitment and understanding. Finally, organizational support and opportunities for professional growth are also frequently missing for teachers serving in remote areas. For example, teachers in small remote schools rarely see supervisors, in-service trainers, and peers (those teaching in the same grade or subject areas). In addition, being far removed from centers of teacher education, they are rarely in a position to upgrade their credentials, and thereby have access to the kind of upward mobility that is often available to mainstream teachers.

Unsuitable School-Classroom Organization

As discussed in chapter 7 by Rowley and Nielsen, school and classroom organization tied to the formal curriculum itself conveys socialization messages. The mainstream school, with its hierarchical organization and its age-graded stratification tends to reflect the "industrial model" and related norms and values. Standard school/classroom organization models, patterned after the assembly line, can lead to ludicrous arrangements in remote village schools, such as a school maintaining a separate classroom for a single second grader (see chapter 2). While the industrial model has its limitations even in large schools in urban areas, it is definitely out of place in rural contexts where there are only a handful of students and teachers spread across the various grades.

In small and distant communities, where both students *and* teachers are few, schools have often resorted to different forms of multigrade teaching, including the "one-room school." Effective multigrade teaching, based on a "family model" of organization, uses the *assets* available in peripheral groups, such as flexible time and space, older children's responsibility for younger, teacher and community resourcefulness, and a social environment containing few community institutions besides the school. Use of such assets in a family model is not generally legitimated by the educational system, however, and teachers are rarely trained in effective multigrade teaching techniques. A few resourceful teachers create viable systems on their own, but, without support, most either resort to modified versions of the conventional classroom or muddled forms of multigrade teaching where very little learning takes place.

Top-Down Inflexible School Management Systems and Scarce Resources
According to Cummings (chapter 8), the modern system of educational management, which has been adopted by old and new nation-states throughout the world, is characterized by a centralized system of top-down management that does not serve well the peripheral groups. As a system of *control*—rooted in the military— "modern" management has emphasized the standardization of goals and management processes even when local conditions and culture have not been receptive or amenable, as in the case of ethnically divided countries. As a system of *efficiency*— grounded in the capitalist manufacturing practices—modern management has a skewed resource allocation to the places where the returns are likely to be high in terms of student numbers and political support, namely the urban, suburban, and prosperous rural centers.

Some governments have attempted to address these limitations by reforming their modern management systems: for example, by drawing parents and community members into limited supporting roles; by developing management information systems; by creating more equitable resource allocation schemes; and by creating local networks or clusters of schools for professional support and resource sharing. Such reforms, however, are still limited and inadequate, since they fail to recognize the extent of the difference between the mainstream communities and those in the periphery, and perhaps more importantly fail, to involve the communities in meaningful ways, and hence "do not capture the energy available there."

School-funding schemes demonstrate the limitations of modern management, even with its recent reforms. Since they allocate the same number of funds per head, they are considered to be equitable. However, given the small size of most peripheral schools, head-count formulas often leave schools short of the critical mass of funds needed for the purchase of essential equipment. Furthermore, such formulas ignore the adverse conditions that often prevail in difficult and remote areas, including high cost of living, expensive and difficult transportation and communication networks, children's lack of readiness for school due to malnutrition, and heavy teacher loads due to the frequent demand to manage more than one grade level at a time. Because of such unequal conditions, "equal" funding in peripheral areas rarely purchases the level of educational services and outcomes that it does in the center.

INTERLINKED NATURE OF CONTRIBUTORS TO SCHOOL FAILURE
In his book on rural development, Robert Chambers (1983) uses the phrase "integrated rural poverty" to describe the interconnected factors which impede the growth of community well-being in the marginal areas. In like manner, the above factors of school failure in the periphery are interlinked and mutually reinforcing in impeding the quality of education for peripheral groups. Examples of this abound: for instance, centralized allocation formulas fail to generate the resources needed to attract good teachers to peripheral areas, let alone to hold and professionally support them there. Furthermore, center-based curriculum dampens community support, which in turn discourages villagers from contributing time and resources to the

school. Moreover, the exclusive use of the dominant language in instruction weakens school-community relations and community participation in children's education.

Top-down management and its standardized rules and regulations also interacts with the other factors, such as a school's inability to set its own priorities and to recruit local people as tutors and teachers; a hesitancy to involve the community in creative ways, and the failure to design local curricular materials and use varied patterns of classroom organization. Finally, teacher policies, in which poorly selected, trained, and supported individuals are placed in peripheral schools, undermine the possibility of establishing innovative instructional strategies, inhibit the development of constructive school-community relations, and constrain the potential for bilingual/bicultural education and multigrade teaching. Many other examples could be cited. The important point is that the determinants of school failure in the periphery interact with and support each other in complex ways, creating formidable barriers to quality education for peripheral groups.

TRANSFORMING THE EDUCATION OF PERIPHERAL GROUPS: TOWARD A COMMUNITY-ORIENTED APPROACH

In our view, adequate teaching for the periphery requires a *community-oriented approach*. By community-oriented approach we mean that *community and center participate as equal partners in planning children's education and making decisions regarding the most important aspects of local schooling.* The problems associated with system management, school-community relations, language policy, teacher policies, curriculum and instruction, and school/classroom management in a center-based educational system can be largely overcome when education is jointly defined and managed by the center and community. Community-oriented education does not imply that education of peripheral groups should rely largely on local resources. On the contrary, sufficient state funds should be allocated to assure access to the same level of quality as available in the mainstream. In addition, the school might expand its resource base to include previously untapped local funds.

We argue that with appropriate reorientation, schools serving peripheral groups can become engaging and innovative centers for individual and community development. For instance, the low population density which characterizes much of the periphery lends itself to the organization of one-room, village schools employing the kind of multigrade teaching that has captured renewed attention and regard among today's educational professionals; the linguistic diversity of peripheral groups enables multilingual education with its potential contribution to higher levels of cognitive development than that available in monolingual schools; a strong vision of community and community development as the aim of education may motivate community support of education and school support of the community. With a community-oriented approach, we maintain that conditions in the periphery, which have until now been counted as impediments to good education, can become assets.

CONTRIBUTORS TO THE RENEWAL OF EDUCATION FOR PERIPHERAL GROUPS

The figure below shows the various features of the "community-oriented school" as an integrated system. Just as the contributors to school failure in the periphery are interlinked and mutually reinforcing, the redeeming features of school transformation are integrated and comprehensive.

Figure 9.2: Features of the Community-Oriented School

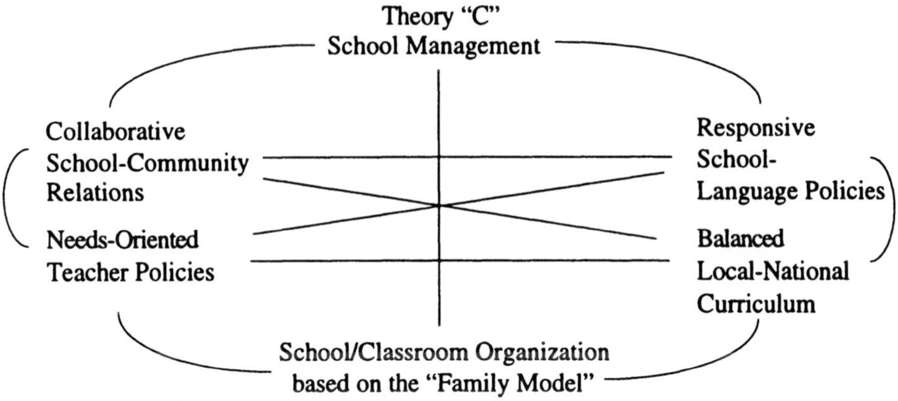

Theory "C"
School Management

Collaborative
School-Community
Relations

Responsive
School-
Language Policies

Needs-Oriented
Teacher Policies

Balanced
Local-National
Curriculum

School/Classroom Organization
based on the "Family Model"

Collaborative School-Community Relations

One core feature of the community-oriented approach is collaborative school-community relations. According to Williams, the new approach calls for abandoning the notion that schooling is the exclusive domain of the professionals in favor of a *collaborative* model. A community-oriented approach calls for governments (a) to identify reasons for lack of community support and work around particular communities' religious commitments, needs, expectations, financial constraints, and schedule of productive activities; (b) to loosen some of the rigid rules and regulations (such as age and attendance rules) that discourage student attendance; (c) to respond to community values (for example regarding public interactions between girls and boys).

In the community-oriented approach, *the government considers the constraints, needs and values of the community and adapts the delivery and content of education accordingly*. For example, governments can facilitate community involvement by providing small grants for innovative projects and/or by training school administrators for their new roles as collaborators with communities that they serve. In return, according to Williams, the community can be actively involved in supporting the school and contribute by generating funds and providing "person power" to help with teaching and tutoring, and designing, constructing, and maintaining school buildings and grounds.

Other variants of the collaborative school-community relations, which we also endorse, view community members, especially parents and leaders, as active and full partners in defining the school's mission and establishing school policies and practices. (Murphy 1991.) In the collaborative model, the traditional barriers between home and school are transformed/redefined, such that parents and the community are more involved in school matters and the school more in community affairs.

Responsive School-Language Policies
The community-oriented approach requires that governments respond to the *particular* educational needs of language communities. Communities vary widely in their views on whether or to what extent the school is responsible for teaching home culture, developing native-language literacy skills, providing bilingual teachers, allowing children to use their native language in school, and so on. In other words, there is no one school-language policy that can respond to the greatly varied educational goals, aspirations, and expectations of language communities throughout the world. School-language policies should be based on the particular needs and preferences of each language community.

Responsive school-language policies involve communities in decisions on language of instruction, development of curriculum and reading materials, and planning and implementation of a language program. Language communities support a school-language policy if it is congruent with their expectations regarding what the school is responsible for teaching their children. Community support for or resistance to a school-language policy has a direct impact on the success or failure of the policy as well as on children's academic performance. When nondominant groups support a particular school-language policy, children are more likely to perform well in school.

If the community supports native language instruction, then the community-oriented approach stipulates the adoption of a bilingual school-language policy and a maintenance bilingual program throughout schooling. In such programs, children are instructed in the native language while gradually incorporating the official language as an additional instructional medium. Bilingual school-language policies *build on* children's language and cultural resources and *develop native-language literacy skills in addition to official-language literacy* skills throughout schooling. Policies aimed at developing full proficiency in both native and official languages positively influence children's academic performance. Such bilingual school-language policies do *not* imply that children's native languages are developed *at the expense* of the official-language literacy skills. The effect of these language policies is "additive," promoting development of literacy skills in the official language in addition to the native language, while instilling pride in children's culture of origin and a favorable attitude toward the mainstream. Children continue to value their native language, local norms, and the cultural life of the community, and add the official language and culture upon their existing cultural base and native language.

If the community supports schooling in the official language, a community-oriented policy would involve the adoption of the modified immersion approach. This approach requires that children be instructed through the official language with continual second-language support throughout the school. In this approach, *bilingual curriculum materials that are locally developed and culturally relevant* should be used rather than monolingual curriculum materials imported from other countries. Teachers should be fully bilingual and encourage children to use their native languages to ask comprehension and clarification questions in class. The use of the modified immersion approach at school could be accompanied by community-based native-language literacy programs after school to develop children's biliteracy skills.

A Balanced Local and National Curriculum

Community-oriented schools must be organized to meet the specific curricular needs of different communities. "Only a curriculum which reclaims the world, language and history of the people in the periphery will be able to persuade parents that schooling is important and useful for their children, and create sustained interest, motivation, and excitement on the part of the student." (Clarke, chapter 5.) This means reflecting in the curriculum, particularly in the textbooks, cultural themes and lifestyle images for those who live in rural areas. Such efforts need to go deeper than the provincial or even district levels: since there are wide local variations, curricular planning must reach the level of the "micro-community."

This kind of curriculum development will require new forms of research and collaboration to identify those cultural traditions. Joint community studies by village teachers, community members and teacher educators can "capture" living and environment conditions, cultural themes, oral histories, and folk knowledge. Similarly, joint curricular-design efforts, involving local people and outside professionals, can enable the development of a balanced curriculum having both local themes and national and international content.

Needs-Oriented Teacher Policies

In community-oriented schools the classroom teacher will have a much greater voice than before regarding the directions and policies of the school. In order to fulfill and find fulfillment in these new professional responsibilities, new approaches to teacher recruitment, training, and professional support are needed. Schools in the periphery need a stable teaching force: teachers who originate from the region, who know the local language and customs, and who are locally recruited, have a much higher chance of remaining in schools in the periphery than teachers from more mainstream areas. Facilitating this may require the government to provide special incentives and supports to local-area teacher candidates, and to bring teacher-education opportunities as close as possible to the peripheral areas. The content of the teacher-education program (including student teaching) will need to be adjusted so as to prepare the teachers for their roles in community schools: addressing/covering different approaches to teaching in non-mainstream schools (e.g., using multigrade teaching and community volunteers), and the enhanced roles of teacher as decision-maker and participant in community-development activities.

Organizational and professional support for teachers consistent with a community-oriented approach would consist of supervision which facilitates and supports teachers in their various roles (as mentioned above), mutual support and professional exchanges within local teacher networks or school clusters, and opportunities for specialized training and career-advancement courses through distance education and/or special institutes during school vacations.

Realistically, none of these innovations will work to attract and retain dedicated and capable teachers unless their social and economic needs are also considered. Teachers need to make a living wage and feel socially accepted and safe. Given the relatively high cost of living in the remote areas, plus diminished opportunities for earning extra income on the one hand, and more demands for involvement in unpaid extra-school activities on the other, teachers in the periphery clearly need special financial incentives and extra benefits. In addition, they need support from the community in terms of housing and social acceptance. The community-oriented model of education, in fact, does not support the idea that all financing should come from the center. The community itself should find ways of rewarding and supporting those who were especially trained for and willing to face the challenges of teaching in non-mainstream schools. The fruits of placing an appropriately selected and trained teacher in a supportive professional and community environment are often remarkable: a quality of instruction and student/teacher satisfaction that is rarely found even in mainstream schools.

School-Classroom Organization Based on the Family Model

The conventional age-graded, batch-processing school is generally ill-suited to the needs of communities in the periphery. In such communities student groups are often small and scattered; curricular resources are limited; buildings are often tiny. But there all also many assets which can be used well within a family-style organizational setting. Flexible time and space utilization, student self-reliance, a student's sense of responsibility for younger siblings, hometown teachers, home-grown teacher-coping strategies, school-centered social life: these are all assets which lend themselves well to multigrade teaching strategies. In fact, multigrade teaching is a fact of life in peripheral areas throughout the world, although often seen as an aberrant condition to be endured until *real* schools can be set up. Recent data, however, is beginning to show that well-organized multigrade teaching can lead to highly satisfactory student outcomes, especially in student attitudes. The community-oriented school, particularly that servicing a relatively small community in the periphery, would do well to capitalize on its assets and adopt a multigrade teaching strategy.

This suggests the need for educational authorities to *legitimate* multigrade teaching in public schools. Having done that, they can then begin to document effective MGT practice—home-grown or imported, produce (or, even better, support the local production of) learning materials suitable for multigrade teaching, and develop teacher-preparation programs for this kind of teaching. At the same time, managers of such schools need to reach out to the community for help of various kinds and develop ways for teachers to get continuous refresher training and support in MGT techniques.

Community-Oriented Management System

The community-oriented management system (Theory C) stipulates that those who understand local needs, commitments, and customs participate in decision-making for their communities. Such collaborative arrangements may not come easily to a school system in which the custom has been to provide a standard packet of educational inputs for all communities. It demands change at the center, both in theory and practice. In theory, the center will need to shed its paternalistic attitude—assuming itself to be the generator of all value and insight—and accept the principle that "local communities have a better understanding of many issues, and particularly concerning the socialization of young people, local authorities should be deferred to." (Chapter 8.) In practice, this means that supervision from the center will shift from a focus on compliance to the support and facilitation of local planning and decision-making.

Theory C also demands flexibility in the rules and regulations that govern school life. As Cummings points out, communities differ widely in their religious commitments, principal economic activities, size, population dispersion, and degree of integration. Each of these features has a bearing on the organization of school life. For example, religious commitments can affect the timing and length of school holidays, the rituals performed at school, the school dress code, and the kinds/extent of interaction between boys and girls. Economic activities can also affect the school calendar—particularly where children are required, at crucial times, to help with planting or harvesting or marketing—and the content of the curriculum. Size and dispersion of the community can affect the number and type of classrooms and class groupings required (e.g., multi- or single-grade). The degree of diversity of linguistic, religious, and cultural groups that need to be catered to are other factors that affect the organization of education.

Finally, under Theory C the provision of material resources will need to be a cooperative venture, with the center being the major source of funding through block grants—in exchange for a local acceptance of certain state or national goals and standards—and the community/school involved in: (a) generating additional resources from within the community; and (b) developing its own school budget and resource-allocation plans according to local need. The level of funding support from the center should take into consideration the *level of difficulty and the high costs* associated with schooling in the periphery, in addition to head counts. The same considerations should be used in developing salary and benefit packages for teachers. In addition, local or regional production/procurement of school books and curriculum materials should be encouraged in order to avoid central-distribution bottlenecks, a feature also consistent with the collaborative view of curriculum development described above.

THE CASE FOR AN INTEGRATED APPROACH TO COMMUNITY-ORIENTED EDUCATION

Just as the contributors to school failure in the periphery need to be viewed as interlinked and mutually reinforcing, the redeeming features of school transformation must be seen as integrated and comprehensive (Goodlad, 1994). The case for bringing these features forth as an integrated, systemic package should be clear. A community-oriented approach cannot be fully realized if it is not accompanied by consistent transformations all the way up the hierarchy, with a willingness at the top to act in facilitating as opposed to controlling roles. Similarly, changes in language policies to match the community expectations will have little impact unless accompanied by local curriculum development efforts that represent the history, as well as physical and socio-cultural realities of the community. Only when introduced as *a full package* do educational policies/strategies reinforce rather than work against each other (Beykont, 1994). Piecemeal strategies, which work on one or two features—such as staff training and/or material development—are not sufficient to transform the education of peripheral groups. A package missing any one of these components will lack coherence and the power to transform (Beykont, 1994).

For example, if every component is in place but the language component, students and their parents still may have trouble accepting and/or flourishing at the school; likewise, the other components cannot contribute to school transformation if ill-suited teachers come in through a revolving door, or top-down educational policies deprive the community of the sense of communal ownership of the school. Likewise, organization of school at the school-community level cannot be fully realized if it is not accompanied by consistent transformations all the way up the hierarchy, with a willingness at the top to act in facilitating as opposed to controlling roles. In short, only when introduced as a full package do policies/strategies reinforce rather than work against each other (e.g. Beykont, 1994, Goodlad, 1994).

Seen in a more positive light, teachers recruited from the community can be trained to teach in bilingual and multigrade classrooms. Children of similar language backgrounds can be put in one classroom to receive instruction through native language with peers from different age groups for part of the day. Teachers can help organize community members as resources for both bilingual education, curriculum development, and fund raising. Community members can support such efforts through their involvement in helping as aids or tutors in schools, and assisting with homework, fund raising, and so on. A flexible management system can further reinforce these changes by allocating extra funds for school-community collaborative efforts to locally develop some curriculum materials and by rewarding exceptional teachers and principals who serve in particularly challenging areas.

Table 9.1 below summarizes the differences between state- and community-oriented approaches to schooling across the various domains covered above. Reoriented towards the community these domains become arenas of school renewal rather than factors in public school failure for peripheral groups.

PUTTING COMMUNITY-ORIENTED EDUCATION INTO PRACTICE

Putting such a comprehensive change package into practice will not be a simple task, particularly given the weight of system inertia and vested interests in the center. It is never easy for the center to devolve power to the periphery, particularly when this also implies the downsizing of the central office and the central control over some resources. Nor is it easy for the center to relax short-term efficiency concerns and emphasize long-term educational goals, such as academic progress and school retention of peripheral groups. Finally, it is not easy for the center to envision major institutional reforms without a corresponding change—namely increase—in funding.

We argue that the community-oriented transformations discussed here do *not* require heavy new financial allocations for education. In fact, in most cases, new funding requirements are counter-balanced somewhere else by new savings. In other words, the community-oriented model requires more of a reallocation of the existing

Table 9.1. Difference between Centrally-Controlled and Community-Oriented Approaches

Domain	Centrally-Controlled Educational Systems	Community-Oriented Educational Systems
1. School-Community Relations	Schooling mainly the domain of professionals; limited roles for parents and community	Education as partnership; collaboration between gov't and community in goal-setting, supporting, and monitoring; school supports community development and vice versa; community collaboration in school construction and upkeep
2. School-Language Policies	No first or second language support; children are placed in mainstream classrooms with native speakers of the official language; exclusive use of official language as the instructional medium; mainstream culture stressed at the expense of nondominant cultures	Based on particular needs of communities. If a community expects native lang. inst. maintenance bilingual programs are offered. If a community expects official lang. inst. modified immersion programs are offered with continual second-language support& bilingual teachers & bilingual curriculum. All cultures stressed.
3. Curriculum	Standardized curriculum preparing children for standardized exams; exclusive emphasis on urban and industrial lifestyle, images, cultural values; the prescribed textbook as the de facto curriculum	Local and regional themes prominent in curriculum; representation of cultural realities, lifestyles, and images of peripheral groups, as well as mainstream cultures

Table 9.1 continued

4. Teacher Policies	Standardized systems of teacher recruitment, training and professional support	Selective recruitment of locals into teaching force; training adapted to circumstances; local organizational support and teacher access to professional development through distance or school-based education
5. School - Classroom Organization	School-classroom organization based on industrial model/age grade emphasized	School/classroom organized "family style" using flexible time and space, teacher resourcefulness, student tutoring & self instruction, and community support as assets
6. Management System	Top-down management oriented toward control and efficiency, characterized by standardized rules, regulations and resource allocation formulas; centralized procurement and distribution	Management starts with needs of the community; resource allocation based on need, includes community-generated resources; local procurement

resources than the commitment of new funds. For example:

- The extra expenses that might go into the selective recruitment and special training of local teachers can be recovered through the lower turnover rate of such teachers;
- The greater time and effort expended in involving the community in planning and decision-making is compensated for by the generation of financial and "in-kind" contributions from the community;
- The training and deployment of bilingual teachers, development of bilingual materials and locally relevant curriculum is more than paid for in terms of lower drop-out rates of students ;
- The use of school clusters or teacher working groups for teacher/school-centered in-service is less expensive than conventional programs based on workshops led by professionals;
- The use of distance education for "teacher upgrading" in remote areas is less expensive (by as much as 1/8) than conventional residential programs or those held during school holidays. (Nielsen and Tatto, 1991.)

SORTING OUT AND PREPARING FOR NEW ROLES: CENTER AND PERIPHERY
Once the commitment has been made for center-periphery collaboration towards a community-oriented approach, the roles of the two main parties need to be negotiated. Our review of literature and practice suggests a simple rule of thumb: *let each party do what it does best*. This theory of "comparative advantage" is most easily applied to financing: the center is best at collecting revenue; the locality is best at determining how to spend it. This implies that the bulk of educational financing should come from the central authority in the form of block grants. Decisions about how to spend the funds should be made at the local (school/community) level, since those closest to the action know where the needs are.

Comparative advantages for the center and periphery are also apparent in other domains, as follows:

Center (National/Provincial)
1. General curriculum standard setting, taking advantage of subject matter and curriculum development specialists.
2. Development of mainstream curriculum content and learning materials.
3. Control of pre-service teacher education and certification standards, either through a network of training institutions or programs of accreditation, to assure uniformity of quality. However, a significant portion of experiential learning and student teaching should happen in schools in the periphery and special supports provided to candidates from peripheral groups, including distance education for both initial certification and upgrading.
4. The establishment of general guidelines related to student and teacher health, safety, non-discrimination/equal opportunity, etc.; namely, all the rights and privileges safeguarded by national/state law and constitutional provisions.
5. Technical assistance and specialized support services should be made available on demand, e.g., in relation to tasks such as setting up school clusters, developing local curriculum, implementing bilingual education, and implementing multigrade teaching.

Locality (School/Community)
In addition to making decisions about the allocation of funds under block grants, our reviews indicate that the local authority has a comparative advantage with respect to the following kinds of decisions:

1. The determination of how the school/classroom should be organized (single grade classrooms or multigrade);
2. Decisions about the school calendar (when to hold holidays; scheduling of classes and activities at the school level, etc.);
3. Selection of teachers (given the fulfillment of general certification requirements);
4. The organization of inservice training and professional support systems for teachers (using school-based or school cluster systems);
5. Determination whether the native language should be a language of instruction;
6. Decisions about different modes of community support (each community to decide best how it can support the school—goal setting; funding, building provision and/or

maintenance; tutoring and skills training; creating support groups, etc.) ; school construction and maintenance (by local firms on contract);

7. The development of the local curricular content and learning materials; printing of learning materials (by local firms on contract).

A second basic principle or rule of thumb would be that of "reciprocity." Those bodies that put something into the schools or teachers are entitled to get something out of them. Thus, in exchange for its heavy financial support, the center would be entitled to set certain curricular guidelines, including the use of the national language as one school language and courses covering national unity and citizenship. Similarly, in exchange for scholarship and other support given, the government can obligate teachers to work in difficult and remote areas at least a minimum number of years.

From the community point of view, a community which invests in the school in various ways can expect help and support from the school (and its students and teachers) in various ways: community-oriented programs and activities (music, dance, literary, commemorative or sports events), community development projects (health, sanitation, reforestation, etc.), educational outreach (adult education and literacy courses), and future workers in the local economy. Returns to parents, who "supply" the learners, could be tangible and useful skills for the home and family; the child's understanding and appreciation of the local cultural; and the capacity for employment (or at least employment training) in both local and mainstream job markets.

PLANNING FOR NEW ROLES

Assuming new roles, both at the center and the periphery, is not something that will come automatically. Extensive training and careful planning will be required at both ends. At local sites principals, teachers, local officials, and community members will need training in goal setting, collaborative decision-making, curriculum development, group relations, and planning and management skills. At the center, managers and inspectors will need training in lump-sum budgeting and in exercising facilitative (as opposed to supervisory) roles in relation to locally developed programs.

An effective way to encourage local initiative in goal setting and local management would be to require schools/communities to develop a feasible management and resource allocation *plan* before block funds can be released. An additional provision might be demonstration of the generation of local resources (financial or "in-kind"). As all schools in the periphery will not be ready for such responsibilities at the same time, a phased-in approach could be taken, in which schools present their plans as they become ready. This may mean working intensively with a few pilot schools until the details and problems of community-oriented schooling are ironed out.

The details of program implementation at exemplary sites could be captured in a series of case studies, which could then be distributed to other sites as a further support towards community-oriented education. A desirable vehicle for producing such studies would be a partnership between community schools teachers/principals and instructors/researchers at regional universities or teachers colleges.

SUMMARY AND CONCLUSION

The proclamation of the World Declaration on Education for All in 1990 created a new sense of urgency and commitment towards the education of peripheral groups. Although the Declaration also encouraged the formation of new partnerships and innovative methods in reaching the periphery, nations have generally responded with designs—often heroic in scope—to bring the conventional school to those in the last frontiers of government outreach. Not surprisingly, such efforts have failed to attract and sustain many students from peripheral groups.

Conventional schools fail in the periphery not just because they are poor—which they generally are—but because they are poorly conceived. Top-down management systems, inappropriate curricula, flawed teacher recruitment/ training/support systems, misguided language policies, unsuitable school-classroom organization systems, and weak school-community relations all conspire and interact to make the conventional school a weak and alien body. Attempts to reform individual components will bear little fruit, since the failure is not simply with components, it is systemic.

Hence, we suggest a radically different approach to extending education to those on the periphery, one which puts the needs of children and their communities first. Ours is not a Robin Hood solution. We do not think that schools in the periphery can be improved simply through a massive infusion of central aid. Rather to move forward peripheral communities need to rebuild their spirit and local initiative, largely subverted in the past by decades of central intrusion. In our proposed community-oriented education, the community will assume a major part of the responsibility for planning where it wants to go and even for financing parts of the journey. Our suggestion for the central authorities is that they take a leading role in activating local initiative by providing funds in the form of block grants and exercising training and facilitation functions. With a substantial reorientation of management, teacher education, curriculum/instructional design, language policy and school-community relations, it will be possible to provide quality education for peripheral groups. This can only be done, however, when changes in the periphery are truly comprehensive, involving not only an integrated set of reforms, but also all levels of the government delivery system.

Community-oriented systemic reform is not meant to push peripheral communities into total self-reliance and further isolation, but instead to create *alternative futures* for the community's children. As an "additive system" the community-oriented school promotes the acquisition of local language, knowledge, skills, and values, *as well as* those prevalent in the mainstream, making it possible for school graduates to function in both kinds of environments. Linked as it is to both worlds, such a school fulfills both the needs of the community and the state. The irony is that for the state to attain its school participation and socialization goals in the periphery it must relinquish direct control of the schools.

Endnotes

1. This term, which was first coined by Lambert (1981) in the context of second-language learning, can be usefully extended to refer to other areas, e.g., curriculum, language policies, etc.

Bibliography

Beykont, Zeynep F. "The Choice of Language Policies and Programs: A Comparative View." In P. Altbach, ed., *Special Studies in Comparative Education*, 31. Buffalo, NY: State University of New York, 1994.

Chambers, Robert. *Rural Development: Putting the Last First.* London: Longman, 1983.

Goodlad, John I. *Educational Renewal: Better Teachers, Better Schools.* San Francisco: Jossey-Bass, 1994.

Lambert, W. E. "Bilingualism: Its Nature and Significance." *Bilingual Education Series,* 10. Washington, DC: The Center for Applied Linguistics, 1981.

Murphy, J. *Restructuring Schools: Capturing and Assessing the Phenomena.* New York: Teachers College Press, 1991.

Nielsen, H. Dean, and Maria Teresa Tatto (with Aria Djalil and N. Kularatne). "The Cost-Effectiveness of Distance Education for Teacher Training." *BRIDGES Research Report Series,* No. 9. Cambridge, MA: Harvard Institute for International Development, 1991.

Index

Achievement, 12, 17, 30 43, 48, 55, 80, 87, 104-105, 184-186, 224-225, 227-229, 232-234
  academic, 17, 30, 156, 187
  cognitive flexibility, 92-95, 109
  concept formation, 92-95, 109
  divergent thinking, 92-95, 109
Adult education, literacy, 222, 262
Affirmative action, 51, 240
Alternative educational program, 49
Assimilation, 96-99, 101-102,104,107
  explicit, 96-98, 101-102
  implicit, 97-99, 102
  cultural, 102, 104
  structural, 101
Australia, 30, 80, 185, 187, 207
Automatic promotion, 46-47, 146, 162, 164

Bangladesh, 42-45, 48-50, 52, 54, 59, 157, 159, 223
Bangladesh Rural Advancement Committee (BRAC), 45-46, 49,52
Belgium, 9-10, 98
Belize, 30-31, 152, 155, 188-190, 193-195, 198-203, 208
Bhutan, 52, 60
Bilingual, bilingualism, 56, 80-99, 102-110, 251, 254, 256, 260-264
  "additive", 103, 254
  balanced, 85, 90, 92, 95, 109
  benefits of, 81, 95,
  critical period for, 92-95

  maintenance, 83, 88-92, 94-99 102-103, 106, 109, 254, 259
  "subtractive", 102-103
  transitional, 83, 86, 88-92, 97-99, 102, 109
  two-way, 88-89, 91, 97, 102
Biliteracy, 95, 110, 255
British colonialism (in India),
  industrialization, 125-6, 132
  modernization, 125-6, 132
  urbanization, 125-126
  westernization, 125
Burundi, 80, 88, 99

Cameroon, 79, 85, 159
Canada, 31, 80, 85, 93, 99
Central Kalimantan (Indonesia), 26-28, 190
Child-care, 46, 66
China, 11, 14, 15, 25-26, 29, 32, 46, 146-147, 149, 151, 158-159, 185
Classroom organization, 183-207, 247, 250, 252-3, 256, 260, 263
Collaborative management, 38
Collaborative model, 39-40, 68-69, 253
Colombia, 46, 54-55, 71, 151, 155, 158, 166-168, 187, 191-192, 198, 201, 205
Common-underlying-proficiency notion, 93
Community
  contributions, 42, 58-60, 161-162, 164, 201-203, 261
  development, 65-67, 234, 252, 259, 262
  donations, 59

funds, 61, 72, 100, 236, 253
    in-kind, 59-60, 67, 201, 203
    labor, 59, 61, 67, 72, 201-203
high-demand, 40-41
involvement, 21, 31, 49, 57-58, 62-67,
        69, 80-84, 96, 101-103 106, 109,
        150, 159, 169, 231, 247, 253, 258
low-demand, 40-57, 215-216, 236
micro-communities, 133, 255
needs, 40-41, 49, 53, 67-69
needs, in India, 124, 133
"ownership," 60-62, 69, 150-151, 155,
        258
participation, 9, 41-42, 62, 67-69, 155,
        169, 223, 234, 252
resistance, 42-43, 62, 68, 103, 105, 109,
        215, 219, 254
self-sufficiency, 125
support, 29, 39-42, 49, 53, 57-69, 80, 84,
        103-110, 147-151, 154, 161-163,
        165, 170, 206, 218, 231-232, 234-
        236, 248-249, 251-254, 256, 258-
        262
values, 8, 31, 40-44, 56-57, 68-69, 99-
        101, 153, 168, 231-232, 235-236,
        238-239, 253
Community-oriented approach to
        management, 231-236
    community as foundation, 232-235
    community-based resource generation,
        235-236
    development of local plan, 235
    diversity of communities, 235
    education and local dev't, 232
Community-oriented educ., 252-261
    balanced curriculum, 255
    collaborative school community
        relations, 253-254
    needs-oriented teacher policies, 255-256
    responsive language policies, 254-255
    school/classroom organization based on
        family model, 256
    systemic approach, 257-258
    "Theory C" school management, 256-257
Congruent goals (re: school language), 103,
        107-108, 110

Constraints to education in periphery
    difficult terrain, 15,
    geographic dispersion, 15
    gov't structure and policy, 16
    language, 15
    social class, 14
Constructivist theory, 167, 169
Cost-effectiveness, 47, 156, 170
Cultural alienation (in India), 132-133
Culture, cultural
    bicultural, 87, 249, 252
    local, 37-38, 40-44, 56, 66, 156, 158,
            202, 215, 231, 238-239, 254-255,
            262
    mainstream, 40, 56, 99, 156, 168-169,
            248-249, 259
    multicultural, 97, 99, 101-104
    "Textbook", 126-127
Curriculum, 31-32, 53-55, 80, 123-134, 166-
        167, 185, 204-205, 226, 248-249,
        255, 259
    balanced, 31, 54-55, 70, 133, 239, 253,
            255, 259
    centralized, 21, 29, 47, 49, 97-98, 123,
            125-133, 191, 216, 261
    decentralized, 27, 31-32, 45, 51, 53, 56,
            87-89, 100-101, 106, 124, 133-
            134, 201, 206, 231
    job-training, 51
    social studies (India), 128-133
        cultural images, 123,128, 133, 149
        portrayal of physical or natural
            environment, 129-130
        portrayal of socio-cultural world,
            130-133
    teacher-constructed, 154-155, 157-158,
            162, 165
    teacher-education, 143, 152-153, 157,
            163

Dalits (of Tamil Nadu, So. India),127, 130-
        131, 135-136
Decision-making, 21, 31-32, 34, 60, 154,
        158, 197, 200, 238-239
    centralized, 154, 238-239
    decentralized, 21, 31, 60, 62, 239, 241

localized/school based, 32, 34, 154, 157-158, 197, 200, 236
Deficiency models (language), 87, 98
Denmark, 10, 85
Dominant culture, 79-80, 85, 87-88, 97, 99, 102-104, 108-110, 165, 168, 249
Drop out, 26-7, 39, 46, 48, 57, 61, 65-66, 70, 81, 83-84, 124, 140, 191-192, 206, 218, 248
Drop-out rate, 45-46, 48, 50, 52, 58-59, 69, 79, 106, 190, 219, 261
Drop-out rate in India, 123-124, 191

Ecuador, 56, 88
Education
    basic, 5, 11, 27-28, 49, 52, 125, 139, 167, 186, 218, 223, 225, 228-9, 233-236, 239, 241
    community-based, 37-38, 44, 84, 87, 95, 254-5
    compulsory, 5, 11, 13, 40
    family model of, 29, 183, 188-190, 192, 206, 250, 253, 256, 260
    higher, 83, 145, 152, 156-158, 182, 187, 189, 204, 218, 227, 250, 260
    industrial model of, 29 ,183, 188-190, 205-206, 247, 250, 260
    mass, 6-7, 12, 37, 54, 125, 167
    modern, 5-22, 43-44, 126, 184, 205, 216-218, 225, 231
    modern, limits of, 18-22, 218-230
    nonformal, 20, 45, 52, 59
    primary / elementary, 8-9, 14, 16-19, 26, 31, 44-45, 49-52, 55, 59, 66-67, 81, 84, 87, 95, 100, 105, 156-157, 160, 185, 193, 196, 199, 205, 218, 221-223, 228, 233, 238
    primary, in India, 123-5, 133
    religious, 8-10, 44, 61, 67, 184, 235-236
    secondary, 8, 16, 26, 49-51, 59-60, 100, 123, 152, 155, 170, 202, 218, 224, 227
    teacher, 9, 33, 45, 81, 83, 142-143, 151-152, 154-164, 165, 167, 170, 206, 250, 261, 263

Education for All, 5-6, 27-31, 33-34, 167, 183, 185, 215-216, 228, 263
Educational systems/approaches
    Anglo and American, 11-13, 216, 243
    French, 8-9, 13, 216, 243
    Japanese, 10-11, 14, 16, 216, 243
    Lowlands, 9-10
    Prussian, 9, 216
    Socialist, 11, 14, 16, 216
Egalitarian values, 5, 8, 11
Egypt, 225, 232-234, 236
England, 80, 98-99, 216
Enrollment (educational)
    decisions, 48-49,52, 222-226, 248
    female, 44, 46, 49
    rates, 13-14, 16-19, 48, 52, 59, 247
    rates, in India, 123-4
Equality, 5, 12-13, 16-7, 169, 221
    of educational opportunity, 10, 12, 16, 27, 39, 43, 45, 79, 97-101, 216, 261
    of funding , 9-10, 21-22, 149, 251, 257
Escuela Nueva, 46, 49, 52, 54-55, 66, 70, 151, 155, 157, 166-167, 187, 191-192, 198, 200-205
Ethnic, 15-17, 154
    complexity, 17
    diversity, 15-16, 40, 95-97, 99, 101, 249, 251
    groups, 15, 80-81
    identity / background, 43, 154
    minorities, 25, 35
Examinations, 29, 31-32, 45, 53-54, 60, 66, 89, 100, 127, 133, 193, 227, 234

Family, 14, 26, 45-46, 57, 100, 104-105, 143, 158-159, 161-162, 193, 197, 201, 204, 232, 240, 249, 262
    "family" model, 29, 183, 188-192, 196, 206, 250, 253, 256, 260
    in India, 127-132
France, 8-9, 85, 185, 190, 216
Funding, 11-12, 167, 218-219, 258
    block grants, 207, 240-241, 257, 261-263
    equalizing formulas, 9, 21, 251
    local-level, 11, 149, 236

national-level, 48,

Germany, 7, 85, 89, 98, 101
Gini index, 16
Globalization, 13, 27-28,165,185
Guizhou Province (China), 25-26, 32

Haiti, 89, 101, 151
Harambee schools (Kenya), 60
Home-school discontinuity, 80, 87, 107-108,
   110, 249, 254
Hungary, 85, 98

Immigration, immigrant groups, 85, 88, 93,
   98, 105
IMPACT, 47-49, 54, 198, 200, 235
Improved Efficiency of Learning (IEL), 48,
   54
Incongruent goals (related to school
   language), 108, 110
India, 5, 13-14, 15, 17, 20, 45, 47, 51-52, 59,
   64, 66-67. 83, 100-101, 123-136,
   185, 191, 223, 236, 248-249
Indonesia, 15, 26-27, 29-30, 32-33, 48-49,
   63, 79, 145, 147, 151-152, 154-
   157, 159-160, 185, 188, 190-191,
   193, 198, 200, 203, 220-222, 236,
   239
InSPIRE, 48
Instruction, 9, 21, 25-26, 29, 34, 45, 48, 53-
   54, 57, 62-68, 70, 83, 85, 98-99,
   109, 155-156, 161, 166-167, 184,
   190-191, 204, 207, 228, 235, 252
   language/medium of, 54, 80-96, 99-100,
      103-105, 107, 109, 152, 161, 170,
      191, 248, 252, 254, 259, 262
   multigrade, 31, 206, 234, 256
   native language, 81, 83-86, 90-91, 98,
      103-106, 207, 254, 258
   public, 8
   self-instruction, 48, 53-54, 70, 191, 195,
      198, 200, 204, 206-207, 260
Instructional materials, 7, 30, 48, 54-55, 70,
   83, 88, 149, 195, 205, 220, 226,
   233, 237

Instructional programs, 57-58, 64, 70, 150,
   233-234
Irian Jaya (Indonesia), 26-27

Japan, 6, 10-11, 14, 16, 86, 89, 101, 216,
   243
Jomtien, Thailand, 6, 27

Kenya, 44, 50, 52, 60, 157

Language
   dominant, 26. 28, 53-54, 252
   dominant language groups, 79-110, 168
   first, 79, 89, 91, 249
   home, 54, 82, 89, 91, 97, 100, 102, 110,
      249
   of instruction, 54, 80-96, 99-100, 103-
      105, 107, 109, 152, 161, 170, 191,
      248, 252, 254, 259, 262
   local dialect, 81
   metropolitan, 21, 81-83
   native, 79-81, 83-95, 98-107, 247-248,
      254, 258, 262
   nondominant, 79-110
   nondominant language groups, 79-110,
      249, 254
   official, 79-103, 107-109, 247, 249, 254,
      259
   partitioning (as in South Africa), 97, 101
   politically neutral, 81
   prestige, 79
   revival, 86-87, 89, 91, 95, 109
   of the school , 207, 249, 262
   school-language policy, 207
   second, 85-95, 98, 103, 191, 259
   standard dialect, 79, 81
   of upward mobility, 79, 81, 83, 101, 105
   of wider communication, 79
Language programs, 80, 83-91, 96-103, 109-
   110, 254
   "additive" bilingual, 103
   balanced bilingual, 90, 92, 95, 109
   comity based immersion, 87, 95
   home-language, 89, 91, 97, 110,
   immersion, 83, 85-87, 89, 91, 254-255,
      259

maintenance bilingual, 88-92, 94-97,
    103, 106, 109, 254, 259
structured immersion, 86, 89-91, 102,
    109
submersion, 83, 85, 89-92, 96-98, 101-
    102, 107, 109
"subtractive" bilingual, 102-103
transitional bilingual, 83. 86-88, 89-92,
    97, 99, 102, 109
two-way bilingual, 88-89, 91, 97, 102
Language skills, 83, 93-95
    context-reduced , 94
    contextualized, 94
    decontextualized, 94
Liberia, 48, 79, 85, 222
Linguistic diversity, 17, 80, 95-97, 252
Linguistic-interdependence hypothesis, 93
Literacy, 6, 18, 66, 81, 83-88, 88, 91-95, 98,
    101, 103-110, 125, 222, 249, 254-
    255, 262
Luxembourg, 79

Malaysia, 46, 48-49, 62, 80, 88, 99, 156,
    160, 223, 230
Mali, 79, 85
Management, 19, 29, 32-34, 39-40, 62-64,
    66, 154, 162, 170, 191-192, 215,
    247-248, 251-253, 256, 258, 260,
    262-263
    accountability, 12, 20, 225, 241
    bureaucratic, bureaucracy, 21, 33, 39,
        48-49, 62-64, 135, 164, 201, 217,
        220, 223, 231, 242
    centralized, 8-11, 19, 142, 145, 165-166,
        169, 216, 238, 242, 251, 260
    community-based, 37-38, 44, 87, 95, 235
    community-oriented approach ("Theory
        C"), 216, 219, 231, 235-242, 245,
        252-263
    decentralized, 8, 11-12, 16, 19, 149, 151,
        165-169, 205, 224, 230, 238
    information systems for, 69, 224, 225,
        228, 251
    localized, 230

modern, 7-11, 12-13, 18-20, 125-126,
    132, 184, 205, 215-217, 222-231,
    236-237, 243, 251
modern, limits of, 218-222
multilevel, 216, 223
problem-solving, 33-34
professional, 12, 62, 69, 150, 201, 217-
    218, 253, 259
reforming, 61, 164, 166, 169, 237-242,
    251, 258, 263
resource management, 151, 224
school-based, 32, 59, 157, 161
strategic role of, 217-231
supervision, and, 33, 54-55, 70, 156-157,
    216, 220, 222-223, 230, 233, 243,
    255-257,
top-down, 149, 216, 247-248, 251-252,
    258, 260, 263
Mexico, 141, 151, 155, 166-167, 223
Morocco, 53, 85, 107, 147
Multicultural orientation, 99, 101-104
Multigrade teaching, 29-31, 48, 55, 70, 149,
    153-155, 162, 163, 167, 183-208,
    250-252, 255, 256, 262
    advantages of, 30, 185-186, 205-208
    classroom conditions, 188-192
    community contributions to, 200-203
    disadvantages of, 185-186
    Escuela Nueva, as an example of, 204-
        205
    learning materials for, 32, 55, 198, 203,
        207, 262
    peer tutoring in, 199-200
    prevalence of , 185
    recognition of, 30, 187-188
    student outcomes of, 29-30, 187-188,
        205-206
    self-directed learning in, 197-199
    teacher coping strategies in, 195-196
    teacher influence in, 196-197
    teacher preparation for, 30, 149, 153-
        155, 162, 163, 195, 207, 250, 255,
        260
    teacher resourcefulness in,194-96
    time management in, 190-192
    voluntary teachers in, 201-203

Namibia, 80, 89
Netherlands, 9-10
New Zealand, 86-87, 98
Nigeria, 43, 54, 59-60, 81, 83, 88, 99, 156, 224
Norway, 85

Pakistan, 15, 42-44, 50, 59, 155, 159-160, 185, 236
PAMONG Project, 48
Papua New Guinea, 83-84, 224
Paraguay, 80, 85, 94
Parent(s), parental
    attitudes, 104-108
    expectations, 104-108
    goals (for child's educ.), 104-108
        congruent with school, 43, 69, 106-108, 110
        incongruent with school, 42-43, 48-49, 104-105, 110, 236, 258
    involvement, 59, 61-64, 67-69, 81, 83, 87, 102-103, 156, 200-204, 216, 253-254, 259
    motivation (to enroll children), 46, 49-50, 52-53, 57, 109, 124, 133-134, 150, 183-184, 236, 247-249, 255
    support, 12, 29, 39, 53, 58, 64, 99, 105, 107, 150, 154, 191, 196, 200-204, 206, 234, 253
Parent-teacher associations, 58-59, 62-63, 206, 231
Partnership, school-community, 63, 102, 156, 158, 215, 236, 253, 263
    Peripheral
    communities, 40, 42, 44, 53, 57, 60-61, 68, 71, 123, 126, 133-134, 193, 216-218, 231-242, 248, 250, 263-265
    groups, 22, 40, 45, 52, 124-125, 140, 155, 168, 247-249, 251-254, 258-261, 263-265
    schools, 12, 40, 44, 53, 64, 70, 145, 147-148, 150, 251-252
Peripheralization, 15, 22, 249
Philippines, 47, 49, 52, 54, 59-60, 63, 94, 185, 190

Policy (re: education in the periphery)
    curriculum, 133-134, 255
    school / classroom organization, 206-208, 256
    school-community relations, 67-71, 253-254
    school language, 109-110, 254-255
    school system management, 232-242, 256-265
    teacher, 160-170, 255-256
Policy making, 12, 16, 42, 63
Population density, 15, 17, 252
Programmed instruction, 46, 48, 198, 200
Prussia, 9, 184, 216
Psycholinguistic
    perspectives, 80, 92-95, 109
    research, 80, 92-95
Puerto Rico, 86, 88, 93, 104, 107-108

Reading
    comprehension, 93, 106, 108, 204
    materials, 84, 254
    skills, 28, 86, 88, 93-94, 106, 187, 197, 229
Repetition (school), 46, 70, 124, 168, 86-187, 219
Repetition rate, 79-80, 108, 205, 218-219, 226

Scholarship programs, 33, 50-51, 155, 160-161, 163, 262
    student, 50-51
    teacher, 33, 155, 160-163, 262
School(s), schooling
    benefits of, 43, 49-53, 81-83, 206-207, 218, 220, 238
    boarding facilities at, 30, 51-52
    clustering, 54, 61-62, 70-71, 150-151, 162, 164-165, 169-170, 224, 230, 251, 255, 261-262
    conventional, 28-29, 31, 48-49, 55, 184, 186-188, 190-192, 196, 197, 200-201, 206-207, 244, 256, 263
    costs of, 43, 48-53, 167, 205-206, 233, 257
    failure, 225

contributors to, 247-252
overcoming, 252-258
fees, 43, 49-51, 130, 159
hidden costs of, 50
one-room, 26, 29-30, 184-185, 188-189,
250, 252
organization, 43, 67-68, 162, 183-207,
242, 247-248, 250-251, 253, 256-
258, 260, 263
private, 11-12, 17, 19, 32, 63, 145, 190
public, 8, 12, 20, 87, 152, 207, 218, 249,
256, 258
purposes of , 38, 43, 166-169, 192, 232-
233
renewal of, 155, 169, 252-258
rural, 12, 54-56, 141, 147, 158-159, 185-
186, 198, 205, 220, 223, 233-234
rural-urban differences, 18, 220
sectarian, 10
single-sex, 43-44
small, 28-29, 51, 149, 184, 188-189, 191,
196, 203, 206, 242
support to community, 31, 38, 40-42, 65-
67, 69, 101, 134, 144, 158-159,
189-190, 192-193, 201, 206, 231-
235, 237, 249, 251, 253, 260, 263-
264
School-community collaboration, 38, 49, 55-
56, 62, 68-71, 147, 156, 254-255,
257-260, 263
School year, flexible, 46-47, 191-192
Segregationist orientation, 97, 99-102
Senegal, 79, 85, 147
Separation (cultural), related
to education, 53, 99, 101, 105
Sierra Leone, 66, 79, 85
Social stratification (in India), 124-124
caste system, 124-126, 127-129, 131-
132, 135-136, 250
high-caste ideology, 126, 129, 250
low-caste, untouchables, Dalits, 124,
127, 130-131, 135-136
twice-born, 124
Sociohistorical
factors, in India, 124-126
perspectives, 103-108, 109-110

Sociopolitical perspectives, 96-102, 109-
110, 250
South Africa, 79, 81-82, 89, 100-101
Soviet Union, 11, 20
Sri Lanka, 50, 54, 59-60, 61, 62-63, 65, 81,
147-152, 154, 156, 160, 169-170,
224, 230, 239, 241
Standardized testing, 31-32, 47-48, 260
Sweden, 6, 85, 93

Tamil Nadu (India), 123-134, 248-249
Teacher(s)
aids (from community), 162, 259
attrition, 150, 156
automatic promotion, 146-147, 164
choice, 140-142, 160, 164, 169
concerns/needs, 142-144, 160-162
economic considerations, 145-148,
161-162
organizational support, 148-152,
161-162
professional development, 152-158,
161-162
social considerations, 158-160, 161-
162
community support of, 57-59, 70-71, 84,
147-151, 154, 159, 163-165, 170,
206-207, 236, 254, 257, 259, 263
deployment, 44, 138, 142-143, 146, 148,
150, 158-160, 162, 164-165, 167,
169-170, 262
differentiated career structure, 153-154,
157
distance education for, 148, 151-153,
156-157, 159-160, 256
education of
access to, 45, 143, 152-153, 155-156,
160-165, 207, 250, 261
costs related to, 55, 143, 162
curricular reform, 45, 149, 154, 157,
163, 207
field-based, 155, 158
site-based, 155
female, 26, 32-33, 44-45
female role models, 26, 32-33, 44-45

health care support, 162, 165
home visit subsidies, 160-162, 165
housing, 143, 147, 158-160, 162, 164-165, 256
inservice education, 105, 143,146-149, 151, 153, 155-156, 158, 161-162, 163-165, 169-170, 193, 207, 224, 262
   curriculum, 143, 149, 151, 153, 155-156, 161-162, 163-165
   distance education for, 153, 156, 163, 169-170, 193
   managed by principal, 150-151, 158, 170
   managed by teachers, 155, 158, 162, 164, 165, 262
job security, 144-147, 161, 163
managerial support of , 151, 154, 164, 169, 237
married couples, 160, 162, 164
morale, 57-58, 147-148, 165, 170
moving cost subsidy, 160-164
new roles of, 144, 152, 154, 157-158, 164, 169, 204, 255
peer support systems, 149, 155, 157, 159, 162, 165, 224
policy, 139-144, 146-149, 150-151, 154-158, 159-160, 161-162, 165-169, 252
preparation programs, 139, 141-142, 145-147, 149, 154-155, 162, 167-168, 207, 250, 256
promotion policies, 141, 144-146, 154, 161-162, 163-164
recognition, 141, 151, 161-162, 163-165
recruitment, 139, 142-143, 148, 150, 155-160, 161, 163, 169-170, 207, 255, 260-261, 263
retention, 139, 142-144, 162, 164-165, 167, 169-170
as role models, 32-33, 44
scholarships for, 33, 155, 160-161, 163, 262
selective recruitment of local youth, 33, 159, 163, 260-261

student teaching, 33, 153, 161, 207, 255, 261
working conditions, need for improvement of , 140, 143-144, 147-150, 153, 158-160, 162, 165, 168-169, 193, 195, 204, 251
Teaching
   multigrade, 29-33, 48, 55, 70, 149, 153, 155, 162, 163, 167, 183-207, 250-252, 255-257
   same-age, 29, 200
   single-grade, 30, 183-185, 186, 187, 189, 192, 196, 206, 257
Textbooks, 9, 21, 25, 29, 31, 48-50, 81-82, 84-85, 97-98, 100, 105, 123, 126-127, 128-132, 134, 136, 149, 151, 153, 162, 165, 190, 198, 237, 249-250, 255
"Textbook culture" (India), 126-127
Tutoring, 155, 160, 161, 163, 186, 191, 199-200, 206, 250, 253, 260
   cross-age, 191
   peer, 186, 191, 199-200

UNESCO, 6, 19, 46, 166, 168, 185, 191, 228
United Kingdom, 11-12
United States, 7, 11-12, 80, 85, 86, 88, 91, 93, 99, 104-105, 107, 108, 140, 157, 167, 184-185, 216
U.S. Agency for International Development (USAID), 30, 139, 166, 168, 170, 225

Vietnam, 58-59, 63, 80

Wastage, 191-192
World Bank, 13, 50, 139, 166-168, 170, 185, 199

Yugoslavia, 11

Zambia, 85
Zimbabwe, 94

REFERENCE BOOKS IN INTERNATIONAL EDUCATION
EDWARD R. BEAUCHAMP, *Series Editor*

EDUCATION IN THE PEOPLE'S REPUBLIC
OF CHINA, PAST AND PRESENT
An Annotated Bibliography
by Franklin Parker
and Betty June Parker

EDUCATION IN SOUTH ASIA
A Select Annotated Bibliography
by Philip G. Altbach,
Denzil Saldanha,
and Jeanne Weiler

TEXTBOOKS IN THE THIRD WORLD
Policy, Content, and Context
by Philip G. Altbach
and Gail P. Kelly

MINORITY STATUS AND SCHOOLING
*A Comparative Study of Immigrant
and Involuntary Minorities*
by Margaret A. Gibson
and John U. Ogbu

TEACHERS AND TEACHING IN THE
DEVELOPING WORLD
by Val D. Rust and Per Dalin

RUSSIAN AND SOVIET EDUCATION,
1731–1989
A Multilingual Annotated Bibliography
by William W. Brickman
and John T. Zepper

EDUCATION IN THE ARAB GULF
STATES AND THE ARAB WORLD
An Annotated Bibliographic Guide
by Nagat El-Sanabary

EDUCATION IN ENGLAND AND WALES
An Annotated Bibliography
by Franklin Parker
and Betty June Parker

CHINESE EDUCATION
Problems, Policies, and Prospects
edited, with an introduction
by Irving Epstein

UNDERSTANDING EDUCATIONAL
REFORM IN GLOBAL CONTEXT
Economy, Ideology, and the State
edited by Mark B. Ginsburg

EDUCATION AND SOCIAL CHANGE
IN KOREA
by Don Adams
and Esther E. Gottlieb

THREE DECADES OF PEACE
EDUCATION AROUND THE WORLD
An Anthology
edited by Robin J. Burns
and Robert Aspeslagh

EDUCATION AND DISABILITY IN
CROSS-CULTURAL PERSPECTIVE
edited by Susan J. Peters

RUSSIAN EDUCATION
Tradition and Transition
by Brian Holmes,
Gerald H. Read,
and Natalya Voskresenskaya

LEARNING TO TEACH IN TWO
CULTURES
Japan and the United States
by Nobuo K. Shimahara
and Akira Sakai

EDUCATING IMMIGRANT CHILDREN
*Schools and Language Minorities in
Twelve Nations*
by Charles L. Glenn
with Ester J. de Jong

TEACHER EDUCATION IN
INDUSTRIALIZED NATIONS
Issues in Changing Social Contexts
edited by Nobuo K. Shimahara
and Ivan Z. Holowinsky

EDUCATION AND DEVELOPMENT
IN EAST ASIA
edited by Paul Morris
and Anthony Sweeting

THE UNIFICATION OF GERMAN
EDUCATION
by Val D. Rust and Diane Rust

WOMEN, EDUCATION, AND
DEVELOPMENT IN ASIA
Cross-National Perspectives
edited by Grace C.L. Mak

QUALITATIVE EDUCATIONAL
RESEARCH IN DEVELOPING
COUNTRIES
Current Perspectives
edited by Michael Crossley
and Graham Vulliamy

SOCIAL CARTOGRAPHY
*Mapping Ways of Seeing Social
and Educational Change*
edited by Rolland G. Paulston

SOCIAL JUSTICE AND THIRD WORLD
EDUCATION
edited by Timothy J. Scrase

QUALITY EDUCATION FOR ALL
Community-Oriented Approaches
edited by H. Dean Nielsen
and William K. Cummings